# Modern Israeli Drama

# Modern Israeli Drama

*An Anthology*

*Edited with an introduction by* HERBERT S. JOSEPH

Rutherford • Madison • Teaneck
Fairleigh Dickinson University Press
London and Toronto: Associated University Presses

Associated University Presses, Inc.
440 Forsgate Drive
Cranbury, NJ 08512

Associated University Presses Ltd
25 Sicilian Avenue
London WC1A 2QH, England

Associated University Presses
2133 Royal Windsor Drive
Unit 1
Mississauga, Ontario
Canada L5J 1K5

**Library of Congress Cataloging in Publication Data**
Main entry under title:

Modern Israeli drama.

Includes bibliographical references.
Contents: He walked through the fields / by Moshe Shamir—The first sin / by Aharon Megged—Difficult people / by Yosef Bar-Yosef—[etc.]
1. Israeli drama—Translations into English.
2. English drama—Translations from Hebrew. I. Joseph, Herbert S., 1920–
PJ5043.M6 1983 892.4′26′08 81-72034
ISBN 0-8386-3104-5

Printed in the United States of America

# Contents

# Introduction

For a number of very obvious reasons, one might consider Israel as a country that is isolated politically, economically, and socially. The population is mixed. People have come from all over the world bringing their own way of life to an already diverse culture. It has been estimated that the population of Israel is made up of people from 102 countries who speak fifty-one different languages.

Because of the cultural and economic isolation and because of political conditions, there is understandably a great deal of tension in everyday life. There is also a great deal of intellectual ferment in Israel. As an indication of this, the arts are well patronized. Tickets to any particular cultural event are usually in great demand.

There is also a great interest in the theater. It has been estimated that 26 percent of the population goes at least once a week to see a live theater performance.[1] The Habimah, one of the major theatre houses in Tel Aviv, played to well over 300,000 people during the 1978–1979 season. The Habimah Theater Building in Tel Aviv houses three theaters. The main auditorium seats 1,000 people. In the same building are two other theaters, a smaller one that seats 300 and an experimental theater, which seats 100. Although these theaters are well patronized, a large establishment such as this cannot exist in Israel without state support. In Israel the legitimate theater is centered at present in five municipal companies. These are also partially state-supported, with the largest theaters, such as those in Tel Aviv and Haifa, receiving the most funds.[2]

These companies have apparently used their support funds to good advantage, for the Israeli theater is an active one and the acting and staging of plays are of high quality and very professional. Not only are plays from the European and American stage (from Shakespeare to Brecht) translated into Hebrew and presented, but all literature is ransacked for suitable subject matter. Any theatre that adapts such difficult materials as Kafka's *Metamorphosis* or Dostoevski's *Notes from the Underground* for stage presentation and communicates such works with any degree of success must surely be considered living theatre.

Concerning the staging of *Metamorphosis* by Kafka, one Israeli commented, "They did it with wires, but it was not so much that he was made up to look like an insect but that all of his movements made him seem like one." All of this leads one to believe that the Israeli theater is actively engaged in serious creative effort on every level.

This is only part of the story, however. Recent developments in theatre practice indicate a trend toward presentation of dramas written by Israeli playwrights. During a recent season, it was estimated that eighty percent of the plays presented in theaters all over the country were written by native authors. This has not always been the case. One has only to turn to the history of Israeli drama to recognize how pervasive the influences from abroad have been.

If one were to trace the history of changes in Western European dramatic taste, one would have to work within a time period covering over 1,000 years. On the other hand, the actual physical history of Israeli drama—the story of its spiritual and economic struggles—covers a relatively short time, from fifty to seventy years. Changes in taste and style, as seen from the perspective of Western European dramatic traditions, have been relatively rapid and changes are still taking place. Israeli drama at present seems to be in the midst of a struggle wherein the native author might come to terms with late developments in dramatic taste in the West, yet still maintain his own voice.

There seem to be three main phases regarding the history of Israeli drama.[3] Those phases might be said to be a period of dramas written and presented prior to statehood, followed by a period of a realistic reaction lasting about ten years, and finally what might be called (with some reservation) a renaissance, during which certain specific characteristics of the first two periods have been modified and used.[4]

The first attempt at producing drama in Israel took place during the 1890s. The subject matter of plays written during this first period of Israeli dramatic history was essentially traditional both in terms of the Jewish literary traditions (as transmitted in the nineteenth century) and of stage practice.

Many attempts were made in the early days (until the late 1930s) to form working theatrical companies, but only a few survived. The main survivor was, of course, the Habimah, which remains the major theater company in Israel to the present day. The Habimah was organized in Moscow in 1917 and achieved a worldwide reputation by the 1920s. This company's major success was the production (in Hebrew) of Anski's play, *The Dybbuk.* The presentation of *The Dybbuk* was essentially impressionistic in the sense that it represented a distinct rejection of naturalism.[5] *The Dybbuk* was performed by the Habimah more than 1,300 times in twenty countries and seventy-eight cities.[6] This company also achieved another major success by presenting a play in Hebrew from the Yiddish stage, *The Golem* by H. Leivick. After many trials and tribulations the Habimah finally settled in Palestine in 1931. During this period, in addition to plays based on traditional Jewish themes, the Habimah and other Israeli theatrical companies presented classical Continental materials including plays by Molière, Shakespeare, Ibsen, Chekhov, etc.

Another theater formed around 1921 in Israel that survived for quite a long time, was the Ohel (tent) Theater. This theater was founded by Moshe Halevy, a former member of the Habimah in Moscow who had emigrated to Palestine at that time with the idea of forming his own company. He approached the Histadrut (labor organization) for money and traveled around the country in search of fresh young talent. The first program that the Ohel presented was an evening of Peretz (a dramatization of seven of his short stories).[7] The second production was a play entitled *Hope,* a workers' drama about poor fishermen and a rich and villainous boat owner.[8] This play was written by a Dutchman named Hijermans. During this early period Halevy and his company presented several biblical plays, including *Jeremiah* and *Jacob and Rachel.* Subsequently, the Ohel turned to classical European materials and in 1935 presented Jaroslav Hasek's work, *The Good Soldier Schweik,* which became one of the theater's greatest hits.

Toward the end of this first cycle in 1944 an experimental theater was founded in Tel Aviv called the Cameri, or Chamber Theater, which is still functioning. Its founder was Josef Millo, who received his training in the Matate Theater (a rather long-lived establishment that began originally in Tel Aviv as a theatre of satire). Millo's first success was Goldoni's *A Servant of Two Masters.*

This brings us directly to the second stage of the development of Israeli drama, for it was Josef Millo in 1948 who contracted with Moshe Shamir to dramatize his novel *He Walked through the Fields* for the Cameri stage. It was the presentation of this play during wartime that helped usher in the change in taste.

Whereas one night characterize the plays written in Hebrew during the first phase in the history of Israeli drama as depending on traditional Jewish themes as well as using biblical and historical materials, the plays written in Hebrew during the second phase might be characterized as realistic and reflecting life situations as they were. As has been noted, the change in taste was inaugurated with Shamir's *He Walked through the Fields* in 1948 during the War of Independence (see page 19). The play was an immediate success and served as a prototype for many others. Among other examples of this type of play one might consider Shaham's *They'll Arrive Tomorrow* as one of the best. The play concerns a group of soldiers stationed in a camp surrounded by mines. The mines have been planted by the enemy and no one in the camp knows where they are. As the play opens there are just seven mines left and anyone venturing out of camp might accidentally step on one of them. Reinforcements arrive. The play's conflict centers around two basic military attitudes, that of Jonah, the first in command, who decides not to tell the new arrivals of the surrounding mine field (and whoever is killed, is killed) and the second in command, who finds Jonah's attitude morally reprehensible. Despite a happy ending, the play was considered essentially realistic.[9]

Additional plays written in this vein include Moshe Shamir's *Kilometer 56* (1949), *The House of Hillel* (1950), and *Stormy Night* (1954). Yigal Mossinson also wrote a successful play in this vein entitled *Plains of the Negev,* which involves a conflict on a kibbutz during wartime. The man in charge wishes to harvest the crops regardless of immediate danger from the enemy, but the army commander wishes to exercise prudence in this matter and withdraw from a hopeless military situation and thus save lives. This play also has a happy ending. Mossinson also wrote a play, *Casablan,* in 1954 which deals with the problems of an immigrant from Morocco and his adjustment to the Israeli social climate.

Aharon Megged wrote several plays, (some comedies and some serious plays) in this vein before going on to other things. The comedies may be typified by *Hedva and I* (1954), wherein the fallible but lovable kibbutznik from the sticks makes a fool of himself in the Big City (everybody out for himself) (Tel Aviv) and then returns home to the life of the kibbutz a wiser and humbler man.

The plays written during this period of Israeli dramatic history not only reflect everyday life in terms of content but in language as well. The language of these plays is less stylized, simpler. The play, *He Walked through the Fields,* is included in this volume to give the reader some historical perspective. From 1948 to 1960 over fifty of these plays were produced and some thirty additional realistic plays were produced by 1972.[10]

In regard to the major theaters in operation during this period in Tel Aviv, the Ohel was the least prosperous. The Histadrut withdrew its sponsorship of Ohel in 1958. The plays produced by the Ohel Theatre during this period met with minimal popular support and scant critical approval. The Cameri and Habimah also had problems, but these theaters continued to operate. The Habimah was recognized in October of 1958 as the Israeli National Theater and, as such, received funds from the government and from the American-Israel Cultural Foundation to assist its operations. The Cameri apparently did not receive outside financial assistance at this time and went through several financial crises. Its financial situation was greatly improved during one of these crises by a long and successful run of *Charley's Aunt* and the theater has continued to operate on a high level. Both the Habimah and Cameri used a great deal of outside material at this time in addition to original, realistic plays. Many plays were adapted from the European and Broadway stages.

During the 1960s the Israeli theater began to develop in many different directions. One critic labels this period of Israeli theatre as the "Explosion of the Sixties."[11] The number of topical plays produced in proportion to other types of drama declines. We have given this period after 1960 a rather arbitrary label, "the renaissance." In this particular case, the term "renaissance" merely means a turning away from a certain theatrical style of presentation and combining many of the forms from the past into a new, less restrictive approach. As Matti Megged states:

> In contrast to the realistic-topical tendency . . . after the establishment of the State, Bar-Yosef . . . (as do, to a greater or lesser degree, other young playwrights such as Nissim Aloni, Hanoch Levin, A. B. Yehoshua and others) created a play whose main thrust is the exposure of the human . . . "condition," and attempted to portray it in a dramatic manner stripped of almost . . . any background of human experience.[12]

An early example of this trend toward a freer, more expressionistic, less realistic type of drama written by a native author may be found in the play, *The Emperor's Clothes,* by Nissim Aloni. This play begins where the children's story by Hans Christian Andersen ends. The play was performed by the Habimah in 1961 and had a cast of more than forty people. In this play everyone is involved in the problem of the emperor's new clothes. Corruption is widespread, and even the emperor himself has appropriated funds from the treasury for the fake garments. This play, as lately indicated by Aloni, remains unedited and is not suitable for publication at this time. Aloni has continued to write plays in the same vein and is still active. His style and approach to materials for the stage carries much from the Theater of the Absurd, Genet, and some existentialist doctrines.

Many other Israeli authors have followed Aloni's footsteps in terms of experimentation. In regard to this, one might consider the plays of Honoch Levin, who is considered the bad boy of the modern Israeli stage. His vision tends to be Swiftian, scatological, and involved with politics. An earlier play, entitled *Jacoby and Leidenthal,* is somewhat akin to musical comedy and features a heroine who appears on stage with an enormous *tochis* (said portion of anatomy made much of in the play.) A later play features an old man trying to peddle a seemingly eternal, much-outdated, and rather extensive store of condoms. These plays are topical and have not as yet lent themselves to adequate translations. Aloni and Levin are only two examples of forward-looking Israeli playwrights. One might include a number of others; for example, Josef Mundy's *It Goes Around,* (a play that takes place in an insane asylum, with one major character thinking he is Kafka and the other thinking he is Herzl) or perhaps social documentaries as assembled by Nola Chilton or the plays of Mittelpunkt.

Theatre companies during the 1960s and 1970s in Israel have proliferated, and many major cities (Haifa being the most notable example) have their own working companies. Ohel has been the only company that has not survived.

In this volume we are attempting to introduce the reader to dramas written during this third period. The plays by Israeli authors included here (with the exception of *He Walked through the Fields*) were all written during the 1970s. This does not mean that the present-day Israeli theater has ceased to use or be influenced by European and American materials. The Israeli theater continues to draw on the latest Continental and American sources of all kinds. However, what one finds most interesting is the manner in which the modern Israeli dramatist comes to grips with the special spiritual and physical conditions involved in living in a particular place at a particular time, and how he has come to grips with the question of Jewish identity and with the human condition in general. The dramatist's response covers a wide spectrum. The present-day Israeli dramatist may turn partially or completely to the use of European traditions and ideas (*Genesis* or *The First Sin* by Megged), or he may turn partially or completely to Yiddish literary traditions and ideas (*Difficult People* by Yosef Bar-Yosef). Israeli playwrights may use a local or historic event to comment on human conditions from an Israeli point of view (*Night of the Twentieth* by Sobol, also *Naim,* adapted from a novel of A. B. Yehoshua). Any combination of these approaches may be found in one play (*Cherli Ka Cherli* by Horowitz). Each of the playwrights included in this volume deals with these matters in terms of his own sensibility and also in a manner that is different from the standard Jewish writer from Europe and America.

NOTES

1. Augustine Zycher, "Israeli Theatre Is Now Developing Its Own Character," *New York Times,* December 3, 1978, pp. 43–44D.
2. Ibid.
3. See Matti Megged, "Israeli Drama during Twenty-five Years of Israeli Statehood" in *Israeli Theatre,* Israeli Center of the International Theatre Institute, (Israel, 1973), pp. 71–72.
Refer to Shimon Sandbank, "Contemporary Israeli Literature; the Withdrawal from Certainty," in *Contemporary Israeli Literature,* edited by Elliot Anderson (Philadelphia, Penna.: Jewish Publication Society, 1977), pp. 6ff.
See also R. Alter's introduction in *Israeli Stories,* edited by Joel Blocker (New York: Schocken Books, 1975), pp. 10ff.
4. Zycher. I would not attempt at this point to offer the reader anything but an outline of Israeli dramatic history. If the reader wishes to correct his perspective and go into further detail, he might refer to the standard work in this area, Mendel Kohansky, *Hebrew Theatre—Its First Fifty Years* (New York: Ktav Publishing Company, 1969).
See also Zara Shakow, *The Theatre in Israel* (New York: Herzl Press, 1963).
5. Shakow, p. 45.
6. Ibid., p. 47.
7. Kohansky, p. 100.
8. Ibid., p. 104.
9. Ibid., p. 159.
10. Matti Megged, p. 72.
11. Kohansky, p. 214.
12. Matti Megged, in the Introduction to *Difficult People* by Yosef Bar-Yosef (Tel Aviv: Institute for Translation of Hebrew Literature, 1975, p. vii).

# A Note on Translation

Translating any literary work from the Hebrew offers a number of problems. Apparently there are many people who read, speak, and understand both Hebrew and English. Many times, however, it is difficult to find the correct English word to fit the spirit of the Hebrew. Several agencies sponsor translations of literary works from the Hebrew into English. The Cultural Division of the Department of Education and Culture in the Diaspora (of the World Zionist Organization) and the Israeli Centre of International Theatre Institute are active in this area.

Many authors also have arranged on their own to have their plays translated into English. However, there are still many good Israeli plays that have not yet been translated. Factors such as exigencies of translation, the amount of time and effort needed for translation, and funding for translations have imposed a limit on dramatic material available. Because of the lack of translated works, the selection of plays is less extensive at present than one might expect. It is hoped that in the future this situation will be remedied and that translations of Israeli plays will be more numerous.

# Modern Israeli Drama

# *He Walked through the Fields*

*by*
MOSHE SHAMIR

The features of this play should be familiar to American audiences. They probably have seen something like it in the movies. However, it is still an interesting play because it recreates time, place, and event from the Israeli point of view. As has been noted, this play is a historical landmark and was prototype for a whole school of dramatic writing "anchored in its entirety—in its story, characters, background and language—in the new generation, the generation of the 'Palmach' (volunteer commando units). For the first time this generation, kibbutz-born pioneers of the struggle for independence and identity, could see itself on the stage as it really was."[1]

This play echoed popular sentiment so directly that it became a social force, as Kohansky indicates:

> The premiere was the first in independent Israel, a fact much stressed by the newspapers which in those heady days were much prone to point out "firsts." On the day of the opening, newspaper headlines read: "Tulkarem, Jenin Bombed," "France Will Take Strong Measures Against Arabs for Damaging French Property in Jerusalem," "Victims of Gas Attacks in Jerusalem Hospitals," and there were columns of announcements of deaths. The subject, plus the timing, made the play a symbol of the War of Independence, a morale builder for the troops who jokingly called it a "secret weapon." Performances were held in army camps, in places where the mortar fire and explosions occasionally drowned out the voices of the actors. The trucks bearing the cast and set rode into Jerusalem in the wake of the troops who had liberated the city after a long siege, and a performance was given the same evening.[2]

The staging and the setting of the play as originally presented seems to have significance in terms of content:

> Millo's staging was as direct and matter of fact as the milieu, the kibbutz and the characters. The acting was devoid of any pathos or sentimentality; the atmosphere of the kibbutz as a place of work was conveyed by a novel feature—actors changing scenery at an open curtain, doing it casually as if they were just going about their regular chores. There was a touch of Brecht in the show; the audience was constantly reminded that they were watching a play, not life. A narrator wandered on and off the stage delivering himself of casual comments. The setting, by Arie Navon, the artist's first, marking the beginning of the most distinguished stage designing career in Israel, consisted of slight, movable objects which only suggested the place of action, and landscape sketches in black on white were projected onto a screen.[3]

During the period of its popularity in Israel, the play was given 171 times and apparently played before 170,000 people. It was revived for the stage in 1966 and in 1967 was made into a film.

Moshe Shamir is a highly successful Israeli novelist and playwright. He is noted for both historical and topical fiction. His best-known historical novels include *The King of Flesh and Blood,* which covers the period of the Second Jewish Commonwealth, and *David's Stranger,* which is the story of Uriah the Hittite. His best-known topical works are *He Walked through the Fields, With His Own Hands,* and *For Naked Thou Art.* These books deal generally with contemporary problems of Israel as seen from the viewpoint of the younger generation.

NOTES

1. Matti Megged, "Israeli Drama during the Twenty-five Years of Israeli Statehood," in *Israeli Theatre, 1971–1972* (Tel Aviv: Israeli Centre of the International Theatre Institute, 1973), p. 3.
2. Mendel Kohansky, *Israeli Theatre, Its First Fifty Years* (New York: Ktav Publishing Company, 1969), p. 157.
3. Ibid., p. 156.

## CHARACTERS

*Uri, young man, member of kibbutz, member of Palmach*
*Mika, young girl, member of kibbutz*
*Ruthka, Uri's mother*
*Willie, Uri's father*
*Avraham Goren, Ruthka's lover*

Members of the Kibbutz:
*Pesach*
*Biberman*
*Ilana (M)*
*Albert*
*Motke*
*Gita*
*Second Mother*
*Veteran Dairymaid*
*Young Dairymaid*
*First Peeler*
*Second Peeler*
*Watchman*
*Chavera*

Members of Palmach:
*Ginger (Commander)*
*Rafi*
*Danda*
*Dinahle*
*Semyon*

*Chorus of voices, Crowd*

*Place: Kibbutz Gat H'amakin*
*Palmach Camp at Ein Yosef*

*Translated by Audrey Hodes*

ACT 1

*Scene 1. In the courtyard of Gat Ha'amakim.*

KIBBUTZNIK: [*A typical kibbutz member—enters, strikes an iron bar hung on a low stand*]: Don't be frightened . . . it's not an alarm. . . . Years ago, we used to ring this gong for every meal. We rang for work to start, for the end of work in the evening, for a general meeting, or a party, or a lecture. . . . During the war we gave up this custom. The gong was reserved for alarms. Sometimes four a day, sometimes ten a day. . . . Tonight, in honor of our Uri, we announced that we would ring it again to call everybody to the memorial meeting. . . . I'll wait a few minutes, and then ring again. Just as we used to do then, when he walked in this very courtyard, taking a shortcut across the lawn on his way to the dining hall, annoying the gardener. . . . I'll ring again, for the third time . . . so don't be frightened. . . . Soon the *chaverim* [kibbutz members] will gather in the dining hall. You can hear the gong clearly in every corner of the farm. I'm sure it even reaches the new cowshed. If Uri were here today, he wouldn't recognize his kibbutz. . . . We've grown right across the ravine. The cowshed stands in the abandoned orchard. From here you can't see. . . . You have to go up to the top of the water tower to see the kibbutz from one end to the other. . . . I hope the dairymen have finished milking.

*Scene 2. In the cowshed.*

VETERAN DAIRYWOMAN: [*Enters*]: What was that gong? A fire or something?

YOUNG DAIRYMAN: [*closing a can of milk*]: No, not a fire. They want us to gather in the dining hall.

VETERAN: If so, it's good that they rang.

YOUNG DAIRYMAN: Of course it's good!

VETERAN: No, you don't understand—I fell asleep, and I'm waiting for a calving. The gong woke me up.

YOUNG DAIRYMAN: I didn't know there's a calving tonight.

VETERAN: What do you youngsters know? Have you got an eye for a good cow? The season of calvings, another birth every night—and he doesn't know about it! The main thing for you youngsters is to finish work—and disappear. Six new heifers this week! If only we had more cowsheds we could increase the herd. We could reach three thousand liters a day. Do you understand? Three thousand!

YOUNG DAIRYMAN: I understand—three thousand.

VETERAN: What do you understand? If you had to milk the whole lot by hand, you'd understand. With a milking machine what's the difference to you if it's one thousand or three? Now what's that gong all about, did you say?

YOUNG DAIRYMAN: It's ten years since Uri died.

VETERAN: Yes, of course! What do you youngsters know? . . . As long as everything goes off all right.

YOUNG DAIRYMAN: What will go off all right?

VETERAN: The calving . . . the calving [*goes out*].

*Scene 3. In the courtyard of the kibbutz.*

KIBBUTZNIK: The members are starting to arrive. Someone gets up from the chair in his room, a couple from a bench hidden among the pines, a conversation breaks off into silence, as it began, and answering steps come out of the quiet. Only the sprinklers continue to water the lawns and gardens, and from the children's houses comes the noise of the last chatter before sleep—tonight the parents are hurrying to put their children to bed early. . . .

*Scene 4. The children's house.*

GITA: [*Rises from her son's bed, smoothes the sheet, finishes her story*]: And then they were married and the king gave them a beautiful house as a present, and they had many children, and they lived happily ever after. . . .

SECOND MOTHER: [*Same actions as Gita*]: And then they were married and the king gave them a beautiful house as a present, and they had many children, and they lived happily ever after. . . .

GITA: And now to sleep, quietly. Look, Yossi is sleeping already. . . .

SECOND MOTHER: And now to sleep, quietly. Look, Noa is sleeping already. . . .

GITA [*To Second Mother*]: I don't know what will become of our children—the way we spoil them!

SECOND MOTHER: We are to blame for everything. We raise them as if the whole world were created for their sake.

GITA: And we've had some experience already. We've learned something. There are grandchildren in the kibbutz already—and it's exactly as it was in the early years—we're ruining the children! [KIBBUTZNIK *strikes the gong a second time.*] Yes. We have to hurry. . . .

*Scene 5. In the courtyard.*

KIBBUTZNIK: Slowly the dining hall fills up with people. In the afternoon we went up with Willie and Ruthka and Mika to the small tombstone. On the hill—between the carob trees. Now they are sitting and waiting for me to call them. The silence in the courtyard grows deeper. Only the people arranging tomorrow's work list in the committee room are still busy. These are difficult days for the work list. . . .

*Scene 6. In the Kibbutz committee room—arranging the work list.*

PESACH: *Chaverim,* silence—this is impossible. . . .

MOTKE: But can you imagine picking cucumbers without mules? Tell me yourself! On the one hand you force me to take the youngsters and on the other hand. . . .

CHAVERA A: But the mules have been promised to me fifty times already. You must give me a cart to take out the rubbish from our yard.

ALBERT: Tsilli and I are going to town tomorrow. We want the day off.

PESACH: But what about Tsilli? Has she the day off tomorrow?

MOTKE: Never mind Tsilli's day off. What about my mules, tell me that?

PESACH: Can't you see what I've got on my head?

ALBERT: Tsilli and I are traveling.

CHAVERA A: But what will happen with the mules—I need two tomorrow.

PESACH [*Hears the third ring*]: The arguments are finished, *chaverim.* I've heard enough.

MOTKE: I won't take the youngsters without the mules. I won't leave the crop out in the open the whole night.

PESACH: I heard you, I heard you! There'll be no changes tomorrow—that's final!

*Scene 7. In the courtyard.*

KIBBUTZNIK: . . . And so, we are starting. On the wall, draped in black, is the picture of the boy. He was twenty when he fell. The school choir. The veteran settlers—sitting beside the windows—the younger members. The door leading to the kitchen is closed. One of the members rises to speak. His voice can hardly be heard. . . . Ten years ago it all happened . . . ten years ago . . . [*The memorial portrait appears in silhouette.*]

*Scene 8. In the showers.*

ILANA [*Shaving next to a mirror*]: Blast! These damn blades! I'd like to make the treasurer shave with one of the blades he buys to save money.

PESACH [*To Biberman*]: Have you a comb perhaps, Biberman?

BIBERMAN [*Runs his hand over his completely bald head*]: Who, me?

GITA [*From the women's shower next door*]: Boys . . . throw us some shower sandals. These are all torn.

ILANA: Who's that?

GITA: Gita.

ILANA: Well, what do you want?

GITA: Shower sandals.

ILANA: With high heels or without?

GITA: I haven't time for wisecracks, *chaver.*

ILANA: My name is Ilana.

GITA: I didn't recognize your voice. Well, where are the shower sandals?

ILANA: One second. [*Bends over and looks.*]

PESACH [*To Ilana*]: Maybe you have a comb, Ilana?

ILANA [*Rises, holds out the shower sandal*]: Will this do?

PESACH: I asked for a comb.

GITA: Well?

ILANA: I'm throwing. [*Throws. Gita screams*]

MOTKE [*Enters, asks*]: Is Avraham Goren in the showers?

PESACH: How much milk tomorrow, Motke?

MOTKE: As usual, twenty cans.

PESACH: And vegetables?

GITA: And the second sandal?

MOTKE: Is Avraham Goren here?

BIBERMAN: He's showering.

MOTKE [*Calls*]: Avraham Goren—telephone.

AVRAM GOREN [*Comes out half-naked*]: What do they want of my life?

MOTKE: There's a telephone call from the District Council.

PESACH [*To Avraham*]: What do they want from you lately?

AVRAHAM: God knows. They're planning a new settlement in the area. They want me to handle it.

URI [*Enters, hangs up his things, starts looking under the bench*].

PESACH: Can we know what you're looking for, comrade?

URI [*Rises*]: I'm looking for shower sandals.

PESACH [*surprised*]: Uri! How did you come? Where did you drop from?

URI: I thought you'd be waiting on the road with the village band.

BIBERMAN: Uri, Shalom, Uri. How did you get here?

MOTKE: Who's that? Hey, Uri! When did you come?

ILANA: Shalom, Uri! How did you get here?

URI: Enough, *chevra!* I'm here, and that's enough! Who has shower sandals?

BIBERMAN: We sent away a child—and a man has come back to us.

URI: Don't be so sure!

PESACH: So, Uri—a doctor of agriculture?

URI: *Doc*tor I don't know about, but *trac*tor for sure. Is there hot water today?

PESACH: Just arrived—and already sure he'll work with the tractor, is he?

URI: Would like to.

PESACH: We'll see how it goes.

URI: If you wait too long—you'll lose me. You know how it is these days. On the night before we finished our course they told us to be ready for action at any time. One day they'll call the boys together—and I'll be off again.

PESACH: Listen, you're starting to sound like your father.

AVRAHAM: Father or son—the same Cahana!

URI: Thanks. I see it's the same with you, too.

AVRAHAM: What you mean, the same?

URI: The same old jokes. And you, Pesach, you're the work manager all the time?

ILANA: With intervals.

URI: And how are things here? What's new at home?

PESACH: As usual—the busy season. We're cutting corn for silage. Willie's in charge of that. Have you seen him yet?

URI: No, I haven't seen my father or my mother yet.

PESACH: Willie's in the fields now, I think. He didn't want to stop work till the last moment.

URI: How do you mean—the last moment?

AVRAHAM: How do you expect him to know about it?

URI: Traveling abroad again for the kibbutz? What's going on here? What are you hiding from me?

PESACH: Willie's joined up.

URI: Dad? Joined up?

PESACH: He simply got up and announced at a kibbutz meeting that he was joining the British Army and had already arranged all his papers.

URI: They won't take him. The English don't need men that age.

PESACH: They've already taken him.

URI [*Sits down, continues undressing, suddenly stops*]: I don't understand it. I've just come home, and everything . . . [*Starts dressing again.*] Joining up is a fine thing, yes, but . . .[*To Pesach:*] Which unit did he join?

PESACH: The Jewish Brigade, I think. Everybody's joining the Brigade now.

AVARHAM: Straight to Italy.

URI [*Rises*]: I'll shower afterwards.

PESACH: Afterwards you won't have hot water. Listen, Uri—after all, we're old friends. Don't start to run before you know why you're running.

URI: On the way it'll become plain to me. [*Tries to go out, but Pesach stops him gently.*]

PESACH: Listen to me a minute. It's a surprise, I know that. It surprised the kibbutz exactly as it surprised you. But you know what we said? We said: You can rely on Willie. He knows what he's doing. There he'll *certainly* be of some use—with his experience, his understanding, his way with people. And here—here we've already grown used to his letters from overseas. Now at least we'll have one Cahana at home. Willie's going, but Uri's come back.

AVRAHAM: The same Cahana.

URI: Where are they cutting the corn?

PESACH: So you've decided to go to him now?

URI: Answer me!

PESACH: So you've decided to go to him now?

URI: Answer me?

PESACH: Go to the machine shed. The tractor drivers will know where to find him. [*URI runs out.*] Yes—the same . . .

*Scene 9. In the machine shed. Willie is sharpening the blade of a reaper.*

URI [*Enters, running, stops*]: Dad!

WILLIE: U . . .

URI: Forgotten my name?

WILLIE: U-ri. Uri. Give me your hand, how're you, how're things? When did you come?

URI: They told me you'd be cutting corn.

WILLIE: Yes, I'm just sharpening some machine blades.

URI: Didn't you know I was coming today?

WILLIE: I think I was just going to have a look to see if you'd come. [*Gives him a friendly look.*] But I didn't manage. You're quicker than me.

URI: I think you're much quicker than me.

WILLIE: Yes, there's one place I'll get to before you.

URI: What's new, Dad?

WILLIE: Don't believe all you hear.

URI: You've joined up?

WILLIE: What? Oh, yes. That happens to be true.

URI: What happened, Dad?

WILLIE: Nothing . . . the blade's blunt. I'll have to sharpen it some more. [*Sharpens energetically.*]

URI: Listen, Dad, without playing the fool. Tell me what happened! Why did you join up so suddenly?

WILLIE: We'll have plenty of time to talk about it, Uri. Let me be happy with you for a while [*looks at him*]. It's simply a pleasure to look at you. A graduate of an agricultural college, eh? With a diploma and the lot?

URI: With a certificate and signature—in my pocket! Well!

WILLIE: Well what?

URI: Tell me something! What happened here. . . .

WILLIE: Things that happened slowly . . . can only be understood slowly. . . .

URI: You call this slowly? Joining up without anybody knowing anything—what's all the fuss about . . . tell me that?

WILLIE: What should I say to you? The work with the youngsters I brought from Teheran is finished. They'll be leaving us in a few days' time, but the war isn't over. That's one reason. Willie's a bit tired; he's getting a bit older. Reason number two. I decided: There's somewhere I can be of more use than in the corn fields of Gat Ha'amakim. In Europe there are enough Jews in the camps to keep Willie and a thousand like him busy! [*Answering Uri's surprised look.*] Do you really think I'm going to join the British Army? Uri—I see you don't know your father!

URI: And Mom—what does she say?

WILLIE: Your mother—that's the third reason.

URI: What?

WILLIE: Not your mother so much as our life together, doomed to loneliness. . . . The strange thing is, away from home I can live without her for years, but at home, here at home I can't stand it for one minute!

URI: What are you talking about, Dad, what are you talking about?

WILLIE: I've told you nearly everything, Uri—from now on you'll have to exert yourself a little and try to understand things for yourself.

URI: And if I won't understand—what will happen? What will I get if I understand?

WILLIE: What's wrong, Uri? What's all this excitement?

URI: I'll tell you, if you want to know. In our course, when we finished, there were two types of fellows. One type went straight to the Palmach. From the school bench—straight to the unit. No home and no kibbutz and no further studies and no security—straight to the unit! And the second type went home. Some to the farms and some to their fathers and mothers and some to help their parents and some to their girl friends, and I don't know what else. I belong to the second type. Understand? A year or six months or two years—but I wanted to be in the kibbutz a bit—to be at home for a while. And now . . .

WILLIE: And now, when you arrived—a surprise like this.

URI: I acted like a child.

WILLIE: You behaved like a sensible man, Uri—continue to act like that.

URI: When are you leaving?

WILLIE: In a few days. I'm waiting for orders.

URI: It's wrong to be too emotional. That's all!

WILLIE: Let me shake hands with you, Uri—you haven't shaken hands yet. How's the mouth organ—do you still play?

URI: When there's time.

AVRAHAM [*Enters*]: I thought he'd be here. Uri, Ruthka wants to see you. We . . . she's been looking for you all over the kibbutz.

WILLIE: Haven't you seen Mom yet, Uri?

URI: I came straight from the road. I wanted to shower first.

WILLIE: Then hurry up and go to her, you young devil. [*Gives Avraham a look which makes him walk a few paces away from the two of them.*] Wait a bit, my precious. Promise me that you won't upset her about this business—my joining up, I mean.

URI: After having upset you such a lot—I've no strength left to upset anybody else.

WILLIE: I didn't mean to imply that you upset me, but . . .

URI: It's better not to talk about it, and that's all.

WILLIE: Allow her to be happy with you—for today at least.

URI: Aren't you coming?

WILLIE: The mower's standing in the fields—waiting for blades.

URI: All right.

AVRAHAM: Are you coming, Uri? Just now she'll be busy again. [*To Willie.*] I told her he'd come—and she didn't know anything about it. She wanted to look for him in the dining hall, but I remembered he'd gone to find you. . . .

WILLIE: I'll be seeing you later, Uri. I'll try to finish work early today! [*Goes out.*]

AVRAHAM: I was afraid you'd already gone down to the fields.

URI: Where's she? In her room?

AVRAHAM: We arranged to meet in my room.

URI [*Is going out, stops*]: In your room?!

*Scene 10. In Avraham's room.*

URI [*Enters, frightening Ruthka with the suddenness of his entrance. She is busy with a kettle of water*]: Hello, Mom. . . . Everyone's scared of me today.

RUTHKA: Uri! You young devil!

URI: Someone already called me that today.

AVRAHAM [*Enters immediately after Uri*]: I found him in the machine shed.

URI: I was with Dad.

RUTHKA: You're a good child.

URI: Well, how are things, Mom?—You look tired.

RUTHKA: Really? I'll have a cup of coffee and I'll feel better.

AVRAHAM: Quite right.

RUTHKA: The water's boiled already.

AVRAHAM [*Searches in a small cupboard*]: Where did you put the cups? I can't find them. Oh, here they are! Some sugar, too.

URI: I see things have progressed at Gat Ha'amakin—an electric kettle, cups, coffee, sugar—even a radio of your own!

RUTHKA: It was a present from the District Council . . . when he ended his term as area commander. They were so grateful.

AVRAHAM: That's enough, Ruthka. It's not necessary to exaggerate.

URI: Yes, I heard something about it.

RUTHKA: Strong, Avraham?

AVRAHAM: As usual.

RUTHKA: Avraham's crazy about black coffee. What about you, Uri?

URI [*With an artificial show of interest*]: Suits me! [*After a slight pause in the conversation.*] Actually, I don't feel like drinking coffee now.

RUTHKA: Drink. It will freshen you up.

URI: I haven't showered yet. [*Gets up suddenly.*] I'll see you later, Mom. I want to have a shower first, to take clean clothes from the laundry.

AVRAHAM: Sit down and drink your coffee. The showers are terribly crowded this time of the day.

RUTHKA: I'll go to the laundry afterwards and bring you a bundle of clothes. . . .

URI: Haven't you told them to get clothes ready for me yet? It's not important. Good, then come to your room. I want to empty this kitbag.

RUTHKA: Not now, Uri. My room's all upside down, you know, with Willie's things—and here it's so quiet and peaceful. Sit a while.

URI: Have you packed his things already?

VOICE FROM OUTSIDE: Avraham, Avraham Goren!

AVRAHAM [*All attention*]: Yes? What is it?

THE VOICE: Telephone!

RUTHKA: Forget about the telephone now.

AVRAHAM: Who's it from?

THE VOICE: From the District Council. Something urgent.

AVRAHAM: All right! At once! [*To Ruthka*] Excuse me. They worry me for nothing—but discipline is discipline.

RUTHKA: Come back at once.

AVRAHAM: I'll try. [Goes out.]

URI: It seems they absolutely love him at the District Council.

RUTHKA: Probably some new job.

URI: A good-looking man.

RUTHKA: What did your father tell you?

URI: He told me . . . you know yourself what he told me.

RUTHKA: What did you say to him?

URI: What could I say?

RUTHKA: All the same—what did you say?

URI: He seems to know what he's doing.

RUTHKA: Avraham told me you were completely taken aback in the showers when you talked to Pesach.

URI: Avraham? Oh, yes! He was there!

RUTHKA: Uri . . . do you know why your father is going away?

URI: He told me something. . . .

RUTHKA: I have the feeling he didn't tell you the real reason—he's going away because he thinks it will make things easier for me.

URI: For you?

RUTHKA: For me and for Avraham.

URI: Avraham—again Avraham.

RUTHKA: You know, don't you, Uri, that lately Willie has had his own room—in one of the huts.

URI: The teacher's room?

RUTHKA: You knew about it?

URI: I know something. Something which takes away from me all desire to know more. That's enough for me.

RUTHKA: That's not good, Uri. From the moment that that's enough for you—the mistakes and errors begin.

URI: That's what they call "separation". I know. Anybody with a bit of brains could have guessed that. You're separated. I understand. I'm old enough for that.

RUTHKA: I want you to tell me exactly what's on your mind. I don't want you to be angry with anybody.

URI: I'm not angry with anybody! This is my first day at home, don't forget!

RUTHKA: All I beg of you is that you should realize that for you, in your life, nothing is changed—that . . . that to you and me, to you and Willie . . . nothing at all has happened.

URI: Very simple—we say nothing happened—so nothing happened—is that it?

RUTHKA: I know it's not so simple. Because of that I thought it better to speak to you before you'd start hearing all sorts of rumors.

URI: Mom, maybe we can stop there?

RUTHKA: All right. . . .

URI: Because if we think this thing out to the end—it can be very bad.

RUTHKA: If we don't think this out to the end—you'll reach the end in other ways, and that's much worse.

URI: Right. We'll think to the end. [*Goes to the middle of the stage.*] Dad—not here. Gone. All right. Mom's not here—all right. She has her own affairs to worry about.

RUTHKA: Uri . . .

AVRAHAM: [*Enters, goes to Ruthka*]: Didn't I tell you this is how it would end!

RUTHKA [*to Avraham*]: It couldn't have been done any other way! [*To Uri.*] Uri! . . .

URI [*Alone in the center of the stage. Behind him the silhouette of the memorial gathering starts to appear. Singing.*]: You wanted me to think till the end. All right. And now there's only one person, *one person* interfering. You've got to persuade him to be reasonable. That's a fellow called Uri.

AVRAHAM: Your obstinacy in wanting to tell him everything the first day!

RUTHKA: There was no other way!

URI [*Alone in the middle of the stage*]: All right. We'll think to the end. Dad's not here. Mom's not here. I've no friends. Here I am, left all by myself. Excellent. Legs, arms—and myself.

AVRAHAM: They telephoned from the District Council. They want to take me.

RUTHKA: Where to?

AVRAHAM: To organize the new settlement at Har Ha'ayalot.

RUTHKA: Can't they find anybody else in the whole valley?

URI: Be a good fellow and make the best of it. If you won't be a sport—they'll put your head under water for you.

AVRAHAM: The truth is—they need a man like me.

RUTHKA: A man like me! Willie was also always "a man like me," and even my little Uri—he's also "a man like me." . . .

URI: So that's that. Outside the whole kibbutz is waiting for me! I'll have a fine life, Mom? You don't think so?

RUTHKA: Everyone's for himself. Everyone has his own troubles—and a woman like me? What's left for a woman like me?

URI: I'll be all right, Mom! You needn't worry about me. I'll find myself a tent to live in. I'll find some decent work. I'll find a girl—don't worry. I'll fix up my life beautifully!

*Scene 11. In the courtyard of the settlement near the tents of the youth group.*

*Mika is washing.* URI *enters with a kitbag over his shoulder.*

URI [*Seeing Mika leave the tap half-open and walk off without her towel*]: Hey, listen!

MIKA [*On the offensive*]: My name's not listen, it's Mika.

URI: What?

MIKA: My name is Miriam, and my friends call me Mika.

URI: Pleased to meet you. My name is Uri, and my friends call me Uri.

MIKA: *The* Uri? Impossible—you don't fit the description.

URI: Look, my child, you certainly make an impression. . . . But allow me to tell you that . . .

MIKA: What?

URI: That at Gat Ha'amakim you don't leave taps half-open.

MIKA: No? I thought you did.

URI: Excuse me, but I spoke in earnest.

MIKA: Yes? I thought you didn't.

URI [*Laughs despite himself, then*]: But after all the wisecracks—the tap still has to be closed.

MIKA: O.K., I'll go and close it.

URI: Don't bother. I can do it myself. [*The two practically collide with one another next to the tap. After a hesitant silence.*] I thought the youth group went on a hike.

MIKA: I didn't feel like going.

URI: A hike—and you didn't feel like going? You don't know what you missed. How long have you been in the country?

MIKA: Nearly two years already. I came with Willie, with the group from Teheran—but in the beginning I stayed with my relations—in town. You're Willie's son, aren't you?

URI: They say so.

MIKA: You're more like your mother. In your eyes, perhaps a bit like Willie.

URI: It seems I'm made up of two pieces put together.

MIKA [*Laughs*]: So strange that Willie should have such a big son. A pity he's going. . . .

URI: Mmmm. . . .

MIKA: Our crowd—all those he brought from overseas—simply couldn't live here without Willie. We still need him.

URI: It seems they need him more somewhere else.

MIKA: Who knows? [*BIBERMAN enters*].

BIBERMAN [*Blankets, a box, paper and pencil in his hand. Strikes out the items as he speaks*]: A bed I've arranged for you, blankets you've got. Sheets you haven't got yet. No chair. Meanwhile you can use this box. A lamp you haven't got. No oil . . . well, you're all fixed up.

URI: I've no complaints. In time we'll arrange the rest.

BIBERMAN [*Continues on his way. URI stops*]: When I complain to the general meeting that it's impossible to make ends meet on the miserable budget they give me, they say . . . Aren't you going to the dining hall?

URI: No. I want to get to know my new surroundings.

BIBERMAN: Shalom, Mika. [*To Uri.*] Maybe I'll find some candles for you for tonight. . . . [*Goes out.*]

MIKA: Have you chosen your tent already?

URI: Not yet.

MIKA: Don't you intend to stay here?

URI: Sure I do.

MIKA: Then it's worthwhile getting a decent tent. There'll be some free soon. We're leaving.

URI: Yes. I heard so. [*Sits down, takes a mouth organ from his pocket.*] I arrive—and everyone starts leaving. [*Plays note or two on the mouth organ.*]

MIKA: Do you play the mouth organ?

URI: No. I eat it. [*Plays a short tune.*]

MIKA: I used to play the piano.

URI: Really? [*Starts playing softly, and doesn't stop.*]

MIKA: But for years I haven't been near a piano. The work in the kitchen ruins one's hands. Where will you work? . . . I suppose with the tractors . . . like your father. I know you can play the mouth organ well—now you can stop for a minute. Where's my towel? Here! Have you eaten already? The sabras don't know what manners are. Couldn't you possibly stop playing when someone talks to you? [*Snatches the mouth organ from his hand.*]

URI: Hey, give me back the mouth organ.

MIKA: And if not?

URI: I'll take it.

MIKA: Just try. [*He gets up and chases her. She runs off-stage throwing the mouth organ behind her.*]

URI [*Picks up the mouth organ. Smiles*]: Hey, listen!

*Scene 12.*

KIBBUTZNIK [*Enters with soft steps, like someone who doesn't want to intrude*]: In the main vineyard, you know where it is, on the slope of the hill, there is a packing shed covered with vines. At night the watchmen are careful not to go inside . . . it's occupied . . . in the orange grove, you know, a week after it's been watered, the ground is soft, cool, and dry leaves rustle under your body. . . .

Uri paid little attention to the changes taking place around him. Willie left, and his first letters came in a green army envelope. He saw Ruthka only at supper. The world was empty and free and infinitely wide, and every day Uri and Mika succeeded in finding a new hiding place—in the vineyard, in the orange grove, in the paths of the forest. One Shabbat they went for a long hike, up the rise of the dry riverbed, as far as the area of the springs. . . .

*Scene 13. Trees beside the spring.*

URI [*Still off-stage*]: Mika, a spring!

MIKA: Who'll get there first? [*Both appear, running. At the last moment* URI *draws ahead of Mika, pushes her aside and sprints to the spring.*] Uri!

URI [*Makes a place for her beside him*]: Sorry.

MIKA: I'm dying of thirst.

URI: Go ahead—the whole spring's at your service.

MIKA: But . . . how can I drink from it?

URI: As usual—on all fours.

MIKA: Sorry, I'm not yet used to it.

URI: You'll have to get used to it! Hold on, I've got an idea. [*Removes his hat, brushes and cleans it, then dips it in the water and hands it, full, to Mika.*] Now hurry without wasting time.

MIKA: Terrific, Uri! Careful, don't wet yourself.

URI: [*As she drinks*]: I'm past that age.

MIKA [*Finishes, returns the hat*]: Enough. Now it's your turn.

URI: What's that? Good idea. I'm going to finish the spring. [*Kneels and drinks for a long time without looking up.*]

MIKA [*Starts getting worried. Shakes him*]:Uri! Uri!

URI [*Lifts up his head*]: Let me drink, what's wrong with you? [*Resumes drinking.* MIKA *goes off by herself, sits on one of the rocks. When* URI *rises, she sighs.*]

MIKA: Ouf—that was quite a run!

URI: [*Sits beside her*]: Want to eat something?

MIKA: Nothing.

URI: Really nothing? Well, we'll see. [*Lifts out of his bag.*] Do you want Kelsey plums? Satsuma? Beiruti grapes, bread, sardines? A penknife? Don't you want a penknife? Yesterday's newspaper? Very tasty. . . . No? Some halva?

MIKA [*With genuine disgust*]: Pooh, don't remind me of that.

URI: What musn't I remind you about—halva?

MIKA: Stop it, Uri.

URI: Oh, halva, did you say? And what do you have against halva? Why? halva . . .

MIKA: Pooh, horrible! On the ship . . . all the way, they gave it to us five times a day. I supposed they didn't have anything else. Persian halva, a horrible brown color, like . . . ugh, I can't even look at the stuff.

URI: What's the use, Mika—you don't know what's good. You simply have no idea.

MIKA: Give me something really good—and you'll see.

URI: For that you'll have to turn round.

MIKA: What?

URI: Face the other way. [*She does so, and receives a kiss.*] How're things, baby?

MIKA: First class! [*Sits thinking.*] I've forgotten so many things. Today is a study day for our youth group. The first time I've missed a study day. The first time I've forgotten that I belong to a youth group. I've forgotten that there's a kibbutz in the world—that there's a world at all . . . [*Noticing* URI, *who is eating energetically.*] Uri . . .

URI [*Mouth full*]: Mmmm?

MIKA: What . . . [*Silence.*] By the way, what about your tent?

URI: All right.

MIKA: What's all right?

URI: It'll be all right.

MIKA: Oh—it *will* be all right.

URI: It'll have to be all right. Biberman said it would be all right.

MIKA: Biberman is the funniest kibbutznik I know.

URI: I've no complaints against him. But I have complaints against the work list. To this day they haven't put me to work on a tractor—isn't that a scandal of the first order? How long can a person put up with picking grapes? The first day it's romantic, the second day you sing, the third day you play the fool—and after that?

MIKA: Work doesn't worry me so much, but a room! It's an absolute joy to have a room of one's own. You can do exactly what you please. . . . I'd hang up some pictures—not many—but big ones, beautiful ones.

URI: Pesach said: In the season you'll be given a tractor to work with, now you can help to finish the grape harvest. But the tractor drivers want me; the tractor drivers themselves . . .

MIKA: And a cupboard with a curtain, not with doors but with a curtain. It's much more attractive. And a vase full of flowers. . . .

URI: But I know Pesach, until I finish the grape harvest I'm wasting my time dreaming about a tractor. He has other problems. . . .

MIKA: And a covering for the bed, embroidered. Even with simple tastes you can make some lovely things.

URI: I see that this doesn't interest you very much!

MIKA: What?

URI: The tractor.

MIKA: I thought we were talking about the room.

URI: What do you want a room for? The whole world belongs to you. Listen—what's on your mind?

MIKA: Come here, idiot. I'm dead. [*Rests her head in his lap.*] How far did we walk today?

URI: Not far. Maybe ten kilometers.

MIKA: It was wonderful looking down from the top of the Carmel. Gat

Ha'amakin is so charming when you look down on it from above. [*URI smiles.*] What are you smiling about?

URI: It struck me that you're also very charming . . . from above.

MIKA: Where from?

URI: Come to think of it—from all angles.

MIKA: That's better.

URI: In a bad mood, Mika?

MIKA: A bit. I was thinking about the meeting of my youth group. Yesterday—no, the day before yesterday . . .

URI: Finding yourself memories!

MIKA: You don't know what happened there.

URI: I don't have to know. Well, have they decided finally when you're leaving? I heard that you're going to some place in the Jordan Valley.

MIKA: They are.

URI: What do you mean, they?

MIKA: They—my youth group—they're moving to the Jordan Valley.

URI: And you?

MIKA: I've left them. I told them yesterday. No—the day before yesterday—that I'm not going with them.

URI: What will you do? [*Noticing Mika's silence.*] Wait, if you're not going—then you're staying. Very simple . . . at Gat Ha'amakim. [*To himself.*] Idiot! Tell me again.

MIKA: I'm staying.

URI: And what will happen if you stay?

MIKA: We'll see.

URI: Do you want another kiss?

MIKA: We'll see.

URI [*Picks her up and puts her down next to him*]: The whole day I've been trying this and rehearsing that, and turning here and hinting there, but didn't have the couarge to tell you, and now—at the last moment—when she's already *said* it—he doesn't understand. [*Kisses her.*] Say something.

MIKA: We'll see.

URI: Stop that "we'll see" business.

MIKA: [*Picks up a piece of wood from the ground*]: Move over.

URI: What happened?

MIKA: I want to write something.

URI: What do you want to write?

MIKA: We'll see.

URI: M-I . . .

MIKA: I want to write Miriam Cahana on the ground. Mika Cahana. And next to that Uri Cahana, and next to that Willie Cahana, and below that Gat Ha'amakim, and below that—the Valley of Jezreel, and beside that, at the end . . .

*Scene 14. Peeling potatoes in the kitchen.*

FIRST PEELER: What do you think of our Uri?

SECOND PEELER: Quite a lad! Less than a month at home, and already wants a family room.

FIRST: What starts quickly ends quickly.

SECOND: What do you mean by that?

FIRST: She's not the girl for him.

SECOND: In which way?

FIRST: Firstly, psychologically.

SECOND: That's all? Then it's nothing.

FIRST: Here no one knows her. But I know that according to her experience she could be his mother. . . . What she's seen and what she's gone through already in her short life—he'll never see and never know. They say that Willie took her out from . . . [*Whispers something to her companion.*] Really, yes, yes . . . he saved many like her. And the boys, they weren't much better.

SECOND: They say she's changed for the better.

FIRST: I wish that was true! But beside her Uri is a child. The first girl he met—and she already turned his head. She's an expert in that. She has experience . . . ho-ho . . . more than both of us together.

SECOND: You're sure she's turning his head? Maybe he's turning hers?

FIRST: Uri? That infant?

SECOND: Yesterday an infant and today a man.

FIRST: She could hold three men like that under her thumb at one time.

SECOND: Why do you make her out to be such a monster?

FIRST: I don't like her. . . . I hoped our Uri would find someone else. [*Holds the basin with the peeled potatoes between her two thumbs and goes out.*]

*Scene 15. In the grain store.*

BIBERMAN [*Loading a sack of grain with the help of* PESACH *onto a low open cart hitched to a tractor*]: At this rate we'll never finish the sowing in time.

PESACH: I'll put Uri on to a tractor this week to help out.

BIBERMAN: He'll be very happy about that.

PESACH: And what about the room? Have you arranged anything for him yet?

BIBERMAN: He's not sleeping outside yet. Let's have some patience.

PESACH: When a boy and a girl want a family room, Biberman—it's a sign that there's no more patience left.

BIBERMAN: And that's just what I don't like. This haste shows something isn't right. It's better we should give them a chance to weigh the matter.

PESACH: I think you'll only increase their nervousness—and especially Uri's. The boy's absolutely eaten up inside—anyone can see that.

BIBERMAN: Are you telling me?

PESACH: The speed of the hands is greater than the speed of the heart, that's all the trouble. The clock outside is running fast, and the clock inside is slow.

BIBERMAN: What can we do? [*Moves the cart.*] I'll come at once for some more sacks.

PESACH: Good. And arrange a room for them—do you hear?

*Scene 16. In the laundry.*

RUTHKA [*Checks the pile of clothes lying on the table*]: You've given him enough clothes to last him for a year.

GITA: When one of our members goes away for a while, I don't want him to be ashamed of his kibbutz.

AVRAHAM: I'm only going for a short time—until they are settled on the land. I think their two tractors have arrived already.

GITA: Wait a minute. Show me what you still need.

AVRAHAM: I rely on you.

GITA: Never trust a woman. See if Avraham's name appears on the towels. Do you have handkerchiefs?

RUTHKA: He has handkerchiefs—I've seen some.

GITA: And socks?

RUTHKA: I don't think so.

AVRAHAM [*Looks in parcel*]: None here.

GITA: Wait a minute—I'll bring you some right away [*Goes out.*]

RUTHKA: When you come home on Shabat don't forget to bring things for washing.

AVRAHAM [*With sudden warmth*]: The moment the first hut will be up, Ruthka—you'll join me.

RUTHKA: But first you must come on Shabat.

AVRAHAM [*Clasps her hands*]: I'll come, don't worry.

RUTHKA: The truth is that I'm worried. Things are happening too quickly for me. They were talking about you not going after all—and now we're already speaking about you coming home once a week. What will we speak about tomorrow? And my Uri worries me more than ever. Have you heard the news?

AVRAHAM: I've heard about it.

RUTHKA: And it doesn't frighten you?

AVRAHAM: Me?

RUTHKA: Before you'll have time to look to the left and to the right—I'll be a grandmother. [*AVRAHAM laughs.*]

URI [*Enters*]: Shalom, Where's Gita?

RUTHKA: She'll come just now.

URI [*To Avraham*]: Two tractor drivers are looking for you outside.

AVRAHAM: What—are they here already? [*To Ruthka.*] Bring me the socks, will you, Ruthka?

RUTHKA: All right.

AVRAHAM [*As he passes Uri*]: Oh, there's a telegram for you.

URI: A telegram?

AVRAHAM: You can get it at the office.

URI: Right. [*AVRAHAM goes out.*]

RUTHKA: How're things, Uri?

URI [*Takes a letter from his pocket*]: I've had a letter from Dad. [*Offers it to her.*] And you?

RUTHKA: Not yet. Does he know already?

URI: Know what?

RUTHKA: About you . . . and Mika.

URI: I haven't written to him. [*See RUTHKA hesitating whether to take the letter or not.*] He sends regards to you at the end. The letter's for you too.

RUTHKA: You should write to your father. He knows her. He was her teacher.

URI: Do you think teachers know the children they are in charge of?

RUTHKA: I think so.

URI: Like parents knowing their sons. You don't like her, do you?

RUTHKA: You have a gift for saying things in the most cruel way.

URI: Look, Mom—if you want to say something about me—please use clearer language.

RUTHKA: You don't know one another well enough.

URI: And after we've known one another for twenty years—will we be an ideal couple? Will we be immune to all surprises?

RUTHKA: [*Hurt and restrained*]: Why don't you try to do better than we did, Uri?

URI: Not better than you and not worse than you, and I don't want to compete with anybody. I'm myself and that's all there is to it.

RUTHKA: Are you angry because I'm interfering too much in your life?

URI: It's your right. [*Silence.* URI *calls to Gita.*] Have you Shabbat clothes for me, Gita?

GITA: Who's that? Uri? [*Enters.*] Yes, the bundle's ready. Where is Avraham?

RUTHKA: We must still talk about it, Uri.

URI: [*To* GITA, *who is handing him the bundle*]: And Mika's bundle—is it ready?

GITA: Yes. Here it is.

URI: I'll take it also. . . . [*Goes out hastily holding both bundles.*]

RUTHKA: As soon as I get near him, he curls up like a porcupine and puts out his quills.

GITA: And perhaps he really loves her?

RUTHKA: If he really loves her, why is he in such a hurry?

*Scene 17. In Uri's tent.*

URI *enters holding two parcels. Holds out a piece of paper to* MIKA, *who is sitting combing her hair. While she is reading the note, he finds a place to put the parcels.*

MIKA [*Reading the note*]: What does it mean?

URI: How should I know?

MIKA: Today?

URI: Wait for me until Sunday. Nothing urgent.

MIKA: Who do you think it's from?

URI: From the unit. I suppose from Ginger.

MIKA: Who's Ginger?

URI: He was in charge of my course . . . one of the boys.

MIKA: Do they want to take you?

URI: Maybe.

MIKA: That's all we need.

URI: Sufficient unto the day is the evil thereof. I spoke to Biberman. We'll be getting a room this week, . . . Aren't you pleased?

MIKA: Yes, of course!—But I thought it would be different.

URI: Different? How?

MIKA: Everything . . . different . . .

URI: Do you miss the rabbi? Or perhaps a table with cakes? A long white dress? White shoes? The parents next to the bridegroom . . . the parents next to the bride . . . and the band? Mainly the cakes, isn't that so? . . . What's wrong with you, Mika—crying? Mika . . .

MIKA: Where are my hairpins?

URI [*Collects them from the bed*]: Here!

MIKA [*Smoothes down her hair. Rises*]: If at least your parents lived with us. We're so alone, so deserted . . .

URI: Lonely and deserted . . . in the middle of the kibbutz? What are you talking about, Mika?

MIKA: Alone and abandoned within the kibbutz. Yes! Perhaps you don't feel like that. But I . . . the last few days they look at me as if I've stolen something from them.

URI: You're imagining things—nightmares.

MIKA: And you haven't noticed it, Uri? The whole kibbutz has to love me before they can agree that one of their boys should love me. That's how it is with them. I have to *prove* myself first. To be good enough to be welcomed into this important family . . . Gat Ha'amakim!

URI: Excuse me, Mika, but you're talking nonsense.

MIKA: Either you're lying or else you're blind.

URI: You don't know what a kibbutz is.

MIKA: I don't know. No! If you'd brought back with you some girl more your type—from one of the kibbutzim—how many days would it take for Biberman to find you a room? How many? And do you think I'm deaf? And haven't I enough sense to understand digs and hints? And don't I see how your mother behaves?

URI: I don't understand you, Mika. I don't understand you.

MIKA: Because you're a good fellow, Uri. [*Picks up her bundle.*] But I'm not so good . . . I have a past, and it's chasing me all the time—here in this place where I hoped to be rid of it—to forget it! Here, of all places—here they won't let me forget anything—anything . . .

URI: Where are you going to now?

MIKA: To put the bundle in my tent.

URI: This is your tent.

MIKA: This is the room they gave us?

URI: This is the room we're taking for ourselves.

MIKA: It's better we should wait till they give it to us.

URI: I'm tired of waiting. . . .

MIKA: Leave me, Uri, don't be so wild!

URI: I'm not as good a boy as you thought I was. Put your bundle on the chair.

MIKA: You're creasing my things, Uri.

URI: Your eyes are still a bit wet.

MIKA: Wait a bit. You don't know what you're doing. . . .

URI: We've stopped waiting. . . .

MIKA: I'm frightened, Uri, I'm frightened. . . .

*Scene 18. In the courtyard outside Uri's tent.*

KIBBUTZNIK [*Closes the flaps of the tent*]: But the man who hurried at this moment along the road to Gat Ha'amakim wanted something else. His power was greater than the power of one love. It was the power of our time. Yes. Those days which tore Willie's life to shreds, the days which tossed Ruthka into the storm, the days which left Mika lonely and forlorn under the heavens—these days did not halt before the doors of Uri's tent. In the early hours of the morning the man who was on his way arrived.

*Scene 19. In the same place.*

GINGER [*Enters, knocks with his stick on the tent flaps*]: Uri, Hey, Uri. Uri Cahana. [*URI's groans are heard from inside the tent.*] Are you still alive? Get up—you've got visitors.

URI [*Comes out of the tent, half asleep*]: Who's that? *Ginger!!* Is that you or just a nightmare?

GINGER [*Strikes him playfully*]: Wake up—then you'll know.

URI: Where did you spring from?

GINGER: From the rich and fertile fields of Ein Yosef. Well said?

URI: First-class.

GINGER: How're you?

URI: Feeling better.

GINGER: Better than what?

URI: Better you don't ask.

GINGER: Did you get my telegram?

URI: I got it, I believe.

GINGER: Then why, I believe—didn't you come?

URI: Were you serious?

GINGER: Where are you living, child? Haven't you heard the news?

URI: I haven't heard a thing.

GINGER: The unit's going into action, friend. We're getting the boys together. We're setting up new companies.

URI: I'm waking up slowly.

GINGER: I suggest you do that quickly. If Ginger's in the saddle—it's a sign we're riding hard. Well said?

URI: Not bad. So what's happening?

GINGER: It's my job to get a new company together in two weeks, and to recruit section leaders anywhere and anyhow—and you're on my list, my boy.

URI: Have you a base already?

GINGER: Ein Yosef itself, no less. A storeroom full of tents is waiting for us. Tomorrow the first people will be arriving. I'm taking you with me tonight.

URI: What else?

GINGER: No time for discussions.

URI: Impossible.

GINGER: What's wrong? Are you a proud father already?

URI: Yes, of half a dozen.

GINGER: A wife? That's all I need.

URI: No, but it's impossible like this— so hastily. We must get permission from the kibbutz.

GINGER: We'll get their permission after you'll be with us already.

URI: There's a recruiting quota and a list. My mother, for example, will go crazy. She'll never agree.

GINGER: Then tell her, for example, that she shouldn't go crazy.

URI: It's no good unless the kibbutz agrees.

GINGER: Do you imagine I'm going to start discussing the matter now with secretaries and nursemaids and committees? Do you know where you're going to, my boy? Without the Palmach there'd be no kibbutz and no anything else either. You take the boys out for training, and after two months you're already in action—in the battlefield. The whole of Palestine is boiling, it's just a battle front—hell, and you come with your discussions.

URI: It's not simple all the same.

GINGER: Listen, the question's a simple one. Are you prepared or aren't you? You, I mean—you by yourself?

URI: Of course!

GINGER: Then that's that! Tell them this: the Bible says—that all a man needs is three things—good friends, good food, and good fighting. Well said?

URI: Hundred percent.

GINGER: So—tonight?

URI: What about tonight?

GINGER: Between eight and nine—wait for me by the gate. I'll go past in my truck and pick you up.

URI: Out of the question. It's impossible to get up and go like that.

GINGER: It's the only way, my friend. They won't have time to cry on your shoulder.

URI: No one's crying on my shoulder.

GINGER: Your mother and your piece. What's her name—Noa, Haviva, Leika?

URI: Go to hell.

GINGER: You're right—I'm going. [*Goes out.*]

URI: Hey, Ginger . . . wait a minute. Have some breakfast. Let's talk about it.

GINGER [*From off-stage*]: Between eight and nine at the gate.

BIBERMAN [*Enters from the other side*]: Good morning, Uri! [*With obvious happiness.*]

URI: Good morning. What's the occasion?

BIBERMAN: Is Mika working today?

URI: No. She's still sleeping.

MIKA [*Pokes her head out between the tent flaps*]: No, I'm not sleeping.

BIBERMAN: Did I wake you?

MIKA: No. I've been awake for some time.

URI: Did you hear?

MIKA: I heard everything.

BIBERMAN: I've good news for the two of you.

MIKA: Someone got here before you.

BIBERMAN: Really? You know already that you're getting a room? Excellent! You can move in tomorrow!

*Scene 20.*

KIBBUTZNIK: Between eight and nine, at the gate. Night comes quickly in the country, and the sky here, you know, starts right over your head. Sometimes you can't be sure: that light—there—is it a window or a star? Will it go out suddenly—or glow till dawn? . . . A star has just disappeared. A tired kibbutznik has gone to sleep. And here—between eight and nine.

*Scene 21. Beside the gate. Night.*

*URI and MIKA are sitting. A WATCHMAN enters.*

WATCHMAN: Who's that?

URI: Uri.

MIKA: Mika.

WATCHMAN [*Confused*]: What? All right. Heavy dew tonight. [*To Uri,*] Have you got a match?

URI [*Takes it out of his pocket and gives it to him*]: What are these tractors doing here?

WATCHMAN: Avraham's taking them to Har Ha'ayalot. It'll take them till morning . . . [*Starts to move away.*]

URI: I'm starting to feel sorry for my mother, so help me . . . listen, if she asks you . . . I told her it's only a matter of a week or two. . . .

MIKA: And what shall I do with your things, Uri?

URI: What things? [*Pats his kitbag.*] All my wordly goods are here. I went into an empty tent, and I left behind me an empty tent.

MIKA: As if you hadn't been here at all.

URI: Possessions aren't everything, Mika.

MIKA: But they're something.

URI: We have a room now.

MIKA: We?

URI: I want you take your things to our room tomorrow.

MIKA: When you come back.

URI: They won't keep the room for you till I come back.

MIKA: What can we do?

URI: What can we do—move over to the room and live in it and wait till I come back.

MIKA: I'll wait in my tent.

URI: I don't understand you, Mika. I don't understand you.

MIKA: Perhaps we really aren't suited to one another—as people say.

URI: Damn . . . you're just in a bad mood . . .

MIKA: No. In fact I'm very happy. Play a polka . . . let's dance a bit . . .

URI: I'm game . . . [*Plays a tune, and* MIKA *covers her face with her hand.*]

MIKA: Stop it. You're making me nervous!

URI: If you don't accustom yourself to be a bit stronger, Mika, to get less nervous and less emotionally upset, it'll be very hard for you to live in this country.

MIKA: I don't want to be a heroine! I've had enough! For years—I've been like a piece of iron, like stone. . . . "Don't get excited, Mika," I used to say to myself, "Don't get nervous" . . . I can't do it any more, . . . I didn't come here for the whole business to start all over again, . . . I've had more than my fair share of troubles. Now I want to be weak, weak. . . .

URI: I think you've got the wrong address—that's my impression.

MIKA: The wrong address?

URI: Gat Ha'amakim—that's the wrong address for being weak.

MIKA: It's the only address I have.

URI: That's what I think. Listen, Mika . . . I understand you . . . A few minutes before our parting . . . but tomorrow morning you'll wake up in a different mood. Biberman will show you the room, and you'll start fixing it up . . .

MIKA: There's nothing to speak about, Uri. I won't go into the room without you.

URI: Are you trying to put pressure on me, Mika?

MIKA: You don't owe me anything, Uri. I want you to be quite clear on that point. You don't owe me anything.

URI: I want to have a room at home—a family room.

MIKA: I know, Uri, I believe you.

URI: Does it help me if you believe me?

MIKA: Stay here.

URI: What?

MIKA: Stay for a month . . . for a fortnight . . . but don't go now.

URI: And so—that's what you want?

MIKA: No, Uri. What I want—that's much more. But I'm prepared to be satisfied with just a little . . . with a drop. . . .

URI: You want me to tell you now that I'm not going?

MIKA: It depends on you.

URI: Tell me what you want?

MIKA: Don't shout—good?

URI: You drive me crazy sometimes. Tell me what you want. Talk straight. What do you want?

MIKA: I want a house which I'll never have to leave. You understand? With big stones . . . with thick walls. I want to get some fun out of life. I want quiet—for myself and it's not much—because once I wanted much more. . . .

URI: In short—you want me not to join up. You want my father to be in Italy and twenty members of the kibbutz in twenty other places, and the boys of my age in the units and in action and in prison, and I don't know where else—and me in some damn hut with pictures on the wall, a curtain—and someone from the youth group . . .

MIKA [*Jumps up*]: I don't want anything! [*An approaching vehicle is heard.*]

URI [*Holds her*]: Mika—say goodbye like a good girl. [*The toot of a horn.*]

MIKA: Leave me alone!

URI: Is that how we're going to part? What are we—children?

MIKA: It seems like it! [*Horn.* GINGER*'s voice:* "Uri, hey, Uri!"] Go, he's calling you.

URI: I want you to say goodbye to me.

MIKA: I don't want him to see me. [*Slips out of Uri's hands.*]

URI: Mika! [*She disappears in the direction of the settlement.*]

CRIES FROM GINGER: Uri, what's happening?

URI: I'm coming! [*Opens the gate and goes to the road.*]

PESACH [*Enters*]: Who's that?

KIBBUTZNIK: Me. Where are we going?

PESACH: To the cauliflowers. The nights are getting darker.

KIBBUTZNIK: Have there been thefts?

PESACH: We have to be on guard. It'll be cold.

KIBBUTZNIK: Yes, it'll be cold tonight.

PESACH: And heavy dew. First-class for the vegetables.

KIBBUTZNIK: And the corn.

PESACH: Of course, of course!

KIBBUTZNIK: Why are the tractors working so late?

PESACH: They're not ours. Those are the four that Avraham's taking to Har Ha'ayalot tonight. Soon you'll hear them moving. It's hard on her.

KIBBUTZNIK: Ruthka's in love with him.

PESACH: Well, he's a good fellow. But he's no match for Willie.

KIBBUTZNIK: By the way, what does Willie write?

PESACH: How should I know? They've been transferred to Egypt. . . . Do you feel the wind?

KIBBUTZNIK: From the wadi. You can smell the oleanders.

PESACH: And the dead camels. . . . [*Soft, silent laughter.*]

KIBBUTZNIK: Well, suppose we'd better move.

PESACH: A fine night. I wish I could sleep a little. Alone all the night.

KIBBUTZNIK: Sleep, my friend. That's the best way to do guard duty. An honest thief doesn't steal from a sleeping watchman.

PESACH: Of course—what would be the point? A man sleeps—and you trick him. Be seeing you.

KIBBUTZNIK: Good night. Careful, there's a hole there.

PESACH: All right. It's about time someone fixed it up. [*Disappears.*]

## ACT 2

*Scene 1. Silhouette of memorial gathering. Kibbutznik beside it.*

KIBBUTZNIK: Two months have passed. . . . That shed in the vineyard is strewn with autumn leaves. The vines have become tinted with gold. Their leaves have fallen. . . . The days are still hot, but at night you can feel the autumn chill. . . . In the clothing store Gita has begun to check the winter blankets. Mika has begun to light the paraffin lamps in her tent, and after work she is seen only at mealtimes. . . . The lengthened evening hours have brought with them sad thoughts. . . . But who had time for these? The country was boiling over. British tanks ruled the roads. In narrow paths along country lanes units drilled, platoons marched and files of men prepared for action. In tents, in huts, in woods—beside the sea, over the face of the whole country—Palmach camps sprang up. [*The picture of the Palmach camp at Ein Yosef begins to appear.*] The arms were still hidden in secret caches, but from time to time dark figures went down to the orchards, dug up the guns and the boxes of hand grenades, and loaded them under vegetables or bales of straw. The units were hidden away, the people were hidden away—but the spirit of the people could not be hidden away. It burst out every now and then in the full flood of youthful joy—as in the evening when the members of Uri's unit celebrated the end of their training—their first leave.

*Scene 2. Palmach camp at Ein Yosef.*

*At the end of the stage on the right, the headquarters tent, and inside it, Ginger, Uri, and Dinahle. The remainder of the stage, tents and a parade ground ready for a party. Wood for a camp fire, etc. Members of Uri's unit sitting and singing. Conversation heard in between the songs.*

RAFI [*To Danda*]: What are they waffling about, do you know?

DANDA: How should I know what's going on inside Ginger's head?

RAFI: Even sergeants aren't allowed to listen.

DANDA: Pride hurt?

RAFI: Doesn't worry me.

[*From the sides:* Shhh . . . sh . . . *In the headquarters tent.*]

GINGER: Have you got a list of your equipment, Uri?

URI: Yes.

GINGER: Let's see it. [*While URI looks in the box underneath his bed, GINGER addresses Dinahle.*] What's the position with your stuff?

DINAHLE: O.K.

GINGER: Have you got plaster and bandages for the first aid kits?

DINAHLE: Enough for a hundred.

GINGER: That's enough. [*To Uri.*] Well?

URI [*Starts reading*]: Guns—ten. Five being repaired.

GINGER: Give me the list. I've learned how to read. [*They bend over the list. Outside, among the crowd, the joy grows greater and greater. Everybody sings; the boys joke with the girls, and above all the noise the cry is heard:* "Tomorrow we're going on leave! Long live leave!" *Soon the general noise resolves into a sort of duet between a solo voice and a choir.*]

SOLO [*In a loud voice, almost singing*]: Where are we going to?

CHOIR: On leave!

SOLO: What do we like?

CHOIR: Leave!

SOLO: What's tomorrow?

CHOIR: Leave!

SOLO: When shall we sleep all day?

CHOIR: On leave!

SOLO: We're going home.

CHOIR: On leave!

[*The scene changes to the headquarters' tent.*]

GINGER [*Slowly, coolly*]: The leave's canceled, of course. But when we are back from the job, we'll give all the boys a day's leave, free—a present from the Palmach.

URI: We owe it to them.

GINGER: As the company nurse, Dinahle, you'll have to see that your officers won't be too upset when they hear we're going into action.

URI: Speak plainly, Ginger—to the point.

GINGER [*To Uri, straight from the shoulder*]: O.K.—to the point. We're all happy—all crazy with joy—pleased as Punch that at last we've got a real job to pull off! Understand?

URI: Who do you think you're talking to?

GINGER: To anybody who's moaning about leave being canceled.

URI: Go right ahead.

GINGER: O.K. The need for silence is plain to you. We'll take your unit as far as . . . as far as Gat Ha'amakim. But don't get any bright ideas, Uri. We'll put you down several kilometers from the kibbutz. It's better that you don't meet anybody, and that no one knows your movements. Clear? And complete silence—understand? You'll go straight into the hills. At Har Ha'yalot you can rest and fill up with water.

URI: There's no water there.

GINGER: There is now. [*Singing starts from outside.*] At night you'll be able to travel over the last part of the mountains and reach the coast . . .

DINAHLE: Where to?

GINGER: That I'll tell you when you leave—as soon as I'll know myself. The orders to move into action will be given to you just before the job's due to start. All clear?

URI: Yes. Can I tell the boys the leave's canceled?

GINGER: Leave them alone now. I don't want to dampen their spirits. When it's time I'll call a parade. Go out and enjoy yourselves with them. I still have some things to fix up here and then I have to contact headquarters. You're free. . . . [*They rise to go. They stop.*] You understand that silence must be observed? [*Outside the singing grows stronger. Everyone is sitting around the campfire and singing.*]

SEMYON [*Enters with a haversack on his shoulder*]: Goodbye, everybody, be seeing you.

RAFI: Hey, Semyon. Where are your legs going to?

SEMYON: To wherever legs will go.

RAFI: Aren't you staying for the party?

SEMYON: Leave me alone. It's no joke.

DANDA: What happened, Semyon?

SEMYON: What happened has happened.

URI [*Comes up to him*]: Where are you off to, Semyon?

SEMYON: We've got leave, haven't we?

URI: No one's yet been given permission to leave the camp.

SEMYON: I have to be in town.

URI: What do you have to do in town?

SEMYON: I had a letter that . . . my girl, my wife . . . she's in the hospital, and I'm worried.

DINAHLE: Have you got a wife, Semyon? And we didn't even know.

SEMYON: Shhhhh . . . I don't want to spoil the party. Goodbye.

URI: One minute. You can't go.

SEMYON: But . . .

URI: No buts.

SEMYON: What you mean, no buts? There *is* a but.

DINAHLE: Let him speak to Ginger, Uri.

URI: All right, let him talk.

SEMYON: Where's he?

DINAHLE: Wait till he comes. And don't worry now. Come sit with us.

[*They join the singing crowd. The singing grows stronger for some time. Then:*]

ONE OF THE CROWD: Uri, let's have a polka.

RAFI: Leave him alone. Can't you see he's thinking?

ANOTHER MEMBER OF THE CROWD: Shame. He'll be without us for three days. Who will he be able to boss now?

ANOTHER MEMBER OF THE CROWD: Uri, take out your mouth organ and show us what sort of man you are.

ALL TOGETHER [*Chanting*]: Uri's playing a polka. Uri's playing a polka. We're all agreed . . . Uri . . .

URI [*Rises. Takes out the mouth organ and starts playing. The crowd dances around him.* DINAHLE *invites him to dance, and he dances one round with her while continuing to play. Then stops dancing.*]

DINAHLE: You aren't exactly helping me to carry out orders. [*URI continues to play while she is talking, but it is obvious that he listens and reacts to her words.*] The Company Commander gave an order for me to cheer you up. . . . What's wrong, Uri. What's happened? Missing somebody? A girl perhaps? *You,* Uri? It's hard to believe. The girls say you have a wall around your heart. Isn't that so? They're always discussing whether you have a girl or not. . . . Do you? A few girls? How many? [*URI plays on, holding the mouth organ in his mouth and showing with his hands that he has many girls.* DINAHLE *laughs.*] Come dance! [*URI dances another round with her.*]

SEMYON [*Approaches and taps Uri lightly on the shoulder*]: Where's Nahum? He's not in the tent.

URI: I told you to wait till he comes.

DINAHLE: He'll come just now, Semyon. Don't be nervous.

RAFI: Boys—the coffee's ready! Where are the cups?

DINAHLE: Drink some coffee, Semyon, it's good for you. [*SEMYON crosses to the other side of the campfire. URI and DINAHLE go into the headquarters tent. URI opens a map on the table and examines it. In the tent.*]

DINAHLE: Is she one of the kibbutz girls?

URI: Who?

DINAHLE: Your girl.

URI: Not exactly.

DINAHLE: A town girl?

URI: Something like that.

DINAHLE: A city girl wouldn't suit you. At least she's born in the country?

URI: No one's like our girls, eh? [*Pulls her towards him.*] Simple, straightforward, girls who know what they're talking about! Don't like complicating things. Brave—sometimes. Would you come into a family room with me?

DINAHLE: Me? Just ask.

URI: And if I joined up?

DINAHLE: I'd join up with you.

URI: That's the spirit!

DINAHLE: Does your girl friend give you a lot of trouble?

URI: No. She's a hundred percent.

DINAHLE: All the same, you haven't seen her since being called up.

URI: How do you know?

DINAHLE: Girls have eyes.

URI: I couldn't get away from here. You know that as well as I do.

DINAHLE: The point is, does *she* know that?

URI: You know, I rather like you.

DINAHLE: Clever boy!

URI: Seriously.

DINAHLE: I can give you some pills against that.

URI: Three a day?

DINAHLE: You must take them at night.

URI: Like this? [*Kisses her.*]

DINAHLE: It's time you went on leave, Uri!

VOICES OUTSIDE: Ginger, Ginger—come and drink coffee.

URI [*Jumps to his feet. To Dinahle*]: Ginger's back.

DINAHLE: No more leave.

[*Outside.*]

RAFI [*To Ginger, who is standing with a cup of coffee in his hand*]: What's new, Ginger?

GINGER: Nothing much.

RAFI: What's cooking?

GINGER: Nothing out of the ordinary.

SEMYON: Here he is, Menachem . . .

GINGER: You can call me Ginger.

SEMYON: All right, Menachem. I want to go to town right away.

GINGER: Now, in the middle of the night?

SEMYON: I'll hitch a lift on the road.

URI [*Who has come up meanwhile*]: His wife is in the hospital.

GINGER: What's wrong with her?

SEMYON: Very sick.

GINGER: I'll tell you what. We're having assembly in ten minutes' time. After that you can decide.

SEMYON: I'm very worried.

GINGER [*Gently, with patience*]: Do you hear what I say? Wait for assembly. *You, yourself,* will decide then. Understood? [*Looks at his watch. To everybody.*] Attention! In another ten minutes, company assembly!

*Scene 3. Kibbutznik, map of 1:100,000, mountains, seacoast.*

KIBBUTZNIK [*Assisted by a stick, which he uses to point to the map*]: And so the leave was canceled, and instead Uri went out with his platoon to see action for the first time. They descended three kilometers from Gat Ha'amakim in the early hours of the morning. At once they entered the mountains, and till late in the afternoon they marched along dry riverbeds, climbed along narrow paths between the rocks, made their way through thorns and prickles. Har Ha'ayalot is here—more or less in the middle of the road between the valley and the sea. The second half of the march—to the lookout post—had to be carried out at night, under cover of darkness. So, when they came to Har Ha'ayalot, they had only a few hours for rest and to stock up with water.

Uri and Rafi collected the flasks from everybody and began to ascend the mountain. Uri knew that a new settlement was about to be established at Har Ha'ayalot, but on reaching the place a surprise awaited him.

*Scene 4. At Har Ha'ayalot. Settlement members planting saplings putting up a barbed-wire fence. PESACH, BIBERMAN, MEMBER A, MEMBER B.*

BIBERMAN [*Toward someone approaching*]: Can't you see where you're going, *chaverim?* Don't you see the plants? *Chaverim* . . . Naphtali . . . No, that's not Naphtali . . . Yes, it is Naphtali . . . No, it's not Naphtali . . . Uri!

SHOUTS: Get off! Can't you be careful? Don't you hear? Uri! Uri!

URI [*Enters loaded with flasks. RAFI after him*]: Biberman. What are you doing here?

PESACH: What are *you* doing here?

URI: Pesach! Shalom. . . . What's this . . . the whole kibbutz?

PESACH: Yes, the whole kibbutz. And not only us, but five other settlements in the area—we came up here today.

URI: First-class!

PESACH: And what about you?

URI: I'm just here by chance. We came to fetch some water.

BIBERMAN: That's a difficult matter. There's a great shortage of water.

URI: When will you ever have enough of anything, Biberman?

BIBERMAN: Worries I have—plenty. As many as you like!

PESACH: Biberman always exaggerates. We have water here in two places—next to the kitchen and next to the watch tower.

URI: Go to the kitchen, Rafi. I'll go to the watch tower. We haven't got time.

BIBERMAN: Aren't you remaining here?

URI: No. We're carrying on.

PESACH: Do you know that Ruthka's here?

URI: My Mom also?

PESACH: Yes, and Mika too.

URI: Where are they?

PESACH: Higher up, I think, in the camp. Maybe you'll find them in the kitchen.

RAFI: Well, if that's so, maybe you want to go there, Uri?

URI [*Hesitates*]: There's no time today. Tell them I was here. I'll soon be home. [*They go out.*]

BIBERMAN [*Calls after them*]: Can't you see where you're going, Uri? Can't you see the plants?

*Scene 5. Next to the kitchen*

*Rafi enters. Opens the tap of the drum—but no water flows out. Climbs up and looks in—climbs down disappointedly.*

RUTHKA [*Enters, supporting* MIKA *lightly*]: Sit down. I'll give you some water. How do you feel now?

MIKA [*Sits down on a stone*]: Please, Ruthka, don't fuss so much.

RAFI [*To* RUTHKA, *who wants to open the tap*]: There's no water here.

RUTHKA: That's very bad.

RAFI: They told me there'd be water here.

RUTHKA: Yes. There should be.

RAFI: And anywhere else?

RUTHKA: I think only in two places.

RAFI: Very poor organization here.

RUTHKA: In this heat the water is finished before it's even been brought.

RAFI: Never rely on kibbutzniks! [*Goes.*]

MIKA: Who's that?

RUTHKA: There're all sorts of people wandering around here today! [*Goes to the drum again. Tries.*] Not even one drop.

MIKA: Never mind. I'm not thirsty any more. Go back to work. I'll rest here a little.

RUTHKA: There's some hot water in the kitchen. I'll make you some tea.

MIKA: Go back to work, Ruthka.

RUTHKA: Don't talk nonsense, child. Perhaps we can get you some first aid.

MIKA [*With sudden anger*]: Don't you dare. I don't want them! No first aid and no doctor and no nurse!

RUTHKA: What's wrong, Mika?

MIKA: I don't need any help, do you hear? Nothing!

RUTHKA: No one's forcing you! I'll get you some tea.

MIKA: I'll go myself. [*Tries to rise, but remains standing with difficulty.*]

RUTHKA [*Holds her firmly*]: You sit here, and I'll bring you tea and arrange a truck to take you home.

MIKA: I don't want to go.

RUTHKA: And at home you'll go straight to a doctor.

MIKA: I won't go.

RUTHKA: I'll go with you.

MIKA: You won't.

RUTHKA: Don't be silly, Mika. Do you still think you can hide anything from me?

MIKA: What are you talking about?

RUTHKA: Both of us know what I'm talking about. [*Puts her hand on Mika's head.*]

MIKA: Leave me alone.

RUTHKA: When will Uri come home, do you think?

MIKA: Is he supposed to come?

RUTHKA: It's nearly three months since we last saw him. I telegraphed to him that Willie is coming.

MIKA: Now he'll certainly come.

RUTHKA: I think we'll both go home today and prepare, don't you think so? Feeling a bit better? [*MIKA nods.*] Some tea won't do any harm. [*Goes out.*]

*Scene 6. The memorial gathering in the background. URI in foreground.*

*Putting up a barbed-wire fence. GITA, CHAVERA A.*

URI: It seems to me this fence never ends.

GITA: Uri! Uri, my boy, it's nice of you to come to see us. Are you looking for your mother?

URI: No. I'm . . . on the way to the watch tower.

GITA: Go straight up. Do you know that Mika's also here?

URI: I know!

GITA: Willie's coming on leave, did you know?

URI: Really? Well, then everything's fine! Be seeing you! [*Goes out.*]

*Scene 7. A group of watchmen beside the watch tower.*

URI [*Enters*]: Hey, Ilana . . . Shalom, there should be water here. Is that right?

WATCHMAN A: There *should* be, but there isn't any.

ILANA: The water truck hasn't come yet.

WATCHMAN B: Try next to the kitchen. Perhaps there's some there. [*URI is about to go.*]

ILANA: Have you seen Ruthka and Mika yet?

URI: Not yet!

ILANA: Willie's coming on leave, have you heard?

URI: What do you say! [*Goes out.*]

*Scene 8. Again beside the kitchen.*

*MIKA is hanging her head, playing with her finger in the dust. URI enters and goes straight to the drum, without noticing Mika. Tries to get water from it, and when he realizes it is empty, bangs it with annoyance. The banging attracts MIKA'A attention. MIKA remains silent. URI is about to go when he notices her for the first time.*

URI: What do my eyes see?

MIKA: The drum is empty, but Ruthka's gone to get water.

URI: Don't you say "Shalom"?

MIKA: Shalom.

URI [*Lifts her on to her feet*]: Come, let's have a look at you.

MIKA [*Stands beside him with difficulty*]: Did you get Ruthka's message?

URI: What message?

MIKA: That Willie's coming on leave!

URI: I heard about it, but I'm here purely by chance!—to fetch water.

MIKA: Just now Ruthka will come.

URI: I don't think I'll wait for her.

MIKA: Are you going?

URI: Am *I* going? *Thirty people* are going.

MIKA: Ruthka will be terribly pleased to see you. She sent you a telegram.

URI: Another time. And how are things here? You look tired. Did they make you work hard, the kibbutzniks, I mean?

MIKA: We traveled the whole night and got here in the morning. When will you come?

URI: It's hard to say.

MIKA: Your father is supposed to be coming any day now. Ruthka will be at home. . . . I'll be . . .

URI: Can you keep a secret?

MIKA: Yes!

URI: Tonight a refugee ship is reaching . . . [*Stops, decides not to say the name*] the seacoast. And we are . . .

MIKA: But tomorrow . . . or *the day after tomorrow?*

URI: I want to come, Mika, but I can't promise anything. It's hard for anybody to understand unless they're there, in the middle of it—but with my job, Mika, Father, mother, relatives, family—are all very nice as long as they don't interfere, you understand?

MIKA: All the same—your father is coming on leave for a while. . . .

URI: I can only be with you for two minutes—do you want to spoil them with an argument?

MIKA: I want to tell you something—something important.

URI: I'm listening.

MIKA: No. Not now—when you come home.

URI: If it's very important, I suggest that you shouldn't wait.

MIKA: If you won't come, it won't be important.

URI: If you think I know what you're talking about . . .

MIKA: You're in a great hurry, I see.

URI: I am, Mika. That's right. But I'm prepared to listen to what you want to tell me. That's also right.

MIKA: It's very nice of you to listen.

URI: I *want* to listen.

MIKA: If someone really wants to listen, they'd act differently. Not like that.

URI: Then we'll have to wait until I'm different. I don't understand you. And you don't understand me. Shalom! [*Starts going rapidly, but stops when* RUTHKA *enters opposite.*]

RUTHKA [*Holding a big cup of water*]: Uri! I didn't know you were here! They just brought some clean water, Mika! [*Offers* MIKA *the cup, but instead of taking it, she gets up and flees.* URI *takes the cup and drinks*]

RUTHKA: Why is she running away?

URI: She's offended, it seems, because I'm in a hurry.

RUTHKA: She told you?

URI: About Dad? Yes.

RUTHKA: Not about your father—about herself.

URI: No. What's happened?

RUTHKA: She's pregnant.

URI [*After a silence, says softly*]: What? [RAFI *enters.*] Tell her I'll come.

RUTHKA: Go to her and say something. She needs you.

RAFI: Where are you, Uri? They've brought water!

URI [*Hurries out*]: Tell her I'll come! Perhaps even tomorrow! Tell her I'll come. . . .

*Scene 9. Same place, at night, in the kitchen.*

*RUTHKA is arranging kitchen utensils. Outside, AVRAHAM'S voice is heard.*

AVRAHAM: Tell the watchmen that they can't take part in the dancing. When the relief comes, they can join in. [*Turns to go in.*] But you, Ruthka—why have you locked yourself up in your kitchen?

RUTHKA: I've only just finished work.

AVRAHAM: I must tell you, Ruthka, you deserve a medal. The way you succeeded in feeding three hundred people with this kitchen—there're no words to describe it. . . . [*The noise of singing and dancing.*] Making merry. A wonderful feeling. In one day—a new settlement.

RUTHKA: Did you arrange about the truck?

AVRAHAM: If it's necessary . . .

RUTHKA: It is . . .

AVRAHAM: I thought you'd stay a few days longer.

RUTHKA: I'm going down tonight with Mika.

AVRAHAM: What's wrong with her?

RUTHKA: She needs treatment. It's impossible to leave her by herself.

AVRAHAM: When will you come back?

RUTHKA: That depends on how she'll feel. At the moment she needs someone close, and I must be that person. There's no one else.

AVRAHAM: Do you mean to say that she's . . .

RUTHKA [*Nods*]: Yes. And it's not at all easy for her.

AVRAHAM: They certainly didn't waste time, I must say.

RUTHKA: It was a complete surprise to both of them, and the truth is that neither was ready for it.

AVRAHAM: Did you speak to them?

RUTHKA: I spoke to Mika—and for some reason I'm worried. The girl is capable of doing something foolish. It's good that Willie's coming on leave. He has a lot of influence over her, and soon Uri will come as well. . . .

AVRAHAM: All the family!

RUTHKA: Yes. All the family—led by the grandfather and grandmother.

AVRAHAM: I see you're starting to enjoy the idea.

RUTHKA: To be a mother or not to be a mother depended to a certain extent on me—but a grandmother! That's like having a *job* to do, and you know I always do my *job*.

AVRAHAM: If so, don't forget that you have another duty to perform.

RUTHKA: I haven't forgotten.

MIKA [*Enters. Stops on seeing Avraham*]: Oh, sorry . . .

RUTHKA: Come here, Mika. We're waiting for you.

AVRAHAM: Ready for the journey?

MIKA: I came to say that I'm not going. I spoke to Pesach. I'm staying with the work unit. [*Seeing Ruthka's consternation.*] . . . I'll explain to you . . . afterwards.

AVRAHAM: I'll get the truck ready.

RUTHKA: All right, Avraham, we've put the trip off long enough. [*AVRAHAM goes.*] What are all these inventions of yours, Mika?

MIKA: No inventions. Twenty people are remaining to help. I'll also stay. Pesach was very happy when I suggested it.

RUTHKA: If he knew your condition, he wouldn't even have listened to you.

MIKA: I wish you would forget my condition—or whatever you call it.

RUTHKA: But you can't forget it.

MIKA: I wish I were dead. Dead!

RUTHKA: You're a stupid little thing, Mika, that's all I can tell you. But I'm sure you'll feel better later.

MIKA: Enough, enough . . .

RUTHKA: If you only knew how sorry I am that I didn't go through it more often. Uri could have had brothers and sisters.

MIKA: It was easy for you. It was your kibbutz. Willie was with you. Everybody loved you . . . you were at home. And I? Who wants me here? Who thinks about me? What do I want a child for? Don't you understand? *What for?*

RUTHKA: Uri asked me to tell you that he'll come home tomorrow or the day after.

MIKA: If he'll have time.

RUTHKA: If he'll have time or if he *won't.*

MIKA: He doesn't belong to himself now. In his job—father, mother, relatives, family—musn't interfere, do you understand? [*After a silence.*] I won't interfere with him. He doesn't need to worry. I won't interfere with him.

RUTHKA: You'll help him.

MIKA: It won't continue like this.

RUTHKA: What won't continue? What are you planning to do?

MIKA: I don't know yet, but it won't continue like this!

RUTHKA: You know what, Mika? Let's not think about it for a while.

MIKA: Let's not think about it for a while! What happens to me doesn't worry you for a second! What do you know about me? What do any of you know about me? You think I'm one of those innocent children of yours? Even Willie—what does he know? Do you think what he told you is the whole story? Do you know what I've gone through in my life?

RUTHKA: Not now, Mika!

MIKA: Yes, now! You'll listen to me once and for all—to all I have to say, and perhaps you'll stop talking to me like you'd talk to a child.

Why do you only have one child? Only Uri? You're not the only one who knows that secret. I've already done it once. I knew all about it. Don't think you can frighten me. You won't be able to frighten me!

RUTHKA: Mika! [*Holds her.*]

MIKA: Ruthka! [*Hugs her.*]

*Scene 10. Kibbutznik. The door of a hut.*

KIBBUTZNIK: Willie arrived. . . . Do you know how? Simple—with the midday bus. Everybody says it's impossible to recognize him in his corporal's uniform. And believe it or not, he's put on weight. Willie always liked beans.

BIBERMAN: Is it true?

KIBBUTZNIK: He's here. He's here.

BIBERMAN: Where is he? [*A group of settlement members round Willie.*]

KIBBUTZNIK: Somewhere among this heap of people. Try to find him!

BIBERMAN: Willie—Shalom, Willie!

GITA [*Enters*]: What a crowd! What a crowd!

PESACH [*Enters*]: Where's our corporal? Hey, Corporal Cahana! [*Come to attention.*] Awaiting orders!

WILLIE: Stand at ease, all of you, stand at ease. What's all the excitement? Anybody would think something had happened.

PESACH: Nothing's happened—never fear. [*RUTHKA enters. Silence.*]

WILLIE [*Puts out his hand, pulls her to him, looks at her*]: This portrait is familiar, unless I'm making a mistake. . . .

RUTHKA: But you, Willie—not the same person! [*To the others.*] He looks wonderful, doesn't he!

GITA: But he'd look much better wearing a kibbutznik's clothes. Isn't that so, Willie?

WILLIE: Quite right! [*Kisses her on the cheek.*]

PESACH: She's blushing just like in the good old days!

GITA [*Feels the material of Willie's shirt*]: Excellent material. You've got a good laundress, I see.

WILLIE: First-class. Her name is Sergeant Isaac Abramowitz.

GITA: Would you like some kibbutz clothes?

WILLIE: Definitely!

GITA: You'll get them right away. [*Goes out.*]

PESACH: Ruthka, I know that you're wishing we would all go away and leave him to you. But you'll have to put up with us a bit longer. The kibbutz comes first.

WILLIE: How are things with you, Pesach?

PESACH: You know how it is. You close a gap somewhere—and a new hole appears somewhere else. The tractor drivers especially are in a bad way. Great shortage.

WILLIE: Why? What's wrong?

PESACH: Neither the old Cahana nor the young Cahana—there's no one available to work.

WILLIE: Well, perhaps you can put me on a tractor for a few days?

PESACH: For my part, with pleasure.

WILLIE: And about you, Biberman, I've heard wonders. They say you managed to accommodate hundreds of people the night before the establishment of Har Ha'ayalot.

BIBERMAN: Three hundred and forty. Of them, a hundred and seventy in beds!

WILLIE: And the rest?

BIBERMAN: In the same beds.

WILLIE: Well, Ruthka, and you?

RUTHKA: You know how it is!

WILLIE: I know and I don't know!

RUTHKA: Till now I've been waiting for you—now I'm waiting for Uri!

WILLIE: Is he coming today?

RUTHKA: He promised me that he would. What's the time, Pesach?

WILLIE: Ten past four.

RUTHKA: Strange—and the bus hasn't come yet!

WILLIE: It will come—it will come. Don't worry!

GITA [*Enters, holding a parcel*]: From socks to cap! And I'd advise you to go straight to the shower room—before the noise starts.

WILLIE: That's a wonderful idea! [*Takes the parcel.*]

RUTHKA: I've got to talk to you, Willie.

GITA: First, let him shower! [*To all*] Come on, come on! Quite enough interference! [*Pulls everybody aside.*] We'll see him at supper! [*All go out except PESACH, RUTHKA, WILLIE.*]

PESACH: Come, Willie, we'll go together! After all, someone has to show you where the shower room is.

RUTHKA: Only don't keep him there too long! At half-past four Uri's coming.

WILLIE: By the way, where is Mika? I haven't seen her.

RUTHKA: I'll speak to you about that!

WILLIE: Isn't she at home?

RUTHKA: She's at home.

WILLIE: I brought her a present. [*Takes out a colored scarf.*] Do you think she'll like it?

PESACH: Listen, Willie, if you'll start with presents now, you won't shower until your leave is over. [*To Ruthka.*] I'll see he's returned to you quickly!

WILLIE [*To Ruthka*]: Don't move from here—I'll come back right away! [*Goes out.*]

RUTHKA: Pesach, one minute. [*PESACH stops.*] Where did Mika work today?

PESACH: She had the day off.

RUTHKA: The day off? I haven't seen her the whole day. Perhaps you could find out where she is now? Tell her to come here . . . that Willie asked.

MIKA [*In the window*]: Can I come in?

RUTHKA: Oh, there she is! [*To Pesach*] Well, hurry Willie up! [*PESACH goes out.*] Where have you come from?

MIKA: From the bus.

RUTHKA: Oh, it did arrive at last.

MIKA: Yes, just now.

RUTHKA: And Uri didn't come?

MIKA: I came.

RUTHKA: From where?

MIKA: I was in town.

RUTHKA: Come in, Mika, come in. [*MIKA enters.*] Willie's here, did you know?

MIKA: I heard about it.

RUTHKA: Why did you go to town? I thought we said you would wait until Uri came.

MIKA: There's no reason to wait.

RUTHKA: I want you to talk to Willie.

MIKA: I came to say "Shalom" to him.

RUTHKA: Sit down. He'll come just now. He brought you a present. [*Gives her the scarf.*] Do you like it?

MIKA [*Takes it*]: He knows?

RUTHKA: I haven't told him yet.

MIKA [*Puts the scarf down*]: Listen, Ruthka. I want to ask you something—don't tell him. Ruthka, you don't know how much I . . . admire him. I beg of you, let it remain between us. If he ever knew that anything had happened—it's not so terrible, but not now, Ruthka, not now!

RUTHKA: What did you arrange in town?

MIKA: I arranged everything. For tomorrow. In half an hour the whole thing will be over.

RUTHKA: You can't do it, Mika.

MIKA: Are you going to tell him? Do you think he can influence me? You're wrong. You'll only add to my suffering. That's all. You'll only make me crazy. That's all.

RUTHKA: All I'm asking is that you wait until Uri comes home.

MIKA: And if I wait, Willie won't know?

RUTHKA: If you wait, Willie won't know.

MIKA: Is that a promise?

RUTHKA: If you wait for Uri, Willie won't know.

*Scene 11. Kibbutznik beside a map of coastal area.*

*Points with a stick. Complete darkness. Uses a pocket flashlight to show where they are situated.*

KIBBUTZNIK: After a forced march, Uri and his men reached their meeting place on the coast after passing [*points to map*] the southernmost spur of the Carmel. But they did not go into action at once. The English seemed to have suspected something. They strengthened their guards, sent reinforcements to the coastal area. Because of this, it was decided to postpone the action to the following night. Uri and his platoon are hidden in one of the dry riverbeds on the Carmel approximately here [*shows with the stick*] . . . about an hour's walk from the coast. There's no moon tonight. Complete darkness. Last-minute instructions are given by torch flashes.

*Scene 12. In the mountains.*

URI *crouching.* RAFI *laying down, sending and receiving messages.*

URI: What do they say, Rafi?

RAFI: Hold on, they haven't finished.

URI: All I need now is a change in instructions.

RAFI [*Deciphering*]: "All previous orders canceled. Await new instructions."

URI: To hell with them! It's maddening.

RAFI: What are you so nervous for, Uri?

URI: What do you want me to do—go swimming? First they postpone the action, then they keep us a whole day in a filthy cave. Then they hurry us up, then they cancel previous orders. . . . Now they're talking again.

RAFI [*Answers, receives, deciphers aloud*]: "Company commander on way to you."

URI: Ginger. I'll give him a piece of my mind! How're things with you? Everything ready?

DINAHLE: Everything—apart from two stretcher bearers.

URI: You'll be attached to headquarters. I'll see to that.

DINAHLE: It'll be too late.

URI: Perhaps you'll stop nagging now? [*She wants to go.*] Wait here.

DANDA [*Enters hurriedly*]: Hey . . . tsssss . . .

URI: Who's that?

RAFI: Danda—if I'm not mistaken.

DANDA: A tank is wandering around on the bottom road.

URI: Never mind. They wouldn't dare to get off the road.

DANDA: They've put out all the lights in the Arab village. They smell something, it seems.

URI: They smell something? They themselves smell—and how! Go back to the lookout point. [*DANDA goes.*] And you, Rafi, take a group out to the road to meet Ginger.

RAFI: And what about the patrol?

URI: What will you patrol when you don't even know the new orders? Move! [*RAFI goes out.*]

DINAHLE: The fact that you're nervous, Uri, isn't my business, but you must realize it's infectious.

URI: It isn't the action that's making me nervous, but the *lack* of action.

DINAHLE: Actually it's the same thing.

URI: It's the same thing for someone who's afraid, but for someone who's itching to do something—to do *anything,* it's not the same thing.

DINAHLE: And so I guessed right.

URI: You didn't guess anything.

DINAHLE: Girls have eyes.

GINGER [*A voice from the darkness*]: Hey, you jackass!

URI: Ginger?

GINGER [*Appears*]: Can you see ginger hair even in the dark?

URI: Even in the dark.

GINGER: Well said?

URI: As usual. [*To Dinahle,*] Go back to your place. [*She goes.*]

URI: Have you brought new orders?

GINGER: Yes. How are things here? How are the boys?

URI: All right.

GINGER: Not nervous?

URI: Doing their best.

GINGER: Now to business—the disembarkation from the ship won't be here.

URI [*Disappointed*]: I knew it. I knew it!

GINGER: You didn't know anything. The ship has been directed to the coast of Galilee, north of Acre. There things are quiet. Here, where we are, we'll make the noise. Understand? Our company has been given the job of distracting their attention on a big scale. Firstly to cut off the army camp and blow up the roads, pipelines and bridges. The division is very simple. South of the camp, one platoon. The camp itself, a second platoon. The bridge north of the camp, that's your job. You know the bridge?

URI: With my eyes shut.

GINGER: Excellent. Send out a party of sappers. Cover their retreat with as much fire as you can give. We want as much noise as possible. The meeting place will be Yagur, on the other side of the mountains.

URI: Zero hour?

GINGER: Hasn't changed. Exactly at midnight.

URI [*Looks at his watch*]: Another hour and a half.

GINGER: Enough for you?

URI [*Puts his finger to his forehead*]: Too much!

GINGER: That's all. I'll be with the other platoon. If you want anything, send a runner or signal.

URI: I won't want anything.

GINGER: Don't be so sure. Any questions?

URI: No.

GINGER: Fine. [*Turns round, then comes back.*] Hold on—I nearly forgot. We had a message from Semyon's kibbutz his girl's in hospital—in a very bad state, it seems.

URI: Do you want me to tell him?

GINGER: No, but take it into account. Let him be among the first ones going back. People like Semyon haven't families or relatives or anything else here. I think they haven't even children.

URI: He could have chosen not to go with us.

GINGER: That's a sign he's all right.

URI: You know what? Take him with you.

GINGER: I won't take him—and you can fix it up for yourself. Put him at the back of the platoon and that's all.

URI: *I'll* put everybody with personal problems at the back—then who will I have left in front?

GINGER: Ouf, what's happened to you, Uri?

URI: I don't like it when our people start acting like saints. One hour a month. Either you're a Palmachnik or you're a husband with a wife—one of the two.

GINGER: I see that you also have personal problems, Uri . . .

URI: I have—of course I have. Perhaps as many as Semyon. So what? Did I ask to be treated differently? Semyon's worried about his girl! Why didn't he go to her? What's he doing here? Why did he join up at all if she's in such a bad way? [*Stops suddenly. With a change of tone.*] Good. That's enough of that. It's getting late!

GINGER: I leave the whole thing to your judgment.

URI: All right.

GINGER: And don't be so miserable. I was also like that before I went into action for the first time. All of us were. All of us were. [*Disappears.*]

RAFI [*Reentering, with others*] Tsssss . . . hey, boys!

SOMEONE: At last . . .

RAFI: Now it's our turn. Listen closely. This time the main job is ours . . . sshhhhhh . . .

URI: Final instructions. Your group has been ordered to blow up the road bridge north of the camp. Do you remember it? [*Motions of assent among the men.*] Fine. We must have a first-class demolition man to do the job quickly and neatly! The other units will provide the cover.

ALL: What's the problem? . . . That's my job. . . . I'm the most experienced. Who wants veterans?

RAFI: Shut up, all of you.

SEMYON: Uri . . . me.

RAFI: Don't talk nonsense, Semyon.

SEMYON: It won't be my first bridge, Uri. I've blown up many bridges. Back in Europe, when the Nazis . . .

RAFI: The same old story.

ALL: General Semyon . . . Look who's talking . . . A new sapper in the country. . . .

SEMYON: Nobody knows me here.

URI: Do you really want the job, Semyon? Very much? Or do you think you have to volunteer?

SEMYON: Yes.

URI: Yes what?

SEMYON: I really want to volunteer.

URI: You're all right, Semyon. He's been through a demolition course, hasn't he, Rafi?

RAFI: Yes, but his methods are very wild, and he has no idea of the conditions here—and, generally, don't you know Semyon?

SEMYON: No. You don't know Semyon.

URI: That's settled. We'll give you the job.

RAFI: I disagree.

URI: I have no reason to rule him out.

RAFI: I'd rather do it myself.

URI: You're in charge of the group, Rafi, and there's no more discussion. Come here, Semyon, we'll finalize some things. Do you hear?

SEMYON: I'm listening.

URI: You remember the bridge?

SEMYON: Concrete. Foundations on both sides. No pillars.

URI: Excellent. Where will you put the explosive?

SEMYON: In . . . [*Searches for the right word, and makes a sort of an arch with his hand.*]

URI: Good. Twice on each side. The approach is through the wadi. An easy approach. So you remember that there's gravel in the middle of the wadi?

SEMYON: I remember.

URI: What's the conclusion from that? [*SEMYON hesitates.*]

RAFI: Not to walk in the middle of the wadi. Else you'll make a noise.

SEMYON: Plain.

URI: It's not complicated. Get the exposives ready as you're supposed to, light fuses of thirty centimeters. That will give you thirty seconds—then run. Your group will wait for you.

SEMYON: Plain.

URI: What do you still need? [*SEMYON hesitates.*]

RAFI: Zero hour.

SEMYON: Zero hour.

URI: 24 zero zero. Exactly another hour. Any questions? No. Fine! Rafi, take the boys. Start moving. I'll come to see you before we start action. [*The men go off quietly. Darkness. Two searchlights probe the background. Afterwards they take the form of two hands. The small hand remains fixed, pointing upward, while the large hand approaches twelve o'clock slowly.*]

*Scene 13. In the wadi.* URI, RAFI, SEMYON.

URI [*Approaches quickly*]: Tssssss . . .

RAFI: Tssss . . .

URI: Rafi?

RAFI: Yes.

URI: All set?

RAFI: More or less. But I wanted . . .

SEMYON: Uri?

URI: What is it, Semyon, something wrong?

SEMYON: No, nothing. Just wanted to ask.

URI: To ask what?

SEMYON [*Removes the magazine from his automatic rifle, takes out a bullet, offers it to Uri*]: Like when we were in the woods at home, the first bullet, for someone we loved. In case, you know, give it to my girl. She's in hospital, you know, in Afula.

RAFI: Stop that nonsense now, Semyon.

SEMYON: Never mind. It happens sometimes, give it to my girl.

URI: All right, Semyon, I'll give it to her.

SEMYON: Now I'm ready!

RAFI: Go back to your place. You've got ten minutes to go. [*SEMYON goes out.*]

DANDA [*Enters*]: Rafi?

RAFI: Uri's also here.

DANDA: The barbed wire runs right down to the wadi.

RAFI: I thought so.

URI: What's wrong?

RAFI: There's a fence in the wadi. We didn't see it because of the bushes.

URI: That's no problem. We have clippers.

RAFI: That's not the job for Semyon.

URI: What do you have against Semyon?

RAFI: Listen, Uri. The tank's here all the time, traveling up and down. They've stationed a patrol here. The searchlights are working like devils. Now we've got the barbed wire—I wouldn't send Semyon out for this job.

URI: Who would you send?

RAFI: Myself.

URI [*After a silence, loads his weapon with a click*]: *Good!*

RAFI: Well?

URI: Send Semyon back. Go with him, take over the command of the platoon. Danda, you take this group.

RAFI: And you?

URI: I'm going to *blow up the bridge!*

RAFI: Are you crazy, Uri?

URI: Listen, Rafi, you're getting a bit out of hand lately. Stop arguing and obey orders. Do you understand?

RAFI: Yes, Uri.

URI: Is everything plain?

RAFI: Yes.

URI: What's the time?

RAFI: We have to go.

URI: Danda, go to your boys. Rafi, look after the platoon. Any questions?

RAFI: No, all O.K.

URI: Right then, let's go! [*URI alone on the stage. A searchlight follows him. He tries to escape, but the searchlight follows him relentlessly. Rattle of machine-gun fire; than darkness.*]

*Scene 14.* KIBBUTZNIK.

KIBBUTZNIK: The ship came. A rope was thrown out to the shore. And in the darkness, bare feet splashed in the water. In the darkness men with heavy boots walked up narrow paths. The covering forces stood ready with loaded weapons on the roads, and the convoys passed. Tired feet stumbled in the darkness. They spread out and disappeared in many directions. By morning they were far from their landing place. All the settlements of the valley received groups of these refugees. They reached as far as the foothills of the Carmel, to the outskirts of Nazareth, to Gat Ha'amakim. No one was prepared for them. This happened early in the morning, before sunrise, and in a few minutes blankets had to be found, meals prepared, places made for the newcomers in rooms, in tents. The children and the infants had to be looked after, the refugees had to disappear inside the kibbutz.

GITA [*Enters carrying blankets, after her comes* PESACH, *also carrying blankets*]: Where to? Where are all of them?

KIBBUTZNIK: To the dining hall, the dining hall.

ILANA [*Enters from the second side with* BIBERMAN, *to whom he is talking*]: I've moved out of my room. You can use it.

BIBERMAN: Excellent. As soon as they come. [*A list in his hands. He reads from it.*] Ilana, vacant. Ruthka, not yet. Naphtali, not yet, Blankets, not enough. Clothes, I must talk to Gita. Well, everything's nearly fixed up. [*Seeing* WILLIE *and* RUTHKA *coming in, holding blankets.*] Have you moved out of your room, Ruthka?

RUTHKA: I've moved out.

BIBERMAN [*Crosses out in the list*]: Another one.

RUTHKA: But where are we moving to?

KIBBUTZNIK: The veterans are gathering in the dining hall. There they'll be shown their new accommodation.

BIBERMAN: Come with me. [*All go out, except for the* KIBBUTZNIK.]

MIKA [*Enters, dressed for a journey, a small bundle in her hand, speaks to the Kibbutznik*]: What's happened? Why is everyone up so early?

KIBBUTZNIK: Don't you know? Refugees are coming soon. They disembarked tonight.

MIKA: I didn't know.

KIBBUTZNIK: With women, with children. Do you have any spare blankets? We're collecting everything in the dining hall.

MIKA: Yes, yes. Later on. Refugees? From where?

KIBBUTZNIK: Who knows? The whole world.

MIKA: Yes . . . yes.

KIBBUTZNIK: We're collecting everything in the dining hall.

MIKA: Yes, I know. [KIBBUTZNIK *goes.* MIKA *is about to hurry off when* RUTHKA *and* WILLIE *return.*]

RUTHKA: Where are you going to, Mika? [MIKA *is silent. Holds the bundle to her breast. Lowers her gaze to the ground.*] And why so dressed up?

WILLIE: She's going with the six-o'clock bus, I suppose.

RUTHKA: Mika! [*No answer.*] We spoke about something. I've kept my promise. [*MIKA is still silent, like a trapped animal.*] I can't be silent any longer, Willie. You have to know.

MIKA: No, Ruthka, no.

RUTHKA: I must tell you.

WILLIE [*Silences Ruthka*]: Wait a minute, Ruthka. Why must you tell me? Mika will do it. [*Waves RUTHKA out, and she goes.*] Come, Mika. Sit next to me. [*MIKA does not move. WILLIE sits.*] You still have time. The bus goes at six. You won't miss it. I promise you. [*Sits down silently beside him.*] I hope you'll come back early, because Uri is supposed to be coming today. Actually, we waited for him, yesterday too, didn't we?

MIKA: She really didn't tell you?

WILLIE: She told me a lot of things. I don't know which ones you're referring to.

MIKA: About me?

WILLIE: About you and Uri? Of course.

MIKA: About me at the moment, about me.

WILLIE: If you won't tell me, Mika, I won't know anything about it.

MIKA: You'll despise me. You'll hate me.

WILLIE: Perhaps. But it's hard for me to believe that you've done anything to deserve that.

MIKA: I haven't done it yet.

WILLIE: A thought can always be changed.

MIKA: It's already too late. I'm going to town now. I have an appointment at eight, with the doctor. I'll come back tonight. It will all be fine, all fixed up. I'll be able to breathe again, to rest, to relax.

WILLIE: I understand.

MIKA: Aren't you going to shout at me?

WILLIE: I hope Uri knows your decision and agrees to it.

MIKA: Uri? Uri doesn't know anything about it.

WILLIE: What do you mean, doesn't know anything about it?

MIKA: Doesn't know anything, and doesn't care anything.

WILLIE: You're mistaken, Mika. He'll never forgive you if you do this.

MIKA: You think so?

WILLIE: I'm certain.

MIKA: How do you know?

WILLIE: I know Uri, and I know how I would have acted myself.

MIKA: Are you trying to influence me? You always knew how to influence me with your speeches.

WILLIE: Mika, to influence you! You know what my method used to be, and still is—the final decision is in your hands—your decision and nobody else's! After all, it's your child.

BIBERMAN [*Dashes in wildly*]: What are you standing here and gossiping for? They've come. They've come. [*People running with blankets in all directions; here and there bewildered refugees are being led by settlement members and Palmachniks.* MIKA *goes out slowly with the bundle in her hand.*]

PESACH [*Enters in confusion and dismay*]: Willie! Ruthka! Willie!

RUTHKA: What's wrong?

PESACH [*To* ILANA, *who enters hurriedly*]: Is your truck available now?

ILANA: Yes, Certainly.

PESACH: Then take them to the hospital at once.

RUTHKA: What's happened? Is it Mika?

PESACH: Not Mika. Uri!

WILLIE: Where? What?

PESACH: You must go there at once.

RUTHKA: But what's happened? What was the message?

PESACH: On that cursed telephone—I couldn't follow exactly what they said. Only his name . . . and the name of the hospital. But you've got to hurry. It seems his injury . . . is serious.

ILANA: Let's go.

RUTHKA: Where to? Where to?

WILLIE: Be calm, Ruthka, be calm.

GITA: I'll bring you something to wear. [*Goes.*]

PESACH: Come, Ruthka, Willie, don't waste time.

RUTHKA: It can't be. They were only hiking in the mountains. He's supposed to come today.

WILLIE [*to* PESACH, *avoiding all concealment*]: What did they tell you Pesach? [*With a movement of his head,* PESACH *makes it clear that Uri is dead.*]

RUTHKA: Willie, what did we do! What did we do, Willie! It can't be!

WILLIE: Get on the truck with Ilana. I'll follow you just now.

RUTHKA: Why? Why? Come to Uri! Come to Uri! Willie!

WILLIE: I want to fetch Mika.

RUTHKA: Leave her alone now.

WILLIE: I want to stop her.

RUTHKA: But why? Why now?

WILLIE: Yes, now, Ruthka. Perhaps . . . Uri's son, his son . . .

RUTHKA: No. [*Breaks down.*] No . . . Come to Uri . . . To Uri. [*ILANA takes her out.*]

WILLIE [*To Pesach*]: You go, Pesach. I must find Mika. Go with them.

PESACH: All right. [*Goes out.*]

WILLIE [*Before PESACH goes out the noise of a departing bus is heard. WILLIE is frozen to the spot.*] Mika . . . Mika . . . [*Runs out.*]

*Scene 15. The bus stop.*

*The pole holding the bus sign, against which MIKA is leaning, her head resting on her arm. A bench. Sound of a departing bus.*

WILLIE [*Enters running, doesn't see Mika, runs on a few steps to the end of the stage. Stops. Turns round, and then MIKA lifts her head*]: You . . . here?

MIKA: I didn't go . . . you see? I didn't go . . . when you said to me: "After all *it's your child,*" my heart started to beat, so that I could hardly breathe. Yours—not Ruthka's, and not the kibbutz's, and not Willie's—yours. Yours, Mika . . . Yours . . . I couldn't get on to the bus. And I began to think about Uri. . . . He'll be very happy. . . . And you'll be a grandfather, Willie. . . . But what's wrong, Willie? This time I'm not lying. I'm not hiding anything. Really, I didn't go. Believe me. Everything's going to be fine, now, Willie. Uri will come, and you'll see how wonderful it's going to be . . . for all of us, Willie . . . for all of us together. . . .

*The memorial scene: The singing grows louder.*

# The First Sin

*by*
AHARON MEGGED

Elaboration concerning exactly what happened in the Garden of Eden has been traditional subject matter in Continental and American literature as far back as Genesis A. Such authors as Milton, Shaw, and Twain have dealt with this subject. *The First Sin* follows this tradition. Megged treats the subject with a light touch. God becomes the landlord, with all that the label implies.

This play is an earlier work of Megged, having been performed in 1962. His later works, novels, throw some light on his treatment of this material. The heroes of Megged's later novels seem to be patterned after the narrator of Dostoevski's novel *Notes from the Underground* in that they "risk their cakes and deliberately desire the most fatal rubbish."[1] A good example of this kind of character may be found in the Megged novel, *Living on the Dead.* The hero has been hired to write a quasi-fictional life of Davidov, one of the heroic early settlers of Palestine, but he cannot bring himself to do so although he has collected all the proper notes. Instead, he drinks the nights and days away in a cafe. He says

> The tyranny of righteousness! I thought resentfully when I sat down at my desk to try to arrange those notes and put them into some kind of shape. The letters I wrote on the paper were dead—compared with them. Ahuva's letters were full of vitality and movement. Why had he lived, why had he died, why was he haunting me, how had he succeeded in invading my life to lord it over me with his vigilant eye, with his surveillance of all my actions, day and night? Of my most intimate desires—which were my own private domain,

> in God's name, my private and personal domain! Didn't I have the right to do as I pleased—to lust, to hate, to get drunk, to make love—without his eyes watching me all the rest of my life?[2]

In Megged's novel, *Living on the Dead,* the hero never does get down to writing as he should. In his play, *The First Sin,* mankind (Eve) throws away everything (Eden) because she cannot stand righteousness and is bored.

There is a distinct difference, however, between Dostoevski's view of this fatal flaw in human nature and that of Megged. Dostoevski, through the voice of the narrator in *Notes from the Underground,* indicates that he finds no pattern in the world and that civilization produces only a greater variety of sensations in man and nothing more.[3] The narrator also feels that regeneration leads only to moral subjugation. Megged, however, feels that life consists of a pattern of sin and retribution, a divine harmony without which the world would be lost.[4]

Aharon Megged was born in Poland in 1920. He emigrated to Palestine at a very early age. He worked on a kibbutz as a farm laborer, fisherman, etc. He made his reputation in the 1960s in Israel as a playwright and has since achieved an International reputation with his novels and short stories. His novels include *Living on the Dead,* 1970, and *A Short Life,* 1980.

### NOTES

1. Fyodor Dostoevski, *Notes from the Underground,* trans. by Ralph E. Matlaw (New York: E. P. Dutton & Company, Inc.), p. 27.
2. Aharon Megged, *Living on the Dead* (London: Cape, 1970), p. 206.
3. Dostoevski, p. 21.
4. Aharon Megged, *The Short Life,* trans. by Miriam Arad unpublished MS (Tel Aviv: WZO Cultural Division), p. 262.

CHARACTERS

*Adam*
*Eve*
*Landlord*
*The Serpent*
*Cain*
*Abel*
*Ishtar*

The roles of Ishtar and Eve are played by the same actress.

Part 1, The First Sin
Part 2, East of Eden
Part 3, The Wind Goes Round and Round

*Translated from the Hebrew*
*by S. Eingad and M. Arad*



## PART 1
## THE FIRST SIN

*A hut in the garden.* ADAM AND EVE, *simply dressed, face each other across a table on which is a bowl of fruit.* EVE, *eating a banana, looks longingly at the Garden through the window.* ADAM *sits with head bent, eyes closed, hands drooping between his knees. He is deep in thought and looks depressed. Outside a bird is heard chirping.*

EVE [*Looking in the direction of the chirping*]: What's that?

ADAM: Sounds like a starling. [*Listens.*] Or maybe a lark.

EVE: A lark?

ADAM [*Drily*]: No. It's a starling. [*Silence.*]

EVE: Why aren't you eating?

ADAM: 'Cos I'm not hungry. [*Silence.*]

EVE [*Throwing the banana peel out of the window.*] Oh, blast!

ADAM [*Looking out of the window*]: You're messing up the Garden with all those peels.

EVE: They'll only rot, like everything else out there. I just can't take this any more!

ADAM [*Without opening his eyes*]: Take what?

EVE: You sitting there all day without opening your mouth.

ADAM: What is there to say?

EVE: Just say something. [*ADAM does not answer. EVE eats a banana and looks at him with a scornful, meaningful smile. Speaking deliberately, looking out the window.*]: You know . . . sometimes he sleeps . . . or goes to the other end of the Garden . . . And then—

ADAM [*Opening his eyes and looking at her forbiddingly*]: Eve!

EVE: Well, why not?

ADAM: He sees everything and knows everything. You know that.

EVE: We could try, couldn't we?

ADAM: I don't want you ever to talk about that again. You understand?

EVE: Bah! You've got no guts.

ADAM: I just want to do the right thing. I don't want to start getting into trouble.

EVE [*Imitating him*]: Do the right thing! All right! We'll just sit here eating bananas for ever and ever, without saying a word. . . .

ADAM: Anyway, what do you find so attractive about that tree?

EVE: Oh, it's so attractive, so terribly attractive. Every time I go near it I come over all of a tremble. I can hardly stop myself from putting out my hand [*with a flash of longing*] and plucking!

ADAM: Be like me. Don't go near it.

EVE: I just can't. Believe me I can't. I keep making up my mind to stay away. . . . I go somewhere else . . . but some force I can't control draws me to that tree like magic. I come closer, stop, then closer still, just to touch it. Or at least to smell it. What a smell!

ADAM: Pleasant?

EVE: Divine! It suddenly makes me so delightfully dizzy. If anything can be called paradise—that's it.

ADAM [*With a smile*]: Oh, women, women, women!

EVE [*Bursts out laughing*]: And what do you know about women?

ADAM: Everything you've revealed.

EVE: Oh, that isn't much.

ADAM: You're completely naked before me.

EVE: That's what you think. There's always something I keep hidden.

ADAM: I know you, Eve.

EVE: You know me? How long have we been living together? Since last Friday. Just one week.

ADAM: A week and a day.

EVE: Oh, of course. Today's the Sabbath day . . . [*remembers, approaches him and whispers seductively.*] Today he sleeps . . . all afternoon. . . .

ADAM *[Shaking himself away*]: Haven't I told you?

EVE [*Bitterly*]: Yes, of course. You want to do the right thing. Not to get into trouble. You want to be the Old Man's good little boy. All the time. To do exactly what he tells you—and nothing else!

ADAM: Aren't you grateful to him?

EVE: Grateful? For what?

ADAM: For having given us life.

EVE: You call this life? Eight days we've been living together and what have we done? Absolutely nothing! One day's so like another I can't even tell them apart. We eat and we sleep. So what makes man so superior to animals, anyway?

ADAM: The animals don't talk.

EVE: Well, you hardly talk either. And when I complain you say there's nothing to talk about. I suppose it's not your fault. What is there to talk about when nothing ever happens?

ADAM: But remember, we have no worries either. Everything is ready-made, on the spot.

EVE: You have no worries!

ADAM: Have you? What is it you want?

EVE: If I only knew what I wanted I think I'd be happy. I only know I want something . . . and I'm sure that it's good . . . that it's marvelous. Something that makes life worth living! [*with desire*] and I want to taste it just once. [*Demandingly.*] Why won't you risk getting into trouble just once in your life? Just once?

ADAM: That would be the end. After that—nothingness.

EVE: How do you know?

ADAM: I feel it. . . . When you talk about it, I get the shivers. I . . . yes—it's true—I'm very much afraid. I feel something dreadful will happen . . . something black and dreadful . . . like that dream I had.

EVE: What dream? When?

ADAM: When he put me to sleep. I dreamt I was lying in a deep dark forest, and suddenly there was a long black snake, slimy and slithery. . . . I ran away from it but it came after me, closer, closer. . . . It caught up to me . . . and suddenly—I was falling into a bottomless pit. . . . I screamed.

EVE: And you woke up and found me there. I remember your scream. It's the first thing I do remember. I was petrified myself. I couldn't understand why you gave such a yell when you saw me.

ADAM [*With an apologetic smile*]: It was in the dream.

EVE: At first . . . I thought it was because you found me ugly.

ADAM: How could you think such a thing? You were—wonderful.

EVE: Tell me. Tell me how was I wonderful.

ADAM: You were . . . oh it was so new . . . so sudden . . . I was completely dazzled.

EVE: Go on!

ADAM: So . . . different . . . [*Searches unsuccessfully for more words.*]

EVE: Go on!

ADAM [*Trying, then giving up*]: Oh . . . you know.

EVE: Of course I know—but I want to hear it from you! You've no idea what pleasure it gives me. It makes me all tingly when you talk about me.

ADAM: I . . . I dunno . . . it's hard for me . . . the words seem to get stuck. . . . When I say something nice to you, it sounds so . . . suddenly—banal.

EVE: Banal? Rubbish! Anything that's true sounds banal . . . but I won't drag it out of you. [*Scrutinizing him.*] You've changed.

ADAM [Surprised]: Me? Changed? In a week?

EVE: Yes . . . the first time . . . you were different. You never stopped talking, mumbling, chattering. I couldn't understand a word, but it was so nice.

ADAM: There's only one first time.

EVE: What a horrible thing to say!

ADAM: Horrible?

EVE: Yes, I want nothing but first times. [*Looks at him pityingly, then provokingly.*] Come on. Why won't you take one little risk? Scared, eh?

ADAM [*Trembling*]: Stop talking about that.

EVE: All you want is to be obedient. The landlord's good little boy! Such a well-behaved little boy, ready to do whatever he tells you. Even before he tells you. What sort of a man are you? Are you a man? You're just a child.

ADAM: Is it so bad—to be a child?

EVE: But I don't want to mother you. [*Heavy footsteps are heard approaching outside.*] Here he comes. Your revered old man. Your God . . . Well, I don't want to see him. [*She jumps out of the window. A moment later the Landlord appears . . . a heavy, deliberate-moving person with a white mane of hair and a white mustache, and a kind, penetrating expression. In his mouth is a pipe.*]

LANDLORD: A very good day.

ADAM [*Jumping up*]: A very good day, sir.

LANDLORD [*Pointing to Eve's chair*]: She gone to pick fruit for lunch?

ADAM [*Embarrassed*]: Looks like it . . . [*Eager to please.*] Shall I go and call her?

LANDLORD: No need. Sit down. She'll come back herself as soon as she feels she's not wanted. [*Looks at Adam carefully.*] Something wrong?

ADAM [*Glumly*]: No, everything's fine.

LANDLORD: Still hurting?

ADAM: What?

LANDLORD: The rib.

ADAM: Yes . . . or rather, no . . . [*Laughs.*] I thought you were referring to . . .

LANDLORD: You've had a row?

ADAM [*Lowering his eyes*]: More or less.

LANDLORD: That's healthy.

ADAM: But it makes me ill.

LANDLORD: I hope you don't regret . . .

ADAM: Regret what?

LANDLORD: My giving her to you.

ADAM: You said she'd be my woman.

LANDLORD: And your woe, Man.

ADAM: Some contradiction!

LANDLORD: The Garden is full of contradictions. Fire, air, water, dust. Take fruit, for example—it decays and at the same time scatters its seeds—the seed is destroyed, but shoots forth new stalks. . . . Woman destroyed one of your ribs—and at the same time brought you new delight.

ADAM: She buzzes around all day like bees round a hive.

LANDLORD [*Laughing*]: Take out the honey.

ADAM: I'll get stung in the process.

LANDLORD: That's the price, Adam. There's no joy without pain. Were you better off before I gave her to you? I felt sorry for you. I saw you walking around the Garden, restless, bored, not happy, not sad, neither enjoying yourself nor suffering. No—man should not live alone.

ADAM: That's what I thought too.

LANDLORD: And now?

ADAM: She's not satisfied.

LANDLORD: With what?

ADAM: With me, I suppose.

LANDLORD [*Bending towards him. In a whisper*]: You have to be the boss.

ADAM: I don't know how.

LANDLORD [*In a strong whisper*]: Tame her! Tame her as you would an animal.

ADAM: But how?

LANDLORD: Be strict! Yell at her if you have to! Force your will upon her! Give her orders!

ADAM: She'll run away.

LANDLORD: Run away? She'll love it. Just try. You'll see her, she'll adore it. Be the boss, her Lord and master.

ADAM: She says I'm a child.

LANDLORD: Of course you're a child if you don't follow my advice.

ADAM [*After a pause*]: I can't . . . I just can't . . . I'm not like that. . . . I'd suffer awfully if I felt I was forcing things on her, if I felt she was living with me against her will . . . what good would that be?

LANDLORD [*After a pause*]: As you wish.

ADAM: I want peace . . . some peace and quiet . . . [*Bursts into tears.*]

LANDLORD: Oho . . . Now you really are a child.

ADAM [*Still crying, hiding his face in his hands*]: Ever since she came . . . every moment . . . there's this sense of responsibility—for her moods, worrying about making her happy all the time . . . seeing she's never bored . . . or sad . . . that she's having a good time . . . and then this constant fear that I might lose her . . . that I might wake up one morning and not find her here . . . as though something terrible was going to happen.

LANDLORD: Oh, Adam. Aren't you ashamed of yourself? You've got your whole life ahead of you.

ADAM: Yes, that's the trouble . . . [*Wipes his tears and looks up.*] Can I ask you a favor?

LANDLORD: Such as?

ADAM: Perhaps . . . perhaps you could give us some place in a distant corner of the Garden . . . far away from everything . . . where we could be alone—just the two of us. [*Pause.*] There's a cave on the other side of the valley . . . all cut off and quiet . . . not a living soul in sight . . . we could live there all on our own.

LANDLORD: How would that help?

ADAM: I think I'd feel quieter . . . more secure.

LANDLORD: And you think she'd agree?

ADAM: If you ordered us to . . . [*EVE appears in the doorway, fuming. She leans against the doorpost with her arms folded.*]

EVE: It strikes me that on this matter I also might have something to say.

LANDLORD [*Laughing*]: I told you she'd come back the moment she realized she wasn't wanted.

EVE: Yes . . . and I heard everything . . . the lot—all your fine advice . . . [*Imitating the Landlord.*] "Be strict with her! Force your will upon her! Give her orders!" Well, you're wrong, Mr. Landlord, he won't boss it over me!

LANDLORD: Of course he won't. He doesn't want to.

EVE [*To Adam*]: And as for your great idea—to live in a secluded cave on the other side of the mountain [*imitating Adam*] "Just the two of us" . . . that's out!

LANDLORD: Why?

EVE: You think I've gone mad? I'm not going to live in some hole at the far end of the Garden, with no one else around, and no conveniences . . .

LANDLORD: Conveniences?

EVE: Yes, conveniences! You want me to walk miles to pick fruit and fetch water? No, sir! I wasn't made for that!

ADAM [*Patiently*]: But it would be so quiet.

EVE: Who wants quiet? I want to enjoy all the pleasures of the Garden. [*Scornfully.*] If you can call them pleasures. . . . But at least you can walk around, you can see, and be seen—yes, be seen—and I'm not ashamed of it! But there? Who would even know I existed? Oh, it'd be great, sitting around all day in some cave, staring at stone walls, and at him . . .

LANDLORD: But he'd like it. Do you think he should give in to you?

EVE: We have equal rights.

LANDLORD: Is this what you call equal rights?

EVE: That's right, Mr. Landlord. I'm the weaker sex, and he's got to give in.

LANDLORD: And if he insists?

EVE [*Shrugging her shoulders*]: We'll get divorced.

LANDLORD [*Bursting out in a roar of laughter*]: And then what'll you do?

EVE: Don't worry. I'll manage.

LANDLORD: And if I order you to live there?

EVE [*Flaring up*]: Great God! Who do you think you are? Just because you breathed life into us, you think you can do what you like with us? You think you can send us here, or there, tell us what we can do and can't do? . . . If that's the price I've got to pay, then you take back your life [*makes a gesture as if taking the life out of her breast*], I don't want it.

LANDLORD: You're getting all worked up over nothing. I wouldn't have ordered you to do it anyway.

EVE: And why not, if I may ask?

LANDLORD: I prefer having you around.

EVE: It'd be boring without us, eh?

LANDLORD: Not exactly . . . but after all, you are quite a pretty creature.

EVE: I always thought that you really created us for your own amusement, not for ours.

LANDLORD: What've you got to complain about?

EVE: I don't like being told not to do certain things! Especially when I don't know why.

ADAM: Eve, he knows best what's good for us and what isn't.

EVE: Sure. You always come up with that one.

LANDLORD: A man can choose only between the things he knows.

EVE: A man, perhaps, but not a woman. . . . Anyway, to tell the truth, I'm bored stiff.

LANDLORD: When you're with him?

EVE: Exactly.

LANDLORD: So soon? After only eight days?

EVE: It's like we've been married eighteen years.

LANDLORD [*Laughing*]: No other creature in the Garden has ever complained of being bored.

EVE: Because no other creature knows how to speak. But I do . . . and anyway you made a lot of the other animals and only two of us.

LANDLORD: Be fruitful and multiply.

EVE: Easily said. . . . And in the meantime?

LANDLORD; Enjoy the beauties of nature.

ADAM [*To Eve*]: Yes, he's quite right.

LANDLORD: Have you seen the buffalo?

EVE [*Disparagingly*]: Yes.

LANDLORD: The Hippopotamus?

EVE: Yes! I've seen all the beasts. Ve-ry interesting! I know the whole damned garden—from the Pishon to the Gihon, from the Tigris to the Euphrates. The gold and the badellium and the onyx and all the rest of it. There's no surprises left.

LANDLORD [*Lighting his pipe*]: But the beauty of these things changes every moment. No moment's like any other.

EVE [*Pointing at pipe*]: What's that?

LANDLORD: A pipe.

EVE: Can I try? [*Takes the pipe, inhales, and starts sputtering.*]

LANDLORD [*Laughing*]: The wages of curiosity.

EVE [*Returning the pipe*]: Still, it's good.

LANDLORD: You see? there still are some things you don't know.

EVE: Which you keep to yourself.

LANDLORD: Come with me.

EVE: Where to?

LANDLORD: I'll show you something never seen since the world was created.

EVE: A fruit?

LANDLORD: You could call it that. In a few minutes the lioness is going to give birth to three cubs. Positively for the first time in history. I myself am quite curious to see how it turns out.

EVE [*Disappointed*]: Not for me! I'll cross that bridge when I come to it.

ADAM [*Rising*]: Yes, I'll come with you.

EVE: [*Mockingly*]: To the end of the world!

LANDLORD [*His hand on Adam's shoulder; to Eve*]: You're going to miss a historic event.

EVE: I'll get a firsthand report from him.

LANDLORD: I like the vulgar way you speak. [*Pinches her cheek.*]

EVE [*Slapping his hand*]: Cut that out! I'm not a little girl! [*LANDLORD and ADAM go out.*]

EVE: [*Calling after them*]: Adam! Come back early!

ADAM [*Offstage*]: Yes, dear.

EVE: [*Looking after them; to herself*]: Like a child cuddling up to his father. As soon as he sees the Old Man, his face lights up and all his confidence returns. Talk about devotion! [*Goes in and sits on a chair, then looks around.*] It's all so damn boring. [*Yawns.*] If there was only something to do . . . [*Playing with fruit in her hand.*] And this vegetarian diet, too . . . [*Pause*] And it can go on for a hundred years, a thousand years, ten thousand years, for ever and ever, the same old routine . . . [*Pause, then bursts out laughing.*] "Enjoy the beauties of nature," he says. For how long? The same old sunrise, the same old sunset. . . . O.K., so they change a bit from day to day . . . but so what? Birds twittering, cows mooing . . . and flowers . . . well flowers aren't bad, but there are so many of them I could puke . . . all that—for ever and ever. . . . Horrible! [*The SNAKE appears through the window, approaching on tiptoe, unnoticed by Eve. He is tall, lean, young, dressed in a tight black sweater, narrow black trousers and black socks. A black peaked hat, His eyes shine with cunning.*]

SNAKE [*Through the window*]: Ssssst.

EVE: [*Lifts her head, startled, puts her hand on her breast*]: Oh . . . you scared me.

SNAKE [*Laughs; gestures with his hand*]: He isn't here?

EVE: He's gone out.

SNAKE: With the old man?

EVE: Who else?

SNAKE: May I?

EVE [*Shrugging her shoulders*]: Why not?

SNAKE: Having a great time?

EVE: Not really.

EVE: Well . . . eating . . .

SNAKE: Bananas?

EVE: Anything.

SNAKE: Anything?

EVE: Mmmm, almost . . .

SNAKE: [*With a cunning smile*]: I saw you this morning.

EVE: Did you? Where?

SNAKE [*Winks*]: Down there . . . by that tree . . .

EVE [*Startled*]: No!

SNAKE: Oh yes. A charming sight. The way you approached . . . looked around you cautiously . . . came closer . . . hugged the trunk . . . looked up . . . and suddenly ran off as if you'd seen the devil! [*Laughs.*]

EVE: I thought I sensed two eyes gleaming among the branches. . . . Was it you?

SNAKE: Could have been.

EVE: Are you following me around?

SNAKE: Well, it isn't every day we see a beauty like you in the Garden.

EVE [*Smiling*]: Where'd you pick up the flattery routine?

SNAKE: The eyes teach the tongue. Your figure is superb! Perfection itself! [*Whistles.*]

EVE: Cut it out.

SNAKE: Really—I didn't think the Old Man had it in him. Excellent workmanship. I take off my hat to him.

EVE: Didn't you admire his workmanship before I came along?

SNAKE: Oh, no! You're something special! And what's more . . . unique! A pearl in the crown of creation.

EVE: Don't overdo it, or I'll stop believing you.

SNAKE: Oh, no, you'll still believe me. But I'm really not exaggerating. Would you like me to tell you something.

EVE: If it's interesting.

SNAKE: Well, then—Before you came on the scene, there were days I thought I'd swallow myself alive out of sheer boredom. God! What can a snake like me find to do in this damn Paradise? This eternal peace! This infinite tranquility! [*Disgustedly*] The wolf lying down with the lamb, the leopard with the kid, the cow with the bear, and the lions carrying on like cattle—[*An agonized cry.*] It's all one great big endless prison! [*Quietly, intimately*] A very pleasant prison, of course, with every modern convenience, lacking in nothing . . . but a prison is always a prison!

EVE: My very words!

SNAKE: But from the moment you came on the scene, it all changed. All at once I was filled with a constant sense of excitement. . . . Shall I call it desire? Passion? Longing? Pain? Unspeakable joy? All of them! Yes, all together! I started hiding behind trees to watch you. I'd see you out walking with Adam, arm in arm, or sitting with him beside the river, or jumping into the water. . . .

EVE: You weren't ashamed of yourself?

SNAKE: No. I admit it. Or—I would see you going out early each morning to pick fruit, alone—

EVE: Funny how I never noticed.

SNAKE: I slid and I slithered. I crawled on my belly—silently, stealthily over the leaves. . . . I knew I could never get you, but still the whole world looked different. [*Laughing*] I even learned to appreciate nature.

EVE: You don't say!

SNAKE: It's strange, but it's true. The dawns and the sunsets . . .

EVE: Interesting . . .

SNAKE: The blossoming of the almond trees, the humming of the bees, the sprouting of grass . . . [*Draws closer to her, whispers.*] I even started writing poetry in secret.

EVE: Very interesting.

SNAKE: Painting, too.

EVE: As bad as all that?

SNAKE [*Pulls out a piece of paper*]: I sketched you coming out of the water after a swim . . . [*Shows her the picture.*]

EVE [*Looking at the picture*]: Is that what I look like?

SNAKE: To me.

EVE: What a beautiful body!

SNAKE: You've never had a chance to see yourself.

EVE: Only in the water, and that was all blurred, I must say it's quite impressive.

SNAKE: It's not finished. "Eve Bathing" I call it. But I still have to work on it a lot more. It isn't impressive enough.

EVE: It's a good likeness.

SNAKE: That's the trouble—it should be more than a good likeness.

EVE [*Looking at him with admiration*]: You talk so . . . so Bohemian.

SNAKE [*Modestly*]: I'm only an amateur. I like color . . . shape . . .

EVE [*Coquettishly*]: Mine?

SNAKE: Yours? Of course! Your eyes . . . your hair . . . your neck . . . your breasts . . . your whole figure . . . [*Draws near, whispers.*] Why didn't you pluck it?

EVE [*Startled*]: What do you mean?

SNAKE: From that tree.

EVE [*Stubbornly*]: It's not allowed.

SNAKE: Who said so?

EVE: Adam. The Old Man's orders.

SNAKE: You do everything he tells you?

EVE: We're grateful to him.

SNAKE: For what?

EVE: For life.

SNAKE: You could try—just once.

EVE: No. It's forbidden.

SNAKE: Pardon my asking, but have you ever wondered why it's forbidden?

EVE: No. It's forbidden and that's that. There's no point in talking about it.

SNAKE: Well then, I'll tell you why. [*Gets up and sits close to her.*] You see . . . he wants to feel that he's the boss.

EVE: But he is the boss! He owns the Garden!

SNAKE: Yes, of course. . . . But how can I explain it to you? . . . Look . . . he's given complete freedom to all the creatures in the Garden—you, me, all the creatures—we're all free to do whatever we want. He doesn't interfere. He is—how shall I put it?—a very liberal landlord, with very progressive ideas. From the outset he decided that the principle of freedom should rule in the garden. I'll put them all in here, he said to himself, give them everything—at my own expense, gratis, no work required in return, so they can all enjoy untroubled lives, and I'll leave them alone to do as they like.

EVE: Surely that was generous of him, wasn't it?

SNAKE: Of course, I wouldn't deny it. Generous, broadminded . . . but look—what's he got left now? He's finished his work. There's nothing more for him to do. He's out on a pension, as it were. A landowner, philanthropist, yes, and a great educator, who's got nothing to do but walk around the Garden watching everyone else. We go about our lives as if he didn't exist, in fact, as if it weren't thanks to him that our lives are so easy. He's being forgotten. We don't need the Old Man any more . . . but he doesn't want to feel that he's not needed. He wants to be the boss! He wants us to remember that he gave us all this. . . .

EVE: Actually, what he demands sounds quite fair.

SNAKE: And quite mean, too. Just so as he can go on feeling he's boss, he's decided to forbid something, anything. It doesn't make any difference what it is, or why . . . just as long as it's forbidden. [*Loudly.*] One tree in the Garden is forbidden!

EVE: But isn't the fruit somehow—dangerous?

SNAKE: Rubbish! It's not the fruit that matters to him, it's the ban! A ban which affects us but not him. With this ban he attains his advantage over us—his only advantage. [*With a poisonous smile.*] Ah, how he enjoys it—the sight of you walking around that tree, not daring to pluck the fruit. He gloats! He drools at the mouth! His mustache quivers with delight. . . . Now I ask you—isn't there malice in that?

EVE: And you—have you . . . tasted it?

SNAKE: Have I? . . . Not just once—dozens of times.

EVE: And . . . is it—good?

SNAKE: Exquisite! Divine! [*Stroking her shoulder.*] Do you want to?

EVE: No . . . no . . .

SNAKE: Afraid?

EVE: Adam would never forgive me.

SNAKE: He'd forgive you—that goodnatured fellow! And anyway—he could also . . .

EVE: You don't know him. He's so devoted to the Old Man, like a puppy.

SNAKE: He needn't know . . .

EVE: But what about the Old Man? He sees everything and knows everything.

SNAKE: So what? Let him know.

EVE: He'd punish me.

SNAKE [*Laughing*]: You? He loves you . . . the old sinner. Haven't you noticed?

EVE: He's never given me the slightest hint.

SNAKE: If you could only see the way he looks at you when you walk through the garden.

EVE [*Laughing*]: Really?

SNAKE: So help me! God! I've seen him. He desires you just as much as you desire the forbidden fruit. [*Laughs.*] Measure for measure eh? He punish you? His heart would break first . . . Ah, what a fruit that is . . . [*Approaches her.*]

EVE: Oh, quit it, will you?

SNAKE: Want to see? I've brought some . . . [*Removes his hat and takes out three rosy apples. Offers her one.*]

EVE [*Shocked*]: Oh . . .

SNAKE: Smell it!

EVE [*Smelling it delightedly*]: Heaven!

SNAKE: Taste it.

EVE: You.

SNAKE [*Bites the apple he is holding*]: See? . . . Nothing's happened to me.

EVE [*Laughing*]: I'm dying to taste it.

SNAKE: Taste it—you won't die.

EVE: Should I?

SNAKE: On my responsibility.

EVE [*Looks longingly at the apple in her hand*]: You won't tell?

SNAKE: You can always say I tempted you.

EVE: Well, just a teeny piece . . . [*Takes a bite. Her eyes open wide.*]

SNAKE: Well?

EVE: Divine.

SNAKE: Now—you see what I meant? Our noble, generous, wise, all-knowing Landlord dreamed up this ban so we wouldn't get the most out of life.

EVE [*Devouring the apple ravenously*]: It's delicious . . . so juicy . . . [*Greedily finishes the fruit.*]

SNAKE [*Offering her another*]: More?

EVE [*Dazedly*]: No . . . no . . . that's enough . . .do you also feel like that?

SNAKE: Like what?

EVE: A . . . a sort of dizziness . . . a sort of pleasant sweetness. [*Laughs.*] What's happening to me?

SNAKE: So something is happening to you?

EVE [*Limply lays her head on his shoulder*]: I've never felt anything like this before . . . everything's going round and round . . . like a dream. [*Laughs.*] Why am I laughing so much?

SNAKE [*Kisses her on the mouth*]: How sweet!

EVE: Not here. [*In a weak voice.*] Adam might come in any minute.

SNAKE [*Whispering*]: Shall we go?

EVE [*In a swoon*]: Where to?

SNAKE: It doesn't matter where.

EVE: Remember—you tempted me.

SNAKE: Of course . . . [*He lifts her, supports her with his arms. They go out, arms around each other. A chorus of birds sing outside.* ADAM *approaches and enters carrying a lion cub.*]

ADAM: Eve? [*Comes in and looks around.*] Must have gone out for a walk. [*Sits on a chair and strokes the cub.*] Cute little cub! How does the world appeal to you? Good? What? You can't see it yet? . . . It doesn't matter . . . in a day or two you'll see it all . . . You'll enjoy the sunrise . . . the dew glistening on the grass . . . the webs of light glinting among the leaves, and the wind whispering in the branches . . . there's a wonderful world ready and waiting for you . . . Will Eve like you? Of course she will—that's why the Old Man gave you to us . . . with you around she'll never be bored. I'm sure . . . she'll be able to stroke you, and pet you . . . You won't bite her now, will you? Of course not! . . . Now close your eyes and sleep, you lazy little thing . . . [*Looks at the table and sees what is there—a piece of paper, a peaked hat, a red apple. Frightened, he puts down the cub, takes the paper and looks with intense hate at the drawing. Takes the hat, examines it, and throws it violently to the ground.*] So he came, the bastard, he finally came here! [*Takes the apple, hesitates then digs his teeth into it. Spits out a mouthful and hurls the apple out the window, picks up the drawing, looks at it, and tears it to pieces. Cries out.*] Curse you! Curse you above every beast of the field! [*Turns to the window with a cry of pain.*] Eve! Eve! [*Bursts into tears.*] I knew this'd happen one day . . . I knew it . . . [*Waits for a reply, sits on a chair with his face in his hands. Outside birds sing again.* EVE *approaches the hut stealthily, stops at the entrance and strokes the doorpost, looking at Adam. Her appearance has changed greatly since she went out. Her face shows traces of a tempestuous experience, mingled with guilt and shame. Her lips are painted scarlet, a necklace of snake-eggs hangs around her neck, she wears a bone bracelet and carries a snakeskin bag. She takes out a cigarette and lights it.* ADAM *raises his head and is amazed at her appearance. Stares at her as though seeing her for the first time.*] You? [*She does not reply. There is a melancholy smile on her face.* ADAM, *in anguish, looks her over from head to toe.*] Why have you done this to me? Why? [*He awaits her reply, but she does not speak.*] Was life with me so terrible? [*She shakes her head.*] [*He looks at her in dismay.*] I don't recognize you any more.

EVE [*Slowly, sadly*]: Perhaps now you're really seeing me for the first time.

ADAM: That red on your lips . . . the handbag . . . the necklace . . . Why did you go with him? Why?

EVE [*Quietly*]: You were too faithful.

ADAM: To you?

EVE: No—to the Old Man.

ADAM: And that's why you went with him?

EVE: If you'd tasted the fruit, you'd understand . . .

ADAM [*With abhorrence*]: Death.

EVE: Perhaps . . . but how are we to know what life is?

ADAM [*Momentarily perplexed—then shouts*]: I'll crush his head in. [*Whispers in fury.*] I hate him! I hate him to death!

EVE [*Her face brightens with a smile*]: Oh-ho, so you've tasted it too.

ADAM [*Holding his head in his hands*]: Oh, God.

EVE: It doesn't matter. Now we can do without him.

ADAM [*In consternation*]: Have you gone out of your mind?

EVE [*Quietly*]: I have tasted knowledge. [*Pause.*] And so have you.

ADAM [*Seething*]: I won't be able to bear it . . . I can't . . . to know that you . . . flesh of my flesh . . . with that . . . [*shouts at her*] with that snake! That damned sly serpent crawling on its belly like a thief! Lurking for you . . . following you around . . . that snake in the grass with the gleam of lust in his eyes and venom in his tongue.

EVE [*With a quiet smile*]: This is how I love you.

ADAM: Me?

EVE: Yes. With your hate . . . your jealousy . . . your longing for revenge . . .

ADAM: Me?

EVE [*Draws near to him and sits beside him; puts her arm on his shoulders*]: Does that surprise you?

ADAM [*Pushing her arm away*]: Leave me alone.

EVE: Now you're a man.

ADAM: And you're—soaked in sin.

EVE: If you like I'll get rid of these. I don't need them any more. [*Takes off the necklace and throws it out of the window, then the bracelet and the handbag.*]

ADAM: But you'll never be rid of him.

EVE: You're wrong. He no longer exists. I just had to taste it once—to know.

ADAM [*With a pained experience*]: But he has known you.

EVE: Oh, that's so unimportant. . . . Don't you understand? Don't you understand that before this I was full of sin and that now I am clean? Before, it haunted me, it gave me no rest. I was with you yet not with you. It pulled at me, like a spell . . . like a snake crawling inside me.

ADAM: Don't ever mention his name to me.

EVE: He no longer means anything to me. . . . But it looks as though you'll never understand.

ADAM: What?

EVE: That I had to know before I could choose. That I had to taste evil to know what good is. I had to choose you. Of my own free will! [*Pause, then with great love.*] Now I'm willing to go with you to the end of the earth. Even to your cave on the other side of the valley.

ADAM [*With a cry of pain*]: But now we won't be alone there! We won't be alone anywhere any more! He'll always be there, everywhere! How will I stand it? Him, the third, haunting me all the time, even when I close my eyes—I'll always see him there, lurking for you! [*Covers his face with his hands and cries.*]

EVE [*Embracing him*]: My man . . . my child . . . it's as though you've been born again for me . . . only this time different—with love and passion and desire and hate—full of sin! [*She notices the cub, surprised.*] What's that?

ADAM [*Turns to it, mollified*]: It's just been born.

EVE: (Picks it up by the neck and looks at it) What a darling! [*To Adam*] Did you see it being born?

ADAM [*Smiling*]: Yes, with a lot of pain.

EVE: Sweet pains, I'm sure . . . how soft it is . . . how sweet . . . God! What a creature! . . . [*From afar comes the voice of the* LANDLORD *calling* "Adam!" *The voice reechoes on all sides.* "A-dam!" "A-dam!" "A-dam!" *The two are terrified.*]

ADAM [*Trembling*]: This is it. I knew it'd come.

EVE: We must be brave.

ADAM: Perhaps we should hide.

EVE: He sees everything.

ADAM [*Glancing at her*]: Are you ashamed too?

EVE: A little, As though I was naked.

ADAM: Shall we tell him the truth?

EVE: Yes, my love. [*LANDLORD approaches with heavy step. Both cringe in anticipation. He stops at the entrance and looks at them for a while in mute reproach.*]

LANDLORD [*Maliciously*]: Was it sweet? [*Waits for a reply.*] Very sweet? [*Waits again, decisively.*] I'm sorry for you . . . you could have lived here forever . . . at my expense, without lifting a finger, without cares. You could have enjoyed this Garden for all Eternity . . . I wouldn't have asked you for a thing—no payment, no service, not even your thanks.

EVE [*Whispers*]: Only obedience . . .

LANDLORD: Rubbish! There was only one tree, out of all the millions in the Garden, that I told you not to touch. Too high a price for all the pleasures I prepared for you, was it? Who do you think I worked so hard for during those six days of Creation? Who did I plant this Garden for? For myself? I'm too old. At my age I could have lived quite comfortably in the void. No, it was for you. Only for you.

EVE: I . . .

LANDLORD [*Stops her angrily*]: Be quiet! Don't tell me the snake tempted you. No creature in this Garden can be tempted without wanting to be tempted. Out of all those trees . . . just one tree . . .

EVE: Why did you plant it all? To test us? To torment us?

LANDLORD: I planted every possible species of tree, and this was one of them. Did you have to taste it?

EVE [*Quietly*]: Yes . . . But what's done is done. Tell us our punishment. That's what you've come for, isn't it?

LANDLORD: You won't enjoy hearing it.

EVE: We'll accept it. Go on, tell us.

LANDLORD [*Imperiously*]: You are to vacate the Garden within 24 hours!

EVE [*Quietly*]: 24 minutes will do. [*Gets up and pulls Adam by the hand.*] Come on, Adam, let's go. [*ADAM does not move. Looks with pain at the Landlord.*] Come along—can't you see he's waiting?

LANDLORD: There's no happiness for you out there.

EVE: But there's freedom. Isn't that enough?

LANDLORD: Yes—and sweat . . . and toil . . .

EVE: Which is better than charity. We don't want any favors.

ADAM: Nor any bans, either.

EVE: Bravo, Adam. [*Taking him by the hand.*] Come on, let's go.

LANDLORD [*Shaking his head*]: All because of one tree . . .

EVE: You could call it the tree of knowledge. We know a lot of things now that we didn't know before.

LANDLORD. You know sin.

EVE: That's a lot. [*Moves away, hand in hand with* ADAM. *Turns her head back.*] And also how to resist it. And love. And good. And evil. [*Pause.*] And I'm not sure who's going to be more sorry—you or us. But in any case you've enjoyed having us around, haven't you? Just a bit, while it lasted? But you expected us to live all our lives without sin. Just like you. Because you can't sin. You're not allowed to . . . You were willing to give us everything—even immortality—as long as we stayed tied to you with silken cords! You envy us, don't you? [*Scornfully.*] Your perfect world! What a bore! [*They both walk away.*]

ADAM [*Whispers to Eve*]: We haven't even thanked him . . .

EVE [*With a mock curtsey*]: Oh . . . thank you very much indeed.

ADAM: Say goodbye.

EVE [*Another curtsey*]: And . . . goodbye. [ADAM *and* EVE *go out. The* LANDLORD *watches them with sorrow. The* SNAKE *appears on tiptoe and stands beside him.*]

SNAKE [*Watching them go*]: Some dish, eh?

LANDLORD [*Startled at seeing him there; furiously*]: Be damned to hell! Go crawl on your belly.

SNAKE: Come now, you did have quite a thing for her, didn't you? . . . Admit it. [*Ironically.*] Oh yes, for him too, of course.

LANDLORD [*Looks at him, then smiles painfully*]: How ungrateful they are . . . and it was I who gave them life.

SNAKE: Didn't you know in advance that this is how it would turn out?

LANDLORD: I suppose so.

SNAKE: You shouldn't have forbidden them the apple. Then they wouldn't have been tempted.

LANDLORD: You want to know the truth? I wanted them to taste this pleasure as well.

SNAKE: You're a cunning one!

LANDLORD: Not the way you think. I still toyed with the hope that they'd be able to resist. [*Laughs.*]

SNAKE: And if they had?

LANDLORD: They would have stayed here for ever.

SNAKE: It'll be dull without them, eh?

LANDLORD [*Sighs*]: Oh, yes, very. You know. I think these were the happiest days I have ever known. I relived myself in those two—in their slightest move, their every disappointment, excitement, discovery—even in their fight with temptation. And now? Whom have I punished? Them? They'll have an exciting life—hard, brief, but fascinating. Full of pain and sin and joy and sorrow. And who am I left with here?

SNAKE: With me.

LANDLORD: You? I know you. You'll sneak out of here—even on your belly.

SNAKE: Only if you forbid it.

LANDLORD: Yes, I'll forbid it . . . and you'll wriggle out and in, and out again. Yes, I've condemned myself to eternal loneliness. [*Takes a handkerchief from his pocket and wipes away a tear.*]

SNAKE [*Glancing at him*]: You crying?

LANDLORD [*Smiles through his tears*]: Nonsense. Just a little upset. These goodbyes, you know.

SNAKE [*With a cunning look*]: Actually, there's nothing to stop you going after them.

LANDLORD [*Comes to himself*]: And leave the Garden to you? No! Not as long as I live!

SNAKE: I'll make trouble for you.

LANDLORD: I know you will . . . and that's my only consolation. Your venom will be my only antidote to boredom. . . . [*Slaps the* SNAKE *on the back.*] Come on, let's go . . . you devil! [LANDLORD *links arms with the* SNAKE *and they both go off through the Garden. The only sound now heard is of the birds.*]

## PART 2
### EAST OF EDEN

*20 Years later. Late afternoon. A stone hut. Sparse rustic furniture; a solid oak table, four chairs, a plain rocking chair. Some work tools in a corner by the door; a hoe, a shovel, a large axe. On the walls, animal skeletons, horned deer's head, cheap landscape print. One entrance leads to the outside, the other to the inner quarters—presumably a kitchen, bedroom, storeroom, etc.* EVE *sits in the rocker knitting a sweater. She looks about forty. Full body, limbs slackening; her face still retains its beauty.*

EVE [*Counting the stitches*]: Two and three and one; two and three and two; two and three and one; [*Stops, lifts her head to look out the window.*] It'll be dark soon and Adam isn't back yet. What can have happened to him today? He didn't even come back for lunch. . . . [*Sighs.*] The men are in the fields all day and you're supposed to just sit around waiting. . . . [*Goes on knitting.*] Two and three and two . . . I've lost count . . . two and three and one . . . two and three and two . . . who knows what he is doing there all day? Anyway, when I went there at lunch time I saw no sign of him . . . strange—[*Pause.*] Of course, it will be more comfortable in the new house—but the same old loneliness, the horrible loneliness . . . not a living soul anywhere in sight . . . [*Sighs, resumes knitting, recites in irony.*] "Who can find a virtuous woman . . . for her price is far above rubies. . . . The heart of the husband doth safely trust in her, etc., etc., etc. [*Enter* ABEL, *about 18, with a smooth sensitive face, tall & handsome. Wears an embroidered shirt, blue work trousers and sandals. A shepherd's bag hangs from his shoulder. He holds a short reed.* EVE *lifts her head, her face brightens.*] Abel! What brings you home at this time of day?

ABEL [*Playfully*]: My heart went out to my mother, so woebegone and forlorn.

EVE: Don't make fun of me. You haven't come home for me.

ABEL: Would my gracious mother have a pair of scissors? Or a razor blade?

EVE [*Imitating his voice*]: What would you do with a pair of scissors or a razor blade?

ABEL [*Shows her the reed*]: I would pierce holes in this yellow herbage.

EVE: Pray, what have you there?

ABEL: A fife I plucked from the banks of the brook.

EVE [*Tiring of the game*]: Oh, cut it out. Call a reed a reed. [*Hands him the scissors.*] and now what?

ABEL [*Blows into the fife, producing a shrill whistle*]: Like it?

EVE [*Doubtfully*]: Not bad . . .

ABEL: But that's nothing. I've discovered that if I pierce holes in the middle, I can make a tune.

EVE: Really? How?

ABEL: Simple. By breathing into it.

EVE: Oh, Abel . . . I see you're on the way to becoming a poet.

ABEL [*Cutting the reed*]: Well, isn't it beautiful to be a poet?

EVE: Beautiful, yes—but not very practical.

ABEL: Oh, mother—in such a family of three practical people, let Abel, for one, be a creator of beauty. In spite of what father always says—what is beauty able to create?

EVE: Beautiful, Abel! I haven't heard anything so poetic for over 20 years.

ABEL [*Catches the slip*]: And who spoke like that 20 years ago?

EVE [*Resumes knitting; evasively*]: Oh, you know . . . we were in Paradise. . . . What does it matter?

ABEL: What was it like there?

EVE: Trees . . . plenty of water . . . all kinds of birds and animals. A garden.

ABEL: And what did you live on?

EVE: We picked fruit.

ABEL: And you didn't have to work at all?

EVE: Of course not. When you can have all you want of anything . . .

ABEL [*Longingly*]: And you could sit by the stream all day—and dream?

EVE: You can dream here as well.

ABEL: And you were turned out?

EVE [*Impatiently*]: Yes, we were turned out.

ABEL: Why?

EVE: The Landlord didn't want us there. That's why.

ABEL: But why didn't he want you?

EVE: "Why-why-why!" You're like a three-year-old child!

ABEL: But I have a right to know! Why do you and father hide it from us?

EVE: There's nothing to hide. The Landlord didn't like us so he sent us away.

ABEL: Wasn't it something to do with—a snake?

EVE [*Startled*]: What put that in your head?

ABEL: Once when you and father were quarreling, he yelled: "Don't think I've forgotten about The Snake Affair!" Then you hushed him up because Cain and I were in the next room.

EVE: Oh, you know your father. He says all sort of nonsense when he loses his temper. . . .

ABEL: No—He's got something against snakes. He hates them.

EVE: Why do you think that?

ABEL: Why do I think that? You want me to repeat all his proverbs against snakes? They're enough to fill a book! "The snake is more cunning than any beast of the field," "A snake in the grass . . ."

EVE [*Laughing*]: Is that what he teaches you?

ABEL: Oh, I could quote lots more. And his eyes flash with fury when he speaks of them.

EVE [*Deprecatingly*]: He's just frightened of their bite.

ABEL: And you're not?

EVE [*Not looking at him; suppressing a memory*]: I'm a stay-at-home, as you know. It's ages since I've seen a snake. By the way, have you seen your father?

ABEL [*preoccupied*]: No. He must be up the hill.

EVE: He hasn't even looked in all day. Not even for lunch.

ABEL: He's working hard. He wants to finish the new house before winter.

EVE: Do you know if he managed to find porcelain tiles for the kitchen?

ABEL [*Absently*]: I think so. . . . Why doesn't the Landlord ever come to visit us?

EVE: "Why" again! Because he never leaves his garden, that's why!

ABEL: You know, if you hadn't told me about him, I'd believe he was just a spirit, with no body.

EVE: That's what your sons and grandsons will believe, I'm sure.

ABEL: I have a tremendous desire to see him with my own eyes.

EVE: I've told you—he never leaves the garden.

ABEL: Then I'll go to him.

EVE: The Garden of Eden is lost, Abel.

ABEL: Forever?

EVE: For ever.

ABEL: There's no way back?

EVE: I've told you time and again—there are guards at the gates with flaming swords in their hands.

ABEL: Couldn't they be . . . bribed?

EVE: Abel, I'm surprised at you. Bribery?

ABEL: You must have committed a dreadful sin to be thrown out for ever.

EVE: Oh, stop it, Abel. That's enough.

ABEL [*Rebelliously*]: But why should *I* suffer for it? Must *I* atone for the sins of my fathers? For some forbidden fruit. . . .

EVE [*Alarmed*]: Who said anything about fruit?

ABEL: It was just a turn of phrase. [*Suspiciously.*] Did you really eat forbidden fruit?

EVE [*Rising angrily*]: We ate nothing . . . and I wish you'd stop all this nonsense.

ABEL: I have a feeling that one day I'll get there and find out the truth for myself. [*Blows through the perforated reed.*] Listen to that!

EVE: Lovely! [*ABEL plays a pastoral love song—preferably a familiar one.*] That would make a charming love song.

ABEL: Which I can play to the sheep.

EVE: Patience . . . one day you'll be playing it to a girl.

ABEL: And where is she going to materialize from?

EVE: He who provided a woman for your father will provide one for you.

ABEL: You mean I should wait for a miracle.

EVE: Abel, you have your whole life ahead of you.

ABEL: Ah, how long will that be? [*Plays a sad melody. CAIN bursts in. Powerful and robust. Wild beard, but a childlike expression. Dusty clothes. Wears long boots and holds a heavy pick.*]

CAIN [*On the threshold, fuming*]: What's going on around here, anyway? Just thought you'd leave the sheep in the field and come running to mother, eh?

EVE: What's happened, Cain? What are you shouting about?

CAIN: What's happened? Where are the sheep? Where are they?

ABEL: I—

CAIN: You what? Go and see what they've done to me. Go on!

ABEL: I left them up on the hill.

CAIN: Sure. You left them up on the hill and thought they'd wait there till you got back! I suppose you forgot that sheep have feet?

ABEL: But what's happened?

CAIN: Go see for yourself! There I am, digging away, and suddenly I see the whole damn flock trampling down the vegetables! All the cabbages are ruined!

ABEL: They were grazing so peacefully when I left them. I never dreamt . . .

CAIN: Never dreamt! You do nothing else! What the hell do you dream about all bloody day, anyway?

EVE: Cain, how many times do I have to tell you to use civilized language in this house?

CAIN: And you're sticking up for him! You think this is the first time it's happened? Only last week I saw the sheep moving toward the barley field, I yelled for Abel—"Abel! Abel!"—not a sign of him. An hour later I found him asleep under some tree . . . with a bunch of lilies in his hand!

ABEL: I was tired—

CAIN: You were tired! Call yourself a shepherd? You're a wool-gatherer. There's one thing I know—a farmer has to be a farmer—and not to dream while he's working, or run off to Mama in the middle of the day.

EVE [*To Abel*]: That was irresponsible of you, Abel.

ABEL: I know, I admit it. [*Turns to the door.*] I'm going back.

CAIN [*Takes him by the arm and stops him*]: You can stay now. I chased them back to the hill myself, and you can't bring back my cabbages. They're completely ruined.

EVE: Cain, really . . . all this fuss about a few heads of cabbage.

CAIN [*Furiously*]: "A few heads of cabbage." What do you know about it? Do you know what it takes to grow cabbage under our conditions? To hoe, manure and rake, to sow, to plant, to water, and then to hoe again and again. . . . Who'm I doing all this for? Myself? No! For all of us! So we can all have food to eat! Wait till father comes. We'll see what he has to say about it.

EVE: Cain, I beg of you. Don't make father angry. He has enough troubles of his own.

CAIN: Don't worry. He won't get too angry with Abel. But I just want him to know. So he doesn't blame me for the poor crop this year.

ABEL: He wouldn't blame you. Anyway, I'll tell him what happened myself.

CAIN [*Scornfully*] Yes, you'll tell him—and you'll be Dad's good little boy again . . . [*Stands the pick on the floor upside down.*] Here, bring me a hammer and a strong nail. I have to fix this.

ABEL: Right. [*Goes into the interior of the house.*]

EVE [*Approaches Cain, gently*] You didn't have to get mad with him like that. He's younger than you . . . and you know how touchy he is.

CAIN [*Without anger but with a certain bitterness*]: If you love him so much, why don't you try to make a man out of him? After all, he's no longer a child. He's got to learn to be responsible for what he does. Looking after sheep isn't a game—it's work. You think he works? He just fools around, believe me, I see him in the fields. If it wasn't for me, half the sheep'd have been dead long ago . . . Sometimes he even forgets to milk them. Do you know what torture it is for a sheep to go around with swollen udders?

EVE [*Putting her hand on his shoulder*]: You're right, Cain. I know you're right. But what can you do? He's like that—a dreamer. Gentle, sensitive, and he has to be taught in the language he understands—through gentleness, not shouting.

CAIN: Well, I'm no psychologist—I'm just a simple farmer, no more.

EVE: But try to understand him. Being a farmer doesn't mean you have to be a crude peasant.

CAIN: Well, I'm a crude peasant. So what?

EVE: So what? A farmer can also be cultured and well-mannered.

CAIN: Where? Have you seen one? And anyway, you lose your temper often enough.

EVE: Me?

CAIN: Not with Abel of course—with father. You think I haven't noticed?

EVE: Noticed what?

CAIN: And you're not in the right. Mostly you're just not in the right. I can tell you that to your face.

EVE [*With a forced laugh*]: Well, it's a lucky father whose son sticks up for him against his wife.

CAIN: I don't want to interfere, but sometimes my heart goes out to him.

EVE: Well, I'm glad to hear you love your father so much. But you inherited that from me—like so many other things.

CAIN: If I was as quick-tempered as you, I'd have killed someone by now.

EVE: Cain, Honor your father—but your mother too.

CAIN: Oh, cut out the preaching, will you? [*Enter* ABEL *with a big hammer and some nails.*]

ABEL [*Giving the nails to Cain*]: Are these all right?

CAIN [*Taking the hammer and a nail*]: Yes, they're fine. You hold the handle. I'll knock it in.

EVE: Shall I fix something to eat, boys?

CAIN: I'm not hungry.

ABEL: Nor am I.

EVE: Perhaps just a bite before you go back to the field. [*Goes into the interior.* ABEL *takes the handle of the pick, and* CAIN *hammers a thick nail into the top.*]

CAIN [*Testing it*]: That's it. Should hold now. I hit a rock and it came loose.

ABEL: Are you digging the channel for turnips?

CAIN [*Laughing*]: I've been irrigating the turnips for the past two weeks, as you haven't even noticed. This is for the tomatoes. I've been experimenting with a new kind—I crossed two strains and developed a new variety—small, round and juicy. [*Proudly*] This evening I'll bring some back to Dad, I can hardly wait to hear what he'll say.

ABEL: It'll be a surprise for him.

CAIN: And how! Would you like a taste?

ABEL: Of course.

CAIN: I'll pick a few when I've finished with the irrigation pipes.

ABEL: Perhaps I could help you.

CAIN: Who'll look after the sheep?

ABEL: We'll be able to see them, won't we?

CAIN [*Thinks; then*]: O.K. Get the spanner and let's go. [*ABEL goes into the interior. CAIN notices the flute. He picks it up, turns it over, tests it, puts it to his lips and blows a few hoarse sounds. ABEL returns, spanner in hand. Showing him the flute.*] What's this?

ABEL: A flute. [*Takes it and plays a tune.*]

CAIN [*Amazed*]: Wonderful! Show me! [*Takes it, blows hoarse sounds again.*] I can't get it to work.

ABEL: I'll teach you. [*Takes the flute.*] You see? There are five holes. Each time you lift your finger off one of them, you get a different sound. [*Plays a tune.*]

CAIN [*With amazement and envy*]: With sound like that you could charm wild beasts. Or even girls.

ABEL: If you knew where there were any.

CAIN: Who knows? Maybe beyond the horizon. Maybe they'll drop out of the sky.

ABEL: Out of the sky?

CAIN: Dad says there are giants somewhere on earth. I've never seen one, but if there are, they must have daughters.

ABEL: I dream of girls almost every night—naked, fair-skinned, with long golden hair. Last night too I dreamed of one. A beauty. She was bathing in a stream. I stood behind a bush and watched her. It was such a delightful feeling. I thought this must be Paradise, the Garden of Eden. Then I woke up—and I saw you standing there. Haven't you ever had a dream like that?

CAIN: I'm so dead beat after a day's work that I just fall into bed and sleep like a log. I never dream. Or if I do, I forget it in the morning. [Pause.] I only remember one dream, because it came back a number of times, and it frightened me. I was standing in a field chopping trees. Suddenly an enormous long fat snake appeared and started twisting and coiling itself around my body, up to my neck. I tried to throw it off, but I couldn't. It raised its head to my face and hissed—ssss . . . sss . . . and its long, sharp tongue shot out of its mouth like a flame. Ugh! [*EVE returns, carrying a plate of sandwiches.*]

EVE: Here, I've brought you something. Sit down and have a bite.

CAIN: We haven't time, mother. We're in a hurry.

EVE: Just for a few minutes.

CAIN: We have some work to finish. It'll soon be dark.

EVE: Well then, take it with you. I'm sure you must be famished. [*Stuffs the sandwiches into Cain's pockets and Abel's bag, despite their protests.*]

CAIN [*Going out*]: See you.

ABEL: Goodbye, mother.

EVE: Goodbye. Don't be back late. [*CAIN and ABEL go out with their tools. EVE hesitates a moment and then turns to the door and calls after them.*] Cain! Abel! Bring back some meat and vegetables. The kitchen's empty. I've nothing to give your father when he comes home. [*From the distance comes Cain's* "O.K., Ma." *EVE paces the room restlessly, and then sits down in the rocker, musing.*] Grown sons . . . so different from each other—just like Adam and me. Cain's got a lot of me in him—and he loves his father. Abel's very close to me . . . Oedipus complex apparently . . . so sensitive. It's tough for him, very tough. The tender hearts get trampled in the struggle to live. He has a delicate, poetic soul—but who can appreciate that nowadays? [*Sighs.*] I should have also had a daughter. Then it would've all been different. She could've helped me round the house, and kept me company, and I wouldn't have been so lonely . . . [*Sighs.*] But at my age . . . I'm over forty. It's too late. [*Laughs. Fumbles in her purse, pulls out a pocket mirror and looks in it.*] My skin's not so smooth . . . wrinkles . . . [*Alarmed.*] What's this? A gray hair?! God! That's terrible! [*Pulls it out and drops it while looking in the mirror.*] Still, one can't say I haven't kept my looks . . . considering the conditions we live in . . . A little makeup and I could still be taken for twenty-five. [*Takes out lipstick, colors her lips, powders her cheeks.*] Not bad. All the same, I would like to be able to go back there once, just once. To walk around, naked as the day I was born, among the trees laden with fruit, and the green foliage, free of burdens, of cares . . . just living . . . enjoying life . . . [*Sighs, closes her eyes.*] Oh well—it's just a dream, anyway. [*Lights dim. Dream atmosphere. Sound of birds singing. The SNAKE appears and peers through the door.*]

SNAKE: Sss . . . sss . . .

EVE [*Waking, alarmed*]: Oh, God!

SNAKE [*Enters the room*]: Wrong. It's the Snake.

EVE: You.

SNAKE: I sneaked out.

EVE: As usual.

SNAKE: Bribed the guards.

EVE: With apples?

SNAKE: With my skin. Snakeskin's very expensive today.

EVE: Just your luck that you can shed your skin.

SNAKE: You can shed your clothes . . . Your body might be more precious than my skin.

EVE [*Laughs*]: You haven't changed, I see.

SNAKE: You've hardly changed either. How old are you now?

EVE: Oh, thirty-five . . . six . . .

SNAKE: Plus two? Four?

EVE: Have you ever known me to lie?

SNAKE: God forbid! Though you might exaggerate a little—one way or the other. Actually, it was my fault—so impolite of me to ask a woman her age. A woman is as old as she looks, they say. And you look like a young virgin.

EVE: You and your honeyed tongue!

SNAKE: And everyone says it's so venomous. Where is he?

EVE: At work.

SNAKE: As late as this? Strange.

EVE: What's so strange?

SNAKE: I don't remember him so industrious.

EVE: Oh, he's completely changed since we left the Garden. Full of energy, enthusiastic, entirely absorbed in his work and his family.

SNAKE: And he never misses it?

EVE: The Garden? Never. He's forgotten all about it.

SNAKE: And you?

EVE: Nonsense! What do I lack here? [*Gestures around the room.*] As you can see. . .

SNAKE [*Looking around*]: Not bad.

EVE: This is nothing yet. In a month's time we'll have a new house . . . three rooms—lounge, bathroom, tiled kitchen.

SNAKE: Excellent!

EVE: I don't need luxury, but I do want decent conditions.

SNAKE: And—you're happy?

EVE: Why not? I have a husband, two grown sons . . . both of them gifted, thank God . . . and there's enough to eat . . .

SNAKE: In short—the picture of bourgeois contentment.

EVE: And what's wrong with that?

SNAKE: You have changed, after all. Once you were a tempestuous, adventurous creature, full of rebellion.

EVE: Life works its changes. We've no time today for fooling around.

SNAKE: I find it hard to imagine Eve domesticated.

EVE: Why?

SNAKE: A beautiful woman like you . . . I can't believe that you don't want to go out and enjoy yourself, to see, to be seen . . .

EVE [*Laughing*]: Be seen? By whom?

SNAKE: By whom? When a beautiful woman goes out, even the angels come down from heaven to see her.

EVE: Adam is enough for me.

SNAKE: But you hardly even see him. He leaves you alone in the house all day, and in the evening he's probably too tired to even look at you.

EVE: Have you come to try to turn me against him?

SNAKE: Certainly not. But a woman's beauty withers when it isn't watered by the dew of men's admiring eyes.

EVE: I haven't heard such a lyrical remark for ages.

SNAKE: Of course you haven't. There's no one here to make one to you.

EVE: Enough of that. What's new up your way?

SNAKE: Oh, the usual.

EVE: How's the Old Man?

SNAKE: No one ever sees him since you left. He keeps out of the way.

EVE [Inquisitive]: Then he gives you a free hand?

SNAKE: To do what?

EVE: Oh, I don't know . . . to tempt, to seduce . . .

SNAKE: To tempt whom?

EVE [:*With suppressed jealousy*]: I'm sure you can find objects for your temptations!

SNAKE: Believe me, since what happened between us, I've been living like a monk.

EVE [*Derisively*]: I'm sure.

SNAKE: I swear it! I just can't work up any interest in any "object"—as you call it.

EVE: Don't lie.

SNAKE: It's the truth. I dream only of you. In a way, I was poisoned by you. I sometimes find myself writhing with desire for you. I shed one skin, put on another . . . but you're stuck to my very flesh, under all the layers of skin.

EVE: Yet in 20 years you couldn't find a moment to come and visit me?

SNAKE [*As if in anguish*]: I didn't have the courage. My conscience has been eating me up . . . this feeling that I've wronged an innocent person.

EVE: You're talking like a priest! [*Laughs.*] A snake with a conscience!

SNAKE: Yes, yes! Strange as it may seem to you, even a snake has a conscience.

EVE: Then why have you come now?

SNAKE [*Approaches her and puts his arm around her*]: Because I couldn't bear it any longer. I was burning with desire for you. You're so beautiful . . . so young . . . so . . . [*Embraces her violently.*]

EVE [*Yells*]: You're choking me. [*Lights go up.* SNAKE *has disappeared. Opens her eyes in alarm.*] What happened to me? I must have dropped off. [*Goes to put the mirror in her bag but glimpses at her face.*] God, what'd I put on all this makeup for? For whom? [*Quickly wipes away the lipstick, looks out the window.*] Evening already, and they're not back yet. I'm so scared of the dark—I'll never get used to it. Shadows closing in on the house, thicker and thicker, like they're about to drown you. And always this dread, as though something terrible was going to happen in the black forest of night. [*Rises and lights a lamp.* ADAM *enters. Black beard. Clothes dirty from plaster and whitewash, trowel in hand.*]

ADAM [*In the doorway*]: Good evening.

EVE: Good evening. Why so late?

ADAM: Congratulate me. I've finished casting the roof.

EVE: Congratulations, but why didn't you come home for lunch?

ADAM: For your information, Eve, when you start casting a roof, you can't stop work even for a moment.

EVE [*Looks at him suspiciously*]: You didn't stop work even for a moment?

ADAM: Of course not. The concrete would have dried up and cracked.

EVE: Try to remember, Adam. You didn't stop at all?

ADAM: I don't understand. Why are you asking?

EVE: Strange. I went up there today. I called your name, but there was no reply.

ADAM: When was this?

EVE: One, one-thirty.

ADAM: Ah—that must have been when I went over to the quarry for gravel.

EVE: And you didn't hear me calling?

ADAM: If I didn't answer, I couldn't have heard you, could I? When you're shovelling gravel, you hardly even hear thunder.

EVE [*Doubtfully*]: Maybe . . .

ADAM: What, don't you believe me?

EVE: I really don't know what to believe and what not to believe.

ADAM: What's happened to you?

EVE: Nothing. But it's strange that the day before yesterday I also went to visit you. I didn't find you then, either.

ADAM: At what time was that?

EVE: Ten, ten-thirty. Were you in the quarry then?

ADAM [*Impatiently*]: You really think I can remember where I was at half past ten two days ago? You know I don't stay in the one spot all day! I have to cart wood, stones, cement . . .

EVE: But still, it's funny that I come there so often and never find you.

ADAM: Have you started tailing me?

EVE: Would you be worried if I had?

ADAM: Worried?

EVE: You sound like you're worried about something. Maybe you just don't want me around at certain hours—to put it delicately.

ADAM: My God, what do you suspect me of?

EVE: How would I know? Maybe you have some rendezvous that I'm not supposed to know about.

ADAM: Rendezvous? With who?!?

EVE [*Carefully*]: Perhaps with someone younger and prettier than me.

ADAM [*Angry*]: God Almighty! You're the only woman in the world. You know that!

EVE: Do I know what's on the other side of the mountain? Or in the forest? Or by the river?

ADAM: What you're saying is ridiculous. The total population of the world today consists of Adam, Eve, Cain and Abel.

EVE: How do I know what you're doing there? [*Bitterly.*] After all, I never get out.

ADAM: What do you want me to do? Stay home all day and do crossword puzzles?

EVE: No. But I just wanted to point out that you never even pop in to see how I'm doing any more.

ADAM: Because I'm working—from sunup to sundown . . . because I have to finish the house before winter. After all, it was you who never stopped nagging about a new house on the hill. Three rooms, a balcony with a view, a tiled kitchen . . . I would have been quite happy to go on living in this hut, and working in the fields. And now you come up with all sorts of crazy accusations! It's for you I'm doing all this!

EVE: For me? The family's welfare doesn't interest you?

ADAM [*Pacing up and down in anger*]: Is there no end to all this nonsense? Whatever I do, you're always finding fault—nagging, suspicious, critical . . . You . . . you . . .

EVE: Go on, say it—You unbearable old bitch!

ADAM: Don't put words in my mouth.

EVE: But if I am so unbearable, why do you go on living with me? Let's separate and be done with it. You go your way, and I'll go mine—and we'll stay friends.

ADAM: Did I say you were unbearable?

EVE: Yes, you did . . . just now!

ADAM: That's a lie!

EVE: So now I'm a liar as well!!

ADAM: I did not say you were unbearable.

EVE: But you thought it . . . and that's even worse! . . . hiding your thoughts and not saying them out loud.

ADAM: Oh, I'm really fed up with all this.

EVE: See? You're really fed up with me!

ADAM: Oh my God. You pick on every slip of the tongue.

EVE: A slip of the tongue is a manifestation of repressed subconscious emotions.

ADAM: You and your psychology!

EVE: Oh, so you've found another fault in me.

ADAM: Will this never end?

EVE: It can end all right, and I've told you how. We separate, and that's that! I release you from the burden of my presence.

ADAM: All right then . . . we'll separate.

EVE: Ah, now you're speaking frankly. This is what you've been thinking of for a long time, isn't it?

ADAM [*Ironically*]: Yes.

EVE: Nice of you to admit it at last. All this time you've been living with me, you've been plotting how to get rid of me. No, my good man, you won't get rid of me so easily . . . not now when I am forty and you know how limited my chances are. I suggested it to you in the Garden, but you refused. And now you want to take advantage of me and throw me out like a worn-out old shoe? Not on your life!

ADAM: All right—we won't separate.

EVE: But you want to!

ADAM: Stop telling me what I want and what I don't want! You're driving me mad! [*Silence.*]

EVE: Adam, I've made up my mind.

ADAM: Now what?

EVE: I've decided to take a holiday.

ADAM [*Stunned*]: A holiday?

EVE: Yes. For two or three weeks. Surely I've got it coming to me after all these years.

ADAM: I don't understand. Where will you go?

EVE: I don't know. Abroad, maybe.

ADAM: Abroad?

EVE: I want to be by myself a bit—to relax, see the world. I can't be shut up at home all my life, and I think it would be good for us if we didn't see each other for a few weeks.

ADAM: And who's going to look after the house?

EVE: You'll manage. The boys are grown up . . . there isn't that much to do. I'm sure Abel will agree to do the cooking while I'm gone.

ADAM [*Flares up*]: Abel! You want to load more work onto him? He's busy enough with the sheep.

EVE: If he agrees?

ADAM: I'll see to it that he doesn't agree. You want him to work overtime while you go off and enjoy yourself?

EVE: I don't understand what you're getting all worked up about. What've you got against me leaving the house for a bit? As far as you're concerned, I practically don't exist anyway.

ADAM: What do you mean by that?

EVE: You never see me.

ADAM: It's quite enough that I hear you.

EVE: What dress was I wearing yesterday? See if you can tell me.

ADAM: Oh, leave me alone.

EVE: You see? You never notice me at all. If I went, you wouldn't know I'd gone.

ADAM: I don't want to discuss this any more. You've decided to go? Then go. I won't stop you. I know quite well where you're going.

EVE: Where?

ADAM: Don't think I've forgotten about the snake!

EVE [*Laughing*]: You think he's still alive?

ADAM: He'll live forever. He'll outlive us all. But go to him—go! I'm immune to his poison by now. Is there anything to eat? I'm famished.

EVE: Don't worry—I'll never get there, even if I wanted to. I'd never get past those flaming swords.

ADAM: I asked if there's anything to eat.

EVE: If there was a chance of me getting to him, you might start taking notice of me again.

ADAM [*Shouts*]: I asked if there's anything to eat!

EVE: There's nothing in the house. I asked the boys to bring something back from the fields. They should be back any minute.

ADAM [*Grumbling*]: A man comes home after working fourteen hours straight, and there isn't even a meal waiting for him.

EVE: I'm sorry, but you didn't come in for lunch so I gave the boys what food was left. Now you'll have to wait. [*Pause. Appeased.*] When do you think the house will be ready?

ADAM [*Reluctantly*]: A month, six weeks.

EVE: And the furniture?

ADAM [*Bitterly*]: All the way you wanted it . . . three armchairs, a divan, Persian carpet, original paintings, a modern table—the lot.

EVE: A telephone?

ADAM: What do you want a telephone for?

EVE: To talk.

ADAM: Who with?

EVE: Oh, just to talk. I'm entitled to at least that much when I'm home alone all day, aren't I?

ADAM [*Sharply*]: There's no trunk line to Eden, you know.

EVE: You off again?

ADAM: I'm sorry, but there'll be no phone. [*Enter* CAIN, *carrying box full of vegetables.*]

CAIN: Good evening.

EVE [*Casually*]: Good evening.

CAIN [*To Adam*]: I said, "Good evening."

ADAM [*Still annoyed by the last conversation*]: Good evening. Where's your brother Abel?

CAIN: Am I my brother's keeper? He's probably chasing the sheep back to the pen.

EVE: You can sit down and eat now, Adam.

ADAM: Thank God. [*Sits at the bare table, pulls a large sheet of paper from his pocket, spreads it out and peruses it.*]

CAIN [*To Eve, whispering*]: Is he angry with me?

EVE: How would I know? Ask him! [*To Adam.*] Do you have to read now?

ADAM [*Does not move the paper*]: This is the building plan.

EVE: Do you have to look at it now, during the meal?

ADAM [*Glancing at the table*]: I see no sign of a meal.

EVE: You could show some interest in your children sometimes. [*She goes out to the kitchen.* ADAM *goes on looking at the paper, which hides his face.*]

CAIN: What's new with the house?

ADAM [*Without looking at him*]: Come and see for yourself.

CAIN [*Surprised at his hostile tone*]: I'd like to help, but there's so much work in the fields at this time of year.

ADAM [*As before*]: I don't need any help.

CAIN: You're doing it all by yourself. I know it's difficult.

ADAM [*As before*]: Nothing's difficult when it's done for love. [Pause.] And when there's peace and quiet at home.

CAIN [*Pained*]: You two been at it again?

ADAM [*Starts to reply but changes his mind*]: Have you prepared the soil for the winter sowing?

CAIN: Not yet.

ADAM: You better hurry. The rain'll come soon and it'll be too late to plough.

CAIN: I know. I've also got to plant the apples pretty soon.

ADAM [*Glances at him*]: What apples?

CAIN [*Surprised at his glance*]: Apples.

ADAM: We don't need any apples. [*EVE comes in, plate, fork, knife in hand. There is a heavy silence. ADAM puts the paper back in front of his face. EVE takes a head of cabbage and some small tomatoes out of the box, puts them on a plate which she places before Adam. ADAM puts down the paper, takes up the knife and fork but drops them almost immediately.*]

EVE: Why don't you eat?

ADAM: What is this anyway? Chewed cabbage and goatdung?

EVE: That's what there is.

CAIN [*Deeply hurt*]: They're tomatoes, Dad.

ADAM: I've never seen tomatoes like these.

CAIN [*Appeasing*]: They're a new variety. Taste them.

ADAM: And the chewed cabbage? It looks as though the rabbits have been at it. [*Silence.*]

ADAM [*To Cain*]: I asked you something. Why don't you answer? [*CAIN cringes.*]

ADAM: Why don't you answer? I've told you often enough to watch out for those rabbits or to kill them off.

EVE [*Tries to appease him—laughs*]: Cain hasn't the heart to kill. He even faints at the sight of blood. Have you ever seen him kill a fly?

ADAM: Well, he'd better get used to it. We must kill wild beasts.

EVE: Rabbits aren't wild beasts.

ADAM: But they're harmful. You want them to eat up all the cabbage?

EVE: Oh, Adam. Don't make a tragedy out of it. Eat your meal and calm down.

ADAM [*Looking at the plate*]: Who can eat this stuff after something else has been nibbling at it?

EVE: You're getting very fussy all of a sudden.

ADAM: I was never wild about vegetarian food.

EVE: Even when prepared with love?

ADAM: What love? [*Enter ABEL carrying a spit with a fat leg of mutton.*]

ABEL: Good evening. Sorry I'm late. I had to kill the lamb, cut it up and roast it. [*Gives the spit to Adam.*] Here you are.

ADAM [*To Eve, taking the spit*]: Now this is what I call food prepared with love.

EVE: You had to wait for it, though.

ABEL: I knew you'd come home hungry. Mother said you didn't even come in for lunch.

ADAM: Bless you, son. Come here; let me kiss you. [*ABEL bends his head and ADAM kisses him on the forehead.*] I was as hungry as a wolf. [*Rips into the meat.*]

ABEL [*Laughing*]: Man is a wolf—to sheep.

ADAM: Is there such a proverb?

ABEL [*Laughs*]: No. The real proverb says man is a wolf to man. I just changed it a bit.

ADAM: Very clever, too. The original one isn't much, though. No man would kill another.

ABEL: As the saying goes—"Love thy neighbor as thyself."

ADAM: You're bursting with knowledge today. [*To Cain.*] You've got a clever brother, Cain.

CAIN [*To Abel, bitterly*]: Dad's been complaining that the cabbage is all chewed up. Tell him how the rabbits nibbled at it.

EVE [*Hastening to save the situation*]: Oh, let's stop talking about food. [*To Abel.*] Show your father the flute you made.

ABEL [*Modestly*]: Oh, it's nothing.

ADAM [*Examining the flute*]: What is it?

ABEL: I made it from a reed. It makes music.

ADAM: Music. I can see you're going to be an artist.

EVE: Artists bring honor to their families.

ADAM: It'll be nice to have music while we work. [*To Cain.*] Have you tried this?

CAIN [*To Abel*]: Tell father what happened to the cabbage . . . go on . . . tell him!

EVE: Oh, not now. Abel, play some music for your father.

ABEL: All right, then. For you, dad. [*ABEL begins to play. CAIN gets up, goes to the corner, picks up an axe and goes to the door. ABEL stops playing. All are amazed.*]

EVE: Where are you going?

CAIN: To chop wood.

EVE: At this time of night?

CAIN: You want a fire in the fireplace, don't you? [*Goes out. Heavy silence.*]

ADAM: What's the matter with him?

EVE: I've never seen him so gloomy.

ADAM: Did you quarrel with him?

EVE: No, not at all.

ADAM: Could *I* have hurt him?

EVE [*Tense, alert to outside*]: I'm worried about him.

ADAM: Abel, go and see where he's gone. [*ABEL gets up to go.*]

EVE [*Holding his arm*]: No, don't go. Better wait here.

ADAM: Why shouldn't he go? [*To Abel.*] Go and tell him I want to speak to him. [*Exit ABEL.*]

EVE [*Frightened*]: It's so dark. He never goes out to chop wood at night.

ADAM: Did I hurt him?

EVE: Didn't you see his face when you wouldn't touch the food he brought you?

ADAM: But I . . .

EVE: He brought you a gift and you rejected it.

ADAM: Oh, he can't be that touchy.

EVE: He's very touchy when it comes to what you think of him. You're like God to him.

ADAM: But I didn't accuse him of anything.

EVE: Yes, you did . . . The cabbage.

ADAM: Exaggerating, aren't you? The cabbage was all chewed, and I only told him he ought to protect it from the rabbits.

EVE: It wasn't the rabbits that chewed it. It was the sheep that got in when Abel left them untended.

ADAM: Then why didn't he say so?

EVE: I suppose he didn't want to put the blame on his brother.

ADAM: So why didn't Abel speak up?

EVE: Abel's tenderhearted, afraid . . .

ADAM: Abel—afraid of me?

EVE: Go out after them, Adam. I feel uneasy.

ADAM: What about?

EVE: I don't know, but go out to them, Adam.

ADAM: What are you afraid of—wolves? [*A great scream is heard from afar. ADAM and EVE rush to the door.*]

EVE: I knew something terrible would happen. [*Calls.*] A-bel!

ADAM [*Calls*]: Cain! Cain!

EVE: Oh, God—he's running . . . he's running away . . . he's—[*Covers her face with her hands.*]

ADAM: Cain! Cain! [*His cry is lost in the wind.*]

## PART 3

### THE WIND GOES ROUND AND ROUND

*20 years after Abel's death. Evening. Storm outside. Adam's living room—spacious, with big table covered with a cloth. On it—flowers in a vase, an empty teacup. 4 upholstered chairs around the table. By the right wall—a couch. Above it—a small paraffin lamp with bright lampshade. Left corner—a large armchair. Against rear wall—small oilstove with kettle on it. Above it, suspended by a leather strap—Abel's flute. Right—the front door. Left—a passage to inner rooms, revealing part of a staircase.*

ADAM, *in thick dressing gown, crouches before the stove, fixing the fire. Rising, his face distorts in pain. He puts his hand to his back, straightening up with difficulty. Looks older than his age; thick white beard, wrinkled face, a bony body, sinewy arms—all betraying his struggle to live. He takes a few steps towards the couch, is stopped by another twinge in his back, then moves on, stretches himself carefully on the couch, covers himself with a rough woolen blanket, lays his head on the cushion and closes his eyes.*

*A cautious knock is heard at the door.* ADAM *opens his eyes for a moment, not sure if he has heard right, then closes them again. The knock is repeated. Surprised, he opens his eyes again. At last he gets up, sticks his feet into his slippers and shuffles to the door. He opens it cautiously.*

*The* SNAKE *appears in the doorway. He is dressed as before, a red kerchief around his neck. His hair and face are wet from the storm outside.*

ADAM [*Amazed*]: You?

SNAKE [*With an embarrassed smile*]: May I? [*There's no reply, with a gentler smile.*] Don't be alarmed. I won't bite.

ADAM [*Regains some composure*]: How did you steal in here?

SNAKE: I knew you were alone. I thought you mightn't object to the visit of an old . . . acquaintance on a cold winter's evening. If I'm not mistaken, it's about forty years since we last met.

ADAM: Must be about that. [*Brings kettle from stove to table.*] You haven't aged at all.

SNAKE [*Ironic smile*]: Time has no dominion over sinners, they say. And I'm a creature of sin—as you well know.

ADAM [*Pours the tea*]: How did you know I was alone?

SNAKE: Oh, I get around. Or, to be more precise—I slither around. I have a pretty good idea of what's going on in the world.

ADAM [*Sits at the table*]: So it appears. Drink up.

SNAKE [*Sips*]: It's hot. I don't know if it's immodest to say this—I'm even not quite sure if it's to my credit—but I think I know more about people and what they're doing than they know themselves. Often I'm with them when they're not even aware of me. I've seen your son, Cain.

ADAM [*Startled*]: Is Cain alive?

SNAKE: I've seen him twice. Once, a few weeks after the . . . incident.

ADAM [*Hides his face in his hands*]: Oh, God . . .

SNAKE: Perhaps I'd better not tell you.

ADAM [*Recovers himself*]: No, tell me . . . tell me!

SNAKE: Shall I get you a glass of water?

ADAM: No, go on. I sometimes get very faint . . . old age, I suppose. All these years I've been sure he'd killed himself, or had been killed by some wild animal.

SNAKE: His fate was worse than that, I'd say. The first time I saw him was in a forest. He was gathering roots and chewing them. He looked terrible. His face was all cut open and he had a big lump on his forehead. The moment he saw me he ran off, as if he'd seen a wild beast. I called his name, but he was gone in a flash, lost in the undergrowth.

ADAM: Oh, Cain . . . Cain . . .

SNAKE: The second time was seven years ago, in the land of Nod. He was sitting by a stream, his feet dangling in the water, his head bent. He seemed to be lost in thought. I crept up stealthily and sat next to him. He got a terrible fright, but it was too late for him to get away. At first he wouldn't speak, but then I told him I knew you and his mother.

ADAM: His mother was no longer alive then.

SNAKE: Yes, I know. I told him. He cried like a baby. Then, slowly, I drew him out. He'd been wandering around all these years, from one country to another, finding no rest. "The voice of my brother's blood cries to me from the ground," he said. "I hear it day and night: 'Where is your brother Abel? Where is your brother Abel?'" I believe his punishment has been much worse than his crime.

ADAM: It was not his crime. It was mine. It was I who should have been punished.

SNAKE: Why?

ADAM: I didn't know how to return his love. Perhaps you won't understand this but bitter experience has taught me that the source of all crime is lack of love.

SNAKE: You didn't love him?

ADAM: Oh, I loved him dearly. But I was hard; I didn't show it. There is an evil streak in me, and it's cost me my two sons and my wife. [*Pause; sighs.*] I probably wouldn't even have held out this long if it hadn't been for the faint hope that I might see Cain again, even just once. I'd give the rest of my life for that.

SNAKE: Perhaps you'll see him yet.

ADAM: No . . . no . . . he's scared of me. He's sure I'd want to punish him for that . . . murder.

SNAKE: Don't say "murder." Legally, at least, it wasn't murder but manslaughter. There's a great difference.

ADAM: What do you mean?

SNAKE: Well, according to his story, which I'm inclined to believe, it happened like this: He went out with the axe. He said he was going to chop wood, and that in fact was his intention—to work off his anger, as he often did. The moment he raised the axe, Abel appeared and tried to stop him by telling him you wanted him. Cain yelled at him to get away, but Abel persisted, holding onto Cain's arm. And then the axe dropped, landing on Abel's head instead of on the tree. That's his story, and I think that in court he'd get the benefit of a doubt. After all, this is a borderline case between intentional and accidental homicide. And it should be said to his credit that he himself doesn't talk of these extenuating circumstances. He torments himself as though it was a murder.

ADAM: And you've never seen him since then?

SNAKE: No. I've lost all trace of him.

ADAM: All these years I've told myself he was no longer alive—but I never really believed it. You know—three or four times I've found wreaths of fresh flowers on his mother's grave, and something inside me has told me it was he who placed them there.

SNAKE [*Quietly*]: You were wrong. It was me.

ADAM: You?

SNAKE: Yes. To this day I cherish her memory. What did she die of?

ADAM [*After a pause*]: Of sorrow, loneliness, and . . . perhaps, to be truthful, of want of love . . . [*Tries to change the subject.*] More tea?

SNAKE: No thanks. I've got something better. [*Takes a bottle out of his back pocket and places it on the table.*]

ADAM: What's that?

SNAKE: Brandy, my constant companion. You've never tasted it?

ADAM: I've never even heard of it.

SNAKE: There's nothing better to warm the heart, to drown the sorrows, to kindle dying fires or to revive your spirits.

ADAM: This is your second try to get me to do something against my better sense. The first time it was with a food—now with drink.

SNAKE: The food wasn't against your better sense—it taught you better sense.

ADAM: Sense, and pain.

SNAKE: And drink obliterates sense and pain. They are two opposites. The food took you out of paradise; the drink returns you there.

ADAM: I'm not so eager to return.

SNAKE: Not literally. My influence is not great enough to open the gates the Landlord has locked. But—it'll give you a taste of paradise. It's true I'm tempting you again—but perhaps with this temptation I atone for the first.

ADAM: It seems you're only capable of atoning for one sin by committing another.

SNAKE: Well, what do you expect from a snake unbearably bored by the perfect righteousness of the Garden of Eden?

ADAM: All right, I'll drink. Just for a little glimpse into that Garden. Just a minute. I'll get two glasses. [*Tries to rise but the pain stops him. He grips his back.*]

SNAKE: What's the matter?

ADAM: Rheumatism. Or perhaps a slipped disc. When I work in the field now I can hardly bend over. [*ADAM goes to inner rooms. Snake surveys the room, goes over to the flute, examines it, tries to blow a few notes. Hearing Adam returning, he hastily puts it back and resumes his seat. Walking to the table with the glasses*]: You see—a pleasant home . . . well appointed . . . but who's to live in it? [*Puts the glasses on the table and sits.*] All these years I've yearned for little but where Eve and I and the boys . . .

SNAKE [*Pours*]: Your health, Adam.

ADAM: Health? Even that's gone. [*Sips, pulls a wry face.*] Bitter as poison.

SNAKE: Wait, you'll only start enjoying it after the third or fourth glass. It's great stuff—made from the same grain as bread. [*Laughs, pours a second glass and drinks.*]

ADAM [*Sipping his second*]: Bitter as death. You say it's made of wheat?

SNAKE: Wheat or barley or rye . . . it's all the same. Just goes to show that the draught of life and the draught of death come from the same source. [*Pours and drinks from the third.*]

ADAM [*Lifts his glass*]: Your health?

SNAKE: Do you feel it going to your head yet?

ADAM: I feel a bit hazy.

SNAKE: Good.

ADAM: It burns, but it's good.

SNAKE: Another?

ADAM: Slowly now. I'm not used to it yet.

SNAKE: The more you drink the happier you'll be. [*Pours again.*] To long life.

ADAM: To joy. [*Sips, becomes merrier.*] It really was nice of you to come. It's hard for a man to be alone. I haven't seen a living soul for ages.

SNAKE: Frankly, I was afraid you wouldn't let me in.

ADAM [*Casually*]: Oh, time heals the deepest wounds.

SNAKE: Still . . . you've never forgiven me all these years.

ADAM [*Thinks*]: Never forgiven you? Pour us another, and I'll tell you what I feel . . .

SNAKE [*Pours another two*]: See what this stuff does? [*They clink glasses and drink.*]

ADAM: Well . . . [*Draws closer to Snake, under influence of drink.*] . . . it's true, I've never forgiven you. But even more I never forgave Eve, may she rest in peace. Even now, ten years after her death, I still have this bitter memory when I think of her.

SNAKE: Still?

ADAM: Yes, yes . . . Still! Just imagine. All these years have passed. We had children, we lived together, we worked together, no strange man ever entered our home, but still—every time I remembered what happened then, the blood would rush to my head. I'll never understand how she could have betrayed me like that.

SNAKE: Come, let's not be so bombastic. Betrayed?

ADAM [*Bangs fist down in fury*]: But it was a betrayal! Because—I trusted her! She was flesh of my flesh. She was mother and sister and companion, and only seven days after our marriage she took advantage of my trust and my innocence, and deceived me—with you!

SNAKE: Forgive my asking—I know it's indiscreet—but man to man, would you never have done such a thing?

ADAM [*Bangs fist*]: Never! Never!

SNAKE: Perhaps it's because you never had the opportunity? After all, she was the only woman in the world.

ADAM [*Shouts*]: That's a lie! I could never have done such a thing. [*More quietly.*] And anyway, if a man does, it's different.

SNAKE [Laughs]: And what would you call it if a man does it?

ADAM: Fun. No more than that. But with her it was betrayal.

SNAKE: You know, Adam, I have a suspicion you never really understood Eve.

ADAM [*Laughs*]: Me—not understand Eve? You really think I could have lived with her for over thirty years without understanding her?

SNAKE: Oh yes. You never understood her, all those thirty years. You know why? Because to understand a woman you have to understand sin. And you never understood sin.

ADAM: What high sounding phrases! Pseudo-philosophy, if you ask me.

SNAKE: Not at all. Allow me to explain. Sin has many faces and many levels, while virtue has only one face and one level. Woman is a deep creature—mysterious, complex, full of contradictions. A simple, innocent man like you could never fathom her depths.

ADAM [*Laughs*]: I object! I'm neither simple nor innocent. [*Loudly, proudly.*] I too have eaten of the apple!

SNAKE [*Laughs*]: I see I have earned my place in the world to come.

ADAM: Sinner! [*Pours two drinks.*] Partake of this nectar! To the first of the Just. [*They clink glasses and drink.*]

ADAM [*Tipsy, in high spirits*]: Bless you, Snake! This drink beats all the apples in the world! I pledge you my eternal friendship.

SNAKE: Careful now. Don't make any promises.

ADAM: No, no. We'll seal a bond of friendship tonight . . . Man and Snake! And you know what? I'll go and fix a special meal for the occasion. [*Tries to get up, but at once drops back into his seat, holding his back.*] Ow! That pain again.

SNAKE [*Gets up and puts his hand on Adam's shoulder*]: Sit down, sit down. When it comes to cooking, there's no one better than me. Where's the kitchen?

ADAM: Upstairs. You'll find meat, eggs and caviar in the fridge . . .

SNAKE: Right. I'll soon have your mouth watering. [*SNAKE leaves with a leap up the stairs. ADAM looks at the bottle, is about to pour himself another, but is stopped by a sharp pain in his chest. He thinks about his pains for awhile. A cautious tap on the door. ADAM is amazed. The tap is repeated. ADAM takes the bottle and glasses off the table hastily and hides them under the bed. Goes to the door and opens it cautiously.* CAIN *appears in the doorway. He still has a beard but is far from disheveled. His beard is trimmed and his clothes are neat and clean. He is dressed like a farmer, with a short sheepskin jacket.*]

ADAM [*Stands speechless a while, then embraces him*]: Cain [*They stand locked in a prolonged embrace.*]

CAIN: Father!

ADAM [*Hugs him lovingly*]: Oh Cain, Cain my son . . . I've prayed for this moment all my life. [*Holds his forehead.*] Forgive me . . . I feel dizzy.

CAIN [*Worried*]: Are you ill?

ADAM: No, no. You are here. Cain, you are here.

CAIN: Forgive me, father. I know you've been alone all this time, but I just couldn't . . .

ADAM: Let's not talk about it. To see you here makes up for all my misery.

CAIN: You must have suffered a lot since mother died.

ADAM: It doesn't matter now. Now you're back again. My lost son. Now you'll stay with me, and we'll never part again.

CAIN [*Embarrassed*]: You've got a beautiful home.

ADAM [*Disparagingly*]: Oh, it's nice enough . . . everything I need. [*With animation, as if revealing a long-kept secret.*] I've willed all my property to you . . . the house, the land . . . everything.

CAIN: What're you talking about a will for? You've still got years and years ahead of you.

ADAM: I'm not as strong as I was . . . pains in the back . . . in the heart . . .

CAIN: I caused it all. . . .

ADAM [*Forcefully*]: Don't talk like that! I want to hear about you. It's twenty years since I saw you! Twenty years!

CAIN: I've seen the world—mountains, forests, deserts. I'm sure I know half of the globe.

ADAM: Worth seeing, eh?

CAIN: If I started to tell you it would take a thousand and one nights.

ADAM: Right, we'll leave it for the time being. What are you doing now?

CAIN: I've found some virgin land and I'm working it. I'm breeding horses.

ADAM: Breeding horses?

CAIN: Yes. I found many wild horses on my travels. I've learned to ride them and tame them. Finally I decided to settle down, and start a farm.

ADAM: And you have . . . woman?

SNAKE [*Calling down*]: Hey, old man, you got any paprika anywhere?

ADAM [*Calling up*]: On the second shelf on the left.

ADAM [*Amazed*]: Who's that?

CAIN: An unexpected visitor . . . Snake.

CAIN: Him?

ADAM: He knocked on the door about an hour ago. Just imagine, I hadn't seen him since . . . that time.

CAIN: And he came to see you?

SNAKE [*Calls down*]: It's O.K., old man, I've found it.

ADAM: He's changed! Completely! He's repented.

CAIN: Did he tell you he'd seen me?

ADAM: Oh, yes. He told me a lot of things. We've become good friends. He even brought a bottle of brandy. [*Gets up, brings the bottle and glass from under the table, apologizes.*] I didn't know who was at the door, so I hid them. Don't want people talking. Will you have some?

CAIN: No thanks. I don't drink.

ADAM: On principle?

CAIN: On principle. I'm a vegetarian.

ADAM: A vegetarian breeding horses!

CAIN: For work, not food. Draught-horses, to plough, to pull carts. I've got a pair for you, too.

ADAM: Oh, leave that for now. You still haven't told me if you're single or . . .

SNAKE [*Calling down*]: Any garlic, old man?

ADAM: [*Calling up*]: Yes, in the cupboard. [*To Cain.*] How did you get here?

CAIN: In a carriage, drawn by two horses.

ADAM: The world's progressing, I see. Wasn't it cold in this storm?

CAIN: The carriage is all closed in.

ADAM: Wonderful. [*Looks at him affectionately.*] Oh, Cain, Cain . . . if your mother had only lived to see you again. . . . She was always thinking of you. You have no idea how much she loved you!

CAIN: [*Smiling bitterly*]: Love covers up all crimes, I see.

ADAM [*Sternly*]: No, don't say that, Cain. Man turns to crime when there is no love! And remember this: the first crime in the history of the world occurred because a father did not know how to love his son!

CAIN: Oh, Father.

ADAM: Yes. Forty years had to pass before we could sit here and talk like father and son.

CAIN [*Amazed*]: All these years I've been pursued by one idea—if only I could turn the clock back just one minute, just that one minute . . that horrible minute . . . in the dark . . . when suddenly . . .

ADAM: The clock can't be turned back. But what we ourselves can't do we can pass on to our children. You'll get married, have children . . .

SNAKE [*His voice from the stairs*]: The food's all ready! [*He comes in, carrying two dishes piled with roast meat, vegetables, etc.; stops in the doorway.*] Well, well, well, look who's here! [*Hurries to the table, puts down the plates and offers his hand to Cain.*] Cain! You've brought your father back to life.

ADAM: This is a great day for me.

SNAKE: [*To Cain*]: Just imagine—we were talking about you only a short while ago, and your father was convinced he'd never see you again. [*To Adam.*] Wasn't I right?

ADAM [*Fondly*]: You sly devil!

SNAKE: You've changed, Cain, and for the better. You look like someone right out of the Wild West.

CAIN [*Laughs*]: The Wild West—where's that?

SNAKE: Oh, wherever people settle in deserts and tame wild animals. [*Turns to the table.*] Well, it looks like my culinary efforts won't be wasted. Eat, my friends. Help yourselves.

CAIN: No, no. You eat. I'm not hungry.

SNAKE: You can't say no to my work. Anyway, I'm superfluous now at this family reunion. I'll be off in a minute.

ADAM: No—I won't hear of it! Sit down and eat with us. You two eat. [*To Cain.*] I want to show you something your mother saved for you all her life. [*ADAM goes out into the inner rooms.*]

SNAKE: So you came back after all.

CAIN: I wouldn't have dared, if it wasn't . . .

SNAKE: Wasn't for what?

CAIN: Well, I haven't come on my own.

SNAKE: No?

CAIN: No. I've brought my . . . wife-to-be.

SNAKE: Really? Congratulations. Where is she?

CAIN: Outside . . . in the carriage.

SNAKE: In the dark? In this cold?

CAIN: Well, you know, I had to . . . prepare him for it.

SNAKE: What is there to prepare?

CAIN: Oh, she's . . . a strange girl, in a way, and I was afraid that . . . Well, you know, my father's a bit old-fashioned.

SNAKE: Nonsense! Where did you find her?

CAIN: She's one of the daughters of the giants. Her name's Ishtar.

SNAKE: What a beautiful name! Did you meet her in the forest?

CAIN: Yes. She suddenly appeared to me, as if rising out of a lake. We loved each other at first sight. She's very beautiful.

SNAKE: So what are you worried about?

CAIN: Well, as I said . . . she's a bit unusual, both in her looks and in her behavior. She might shock father.

SNAKE: You don't know your father. He's still young in spirit.

CAIN: No! I do know him. He'd expect a quiet, sedate woman like my mother. But I've told Ishtar that we won't get married until Father's seen her and given us his blessing. [*Laughs.*] You know? The truth is that if it wasn't for her I'd never have found the courage to face him again.

SNAKE: Would you like me to speak to him? We're the same age.

CAIN: No. I have to do this myself. I'll explain to him. I'm sure that once he gets to know her a bit he'll grow very fond of her. [*A faint sound outside.* SNAKE *pricks up his ears, and makes a movement as though he has come to some decision.*]

SNAKE: Yes, you're quite right. You must speak to him yourself. [*Propels* CAIN *towards the inner quarters.*] Go on . . . tell him! It'll make tonight a double celebration for him. [CAIN *goes out.* SNAKE *glides to the window and looks out. A strong knock at the door.*]

SNAKE [*Vigorously*]: Yes? [ISHTAR *appears in the doorway. She is young, voluptuous and wild.*]

ISHTAR [*Surprised at seeing Snake*]: Wow! I wasn't expecting this!

SNAKE [*Bows gallantly*]: Mademoiselle!

ISHTAR: And my financé said the old man lives here alone.

SNAKE [*Approaches, extends his hand*]: May I introduce myself? I'm Snake.

ISHTAR [*As though trying to remember; her hand in his*]: Snake . . . Snake . . . Snake . . . Haven't we met somewhere before?

SNAKE: I think not. Such beauty as yours would have remained enshrined in my memory forever. Your name is Ishtar, if I'm not mistaken.

ISHTAR: How did you know?

SNAKE: Cain has just been telling me about your . . . romance.

ISHTAR: He's got a cheek, hasn't he—leaving me out in that lousy carriage in the cold, until his old man graciously agrees to recognize my existence!

SNAKE: [*Finger on lips*]: Shh—shh—shh—. They're in the next room. A very moving reunion, after all they've gone through. Won't you sit down?

ISHTAR [*Looking around*]: What a grand apartment! Modern furniture, carpets. I expected to see an old shack. Looks like the old boy's pretty well off, eh?

SNAKE: After 40 years of hard work, a man can get somewhere . . . [*Laughs* ] . . . specially when he doesn't have to pay income tax.

ISHTAR [*Laughs with him*]: Yeah, I guess so. And you? You a friend of the family?

SNAKE: Yes. A very close friend. We grew up together. I've just dropped in for a short visit.

ISHTAR: Do you live far away?

SNAKE: Not so far, but the transport's a problem.

ISHTAR: Oh, you're from the city?

SNAKE: What makes you think so?

ISHTAR: Just a guess. Your looks, your manners, your clothes . . . that scarf suits you! Where'd you get it?

SNAKE [*Takes it off and hands it to her with a bow*]: It's yours!

ISHTAR [*Pushes his hand away; laughs*]: No, no, no! Thanks all the same.

SNAKE: I am deeply offended.

ISHTAR [*Pats his head nonchalantly*]: You poor thing. At any rate—not now. You an artist?

SNAKE: Hmmm—in a way.

ISHTAR: I thought so the moment I saw you. You wouldn't be a photographer?

SNAKE: I'm afraid not. Why do you ask?

ISHTAR: 'Cos my life's ambition is to be a model . . . [*Plaintively.*] . . . but can a gal be a model when there's no photographer in the whole goddamn place? [*Gestures coquettishly.*] Don't you think I'd make an ideal model?

SNAKE: Undoubtedly. Is Cain aware of your ambitions?

ISHTAR: Yeah, but he's dead set against it. He wants to fence me in the ranch where I can help him raise horses.

SNAKE: Raise horses?

ISHTAR: Didn't he tell you we have a ranch? Oh, I'm nuts about horses—riding them, I mean—but when it comes to feeding them and cleaning their stables . . . [*Laughs.*] I'm spoilt, aren't I?

SNAKE: Nothing natural can be spoilt.

ISHTAR: You're pretty sharp, you know? [*Sighs.*] But we're spoilt in my family. And Cain's always telling me how wonderful I am, but he says I'm a bit short on knowledge.

SNAKE: That's nothing to get upset about. Too many women have been ruined by knowledge.

ISHTAR: How would you know?

SNAKE: I'm quite an expert on knowledge.

ISHTAR: You don't say? And on women?

SNAKE: An amateur.

ISHTAR: (Bursts out laughing). Great! You're real fun, you know? Has anyone ever told you that before?

SNAKE: Er—yes. I once lost my legs for being too much fun.

ISHTAR: You poor thing. But they've grown back, I see.

SNAKE: Oh, yes. Fortunately I'm able to change my legs, shed my skin, etc. . . . all according to circumstances.

ISHTAR: Circumstances. That's a new word for me. You know, I do think I've seen you some place. [*ADAM and CAIN come back. CAIN holds a red sweater. Runs to Adam and embraces him.*] Dad! [*Kisses him on both cheeks; to Cain.*] I'm sorry, Cain. I couldn't wait any more. [*To Adam.*] Has he told you about me?

CAIN [*Perplexed*]: Father—I'd like you to meet—this is Ishtar. We met not long ago, and now . . .

ISHTAR [*Pulling the sweater from Cain*]: What a lovely sweater! Who gave it to you, Cain?

CAIN: My mother knitted it for me, but I—

ISHTAR [*To Adam, impatiently*]: A present?

ADAM: She kept it for him all those years, hoping he'd come back one day. But she didn't live to see him again. . . .

ISHTAR: What a pity. It's a beautiful present, Dad. Thanks a lot. [*Kisses him on the forehead.*]

ADAM [*Confused*]: But I don't understand . . . Where . . .?

ISHTAR: Cain! Haven't you told him yet? [*To Snake.*] He's so slow, my fiancé.

SNAKE [*Takes up the plates*]: I'm afraid the food's got cold. I'd better go and warm it up again. [*Turns towards the stairs.*]

ISHTAR: Are you the cook here?

SNAKE: Cooking's one of my hobbies.

ISHTAR: Great! I'll come up with you! You don't mind, do you Cain? [*Pecks him on the cheek.*] And meanwhile, tell Dad everything. [*SNAKE and ISHTAR go out.*]

ADAM: Is she a friend of yours?

CAIN: I'm sorry, Father. I was meaning to tell you.

ADAM: I don't understand a thing. Who is she? Where was she hiding?

CAIN: I left her outside in the carriage. I wanted to prepare you . . . I knew you'd be surprised. . . .

ADAM: I'm extremely surprised, if you want to know.

CAIN: I understand. She's a bit unusual.

ADAM: That's putting it mildly. I got the shock of my life. She came in here like a whirlwind.

CAIN: Yes, she is a little wild.

ADAM: What do you know about her family?

CAIN: She's the daughter of the giants. They're all like that—wild, I mean. But as you know, Father, they're the only women in the world.

ADAM: Do you . . . love her?

CAIN: Very much. I fell in love with her the minute I saw her.

ADAM: And she loves you?

CAIN: Otherwise she wouldn't want to marry me.

ADAM: So you've made up your minds?

CAIN: Yes. She's already living with me. But we've put off the wedding because I wanted to see you first.

ADAM: You mean you're living with her . . . just like that . . . without the blessing of Holy Matrimony?

CAIN: Father, things have changed since your day.

ADAM: Well, well, well. What's the world coming to? And what about her parents? Do they agree?

CAIN: That's the point. She has no parents.

ADAM: What happened to them?

CAIN: She doesn't know herself. She never knew her father, and her mother left her in the forest years ago and disappeared.

ADAM: And you want to marry a girl of such dubious origins?

CAIN: Really, father! Are origins all that important?

ADAM: Yes, very important. You must remember, son, that our family is of pure, aristocratic descent. The Family of Man. And the Giants? Who knows who they even are?

CAIN: I'm surprised at you sticking to these prejudices, father. After all, it's the character that really matters, isn't it?

ADAM: Well, I can't say I'm very impressed with her character. You can see straight off that she's ill-bred, uneducated and bad-mannered.

CAIN: But father, this is the new generation! You've got to get used to it.

ADAM: The new generation! The new generation! There's nothing new under the sun. If you ask me, a woman has to be quiet, modest, hardworking and faithful to her husband—in every generation!

CAIN: I understand, father. You're thinking of Mother. I also worshipped her. But things are different today. Concepts have changed. Women are freer.

ADAM: Freer? What does that mean? That they can run wild, be unfaithful, do whatever they like?

CAIN: Why do you say that, Father? You don't even know Ishtar yet. True, she's cheeky, she's a chatterer, she likes to show off—but she's good at heart.

ADAM [*Warningly*]: A woman's heart is very fickle, Cain, very fickle.

CAIN: But she loves me.

ADAM [*Pause*]: And you don't think the difference in your ages should make you think twice? After all, you're forty, and she's what—eighteen?

CAIN: Oh, what does that matter? You should see us at home—on the farm. We haven't had a single quarrel during all these months.

ADAM: Look, son. You're not a child any more, you're a grown man, and I won't try to force my opinion on you. All I want to ask of you is this: think it over very carefully. All that glitters isn't gold, and a family isn't like a desert island, cut off from the rest of the world. There are always all sorts of surprises; I know from experience. You think everthing is fine, when all of a sudden . . . [*Stops and listens to sounds from above.*] Why does it take them so long to heat up a bit of food? [*Calls up.*] Snake!

ISHTAR [*From above.*] We're coming, Dad. [*Coming downstairs.*] He's some cook, your Snake! Knows all the spices! [*ISHTAR and SNAKE come in, each carrying two plates. On the way to table; to Adam.*] Has Cain been telling you about how I'm modest and gentle and say my prayers every night? [*Puts food on the table and notices the bottle.*] Oh, brandy! What is it . . . Courvoisier?

SNAKE: No. Local . . . Old Eden.

ISHTAR: I never heard of it. What's it like?

SNAKE: Taste it! Ladies and gentlemen—with the kind permission of our gracious host, I propose a toast to the young couple. [*Pours two glasses—gives one to Ishtar and one to Cain.*]

CAIN: Thank you, no. I don't drink. [*To Ishtar.*] And I think it'd be better if you didn't either.

ISHTAR: Oh, really Cain! You don't get married every day.

CAIN: You know my views on the subject.

ISHTAR: But after all . . . I'm getting married for the first time in my life! Don't be so mean.

CAIN: I've said all I have to say.

ISHTAR: O.K. then—I'll drink with Snake. [*To Snake.*] Where's yours?

SNAKE [*Reaches for Cain's glass*]: You sure you won't drink?

CAIN: Quite.

SNAKE [*To Adam*]: And you?

ADAM: No.

SNAKE [*Lifting the glass to Ishtar*]: Well, then . . .

ADAM [*To Ishtar as she lifts the glass*]: Young woman, there is a saying: Thy desire shall be to thy husband and he shall rule over thee.

ISHTAR [*Fluttering her eyelashes*]: Come again?

ADAM: It means that a wife must obey her husband.

ISHTAR [*Bursts out laughing*]: You're a scream, Dad. Cain proscribes and the woman imbibes. [*To Snake.*] How's that for a rhyme?

SNAKE: Terrific!

ISHTAR: And I made it up, just like that. [*Snaps her fingers. Raises her glass.*] Here's to you, Dad, and to you, love of my life, and of course—to you.

SNAKE: To the first couple ever to enter the bonds of Holy Matrimony. [*SNAKE and ISHTAR drink.*]

ISHTAR [*Drinks and screws up her face*]: Great stuff. Old Eden, you said?

SNAKE: Yes, very special. Year One of Creation.

ISHTAR: Real prehistoric. [*To Cain, coaxing.*] Cainy, have one too, please . . . [*approaches him, embraces him, pleads*] . . . come on, Cainy, just for me. . . .

CAIN: No.

ISHTAR: Why not? It's good.

CAIN: Not everything that muddles the brain is good.

ISHTAR: Oh, come off it. Why must you be such a goddamn Puritan.

ADAM [*Sternly*]: You shouldn't try to tempt your husband. If he doesn't drink it means it's a matter of principle with him.

ISHTAR: Oh, God. I've got myself into a family with principles. Pour another glass, Snake, or I'll start getting desperate.

SNAKE [*Pours for the two of them*]: Well, ladies and gentlemen, let's eat. We can't have this food getting cold again. [*Lifts his glass.*] To your happiness.

ISHTAR [*Lifts hers*]: To a brilliant future for us all. [*To Cain, pointing out his plate.*] You see? We fixed a special vegetarian dish for you.

CAIN: That was nice of you.

SNAKE: Bon appetit! [*All take up knives and forks and begin to eat,* ISHTAR *and* SNAKE *with obvious relish,* CAIN *because he is hungry, and* ADAM *morosely, as if forced to eat. As they eat the following conversation ensues.*]

ISHTAR: Snake really is an excellent cook. It's so spicy. Where'd you learn to cook so well?

SNAKE: Oh, I get around in the world, tasting a bit here and there, learning how to put tastes together.

ISHTAR: You don't have a kitchen of your own?

SNAKE: No, I never had one. I prefer to peep into other people's kitchens, and occasionally I help out young couples who haven't yet learned to cook. I advise them about food, drink, spices. . . .

ISHTAR: Adorable! But don't you ever feel like getting married, having children, a home of your own . . .

SNAKE: Yes, I've felt like it. But I've no talent in that direction. Unfortunately it just isn't my nature.

ISHTAR: What a pity! Haven't you ever been in love? Or perhaps I shouldn't ask such an indiscreet question.

SNAKE: I was in love once, but it was a very unfortunate affair.

ADAM [*Pushes his plate away*]: Too much garlic. [*Gets up.*] I must go and get some water. [*Goes out.*]

ISHTAR [*To Snake*]: Who was she?

SNAKE: You wouldn't have heard of her. I met her in the forest.

ISHTAR: In the forest! How romantic! I was born in the forest too. What was her name?

SNAKE: Lilith.

ISHTAR: Lilith—Lilith . . . Lilith who?

SNAKE: Asmodeus.

ISHTAR: Lilith Asmodeus. No, I've never heard of her. But it's a lovely name. So—what happened? Didn't she love you?

SNAKE: As a matter of fact, she did.

ISHTAR: Just didn't work out, eh?

SNAKE: A bit too well.

ISHTAR: I don't get you.

SNAKE: We were too much alike. Blazing lights. And when two such flames come together, the whole world can be burned to a crisp.

ISHTAR [*Laughs*]: Wonderful! So how did it end?

SNAKE: She went off with someone else.

ISHTAR: With who?

SNAKE: Someone called Lucifer.

ISHTAR: She sounds quite a type. Be interesting to meet her.

SNAKE: She was a little devil. [*Pours another two.*] Here's to you! [*Clinks her glass and drinks.*] We had a wild time together . . . but what I didn't like was the tricks she used to play on children. She used to sneak into their houses at night, through the windows, and put a curse on them. I'd make her promise to stop, but she never kept her promises. I couldn't stand it, for although I have quite an amount of venom in me myself, I mostly love people. I'm a humanist, so to speak, and so I left her.

CAIN: Someone like her shouldn't be left on her own. God knows what damage she could do!

SNAKE: Yes, you're right. But after all, I'm not the ruler of the world . . . I'm just a Snake.

ISHTAR: And ever since, you've remained a bachelor.

SNAKE: Yes . . . an eternal bachelor.

ISHTAR: But you don't look more than twenty. Any girl could fall in love with you.

SNAKE [*Laughs*]: Fall in love with me! Perhaps—but not live with me. [*ADAM comes in with a glass of water.*]

ISHTAR: You have a charming friend here, Dad. You should hear the stories he tells.

ADAM: God protect me from my friends. From my enemies I can protect myself.

ISHTAR [*To Adam and Snake*]: Why? Aren't you two on good terms?

SNAKE: God forbid! This is just our manner of speaking. We enjoy teasing each other.

ADAM: I thought you'd changed. It appears I was wrong.

SNAKE: Can the leopard change his spots?

ADAM: Probably not. But a snake, as far as I know, can change his skin . . .

SNAKE: . . . but he stays a snake!

ISHTAR: That's a good one.

ADAM: Hold your tongue while men speak.

ISHTAR: I . . .

ADAM: And show some respect for your elders, you . . . you . . . Giant's Daughter!!

ISHTAR [*Rises*]: I haven't come here to be insulted. I'm leaving. Coming, Cain?

CAIN: Ishtar!

ISHTAR: No. I've got feelings too.

ADAM: Sit down, please. I'm terribly sorry.

ISHTAR: No, it's getting late in my case. We've a long way to go and as it is we won't be home before sun-up.

SNAKE [*Picks up the bottle*]: One for the road?

ISHTAR: No thanks. Come on, Cain. Let's go.

CAIN [*Rising*]: Yes, we really must. [*To Adam.*] Sorry, father.

ADAM: I'm sorry I lost my temper. Stay a while longer.

CAIN: No, we'd better be going. She's a little thoughtless, that's all.

SNAKE: Could you give me a lift?

CAIN: Which way do you go?

SNAKE: Whatever way you're going. All roads take me home.

ADAM [*Tries to save the situation; to Snake*]: You'd better stay here. Traveling by night isn't very pleasant.

SNAKE: I'll protect them on their way. My eyes glow in the dark and I'm very good at keeping evil spirits away.

CAIN [*Approaches Adam and grasps his hand*]: Goodbye, father. We'll be back in a few days.

ADAM: Look after yourself, son. There are robbers around, and wild animals too.

CAIN: I'm used to the roads, Father. Keep well.

ISHTAR: G'night, Dad. It was nice meeting you. [*Kisses him on the cheek.*]

ADAM: God be with you.

ISHTAR [*Takes Cain's arm*]: See you! [*Goes to the door but returns.*] Oh, Cain, we almost forgot to take the sweater. [*Runs back, takes sweater, kisses Adam.*] Thanks Dad. . . . Bye now!

SNAKE: Goodbye, Adam. [*Adam does not reply. He glowers at them.* CAIN *and* ISHTAR *go first, followed by* SNAKE. *Returns, goes to Adam, pats him on the shoulder.*] Don't worry, Adam. I'm not as dangerous as you think. I only flutter around a bit . . . never stay for good. My place in paradise is always waiting for me. [*Dashes out. From outside comes Ishtar's voice:* "It's so dark! Hold me tight—both of you!" ADAM *stands looking painfully at the closed door, then sinks down on the chair.*]

ADAM: Lord God, be with them on their way, guide their steps, and lead them in joy and peace unto their destination. For thou hearkenest to thy servant's prayers, and [*a sudden pain in his chest; he rises and wants to go inside but the pain stops him*]. What's this? Why did they go? [*Turns to outer door and calls in a broken voice.*] Cain, Cain! [*Closes the door and reenters.*] They've gone. . . . [*Moves with difficulty towards the interior, climbs a step but can't go on. Goes back to the room, closes his eyes and fights the pain.*] Oh my God, my God! [*Door opens silently,* LANDLORD *enters. Appearance as in Act 1. Comes in silently, takes a chair, carefully puts it by the sofa near Adam's head and sits down. Adam opens his eyes in terror.*] O, my God! [*Tries to sit up, supporting himself on one elbow.*]

LANDLORD: Don't get up. It is I!

ADAM [*Head on pillow*]: Forgive me. The pains . . .

LANDLORD: Don't be afraid. I shall soon relieve you of them.

ADAM [*In pain*]: All my strength is leaving me. I can feel it ebbing away.

LANDLORD: Be brave. It's the fate of every man.

ADAM [*Groans*]: Oh, God! [*Suddenly rouses himself.*] Why did you create him then . . . Why?

LANDLORD: If I hadn't created him, who would have known me and my creation?

ADAM: And for that man has to toil and suffer all his life?

LANDLORD: Haven't you also known some joy and happiness?

ADAM: A moment of joy for every ten of sorrows.

LANDLORD: If not for the sorrows, you'd never have appreciated the joys. Did you regret leaving the Garden?

ADAM: No, not for a minute. I was only sorry that you left us all on our own, never intervening, never preventing what you could have prevented.

LANDLORD: I gave you free choice. . . . a gift I've given to no other creature.

ADAM: Free choice? To do what?

LANDLORD: To love, to hate, to sin, to forgive. You did well to forgive Cain. I saw how happy you were when he came to see you.

ADAM: But even that joy contained a poison.

LANDLORD: Because of the Snake?

ADAM [*From the depth of his heart*]: Why don't you lock him up? Why do you always send him out against us?

LANDLORD: So that you can fight him.

ADAM: Have you given us the strength to defeat him?

LANDLORD: There is neither victory nor defeat in this struggle.

ADAM: Why?

LANDLORD: Because if you won, the world would again be the Garden of Eden. If he won, it would return to Chaos. And either possibility means death. This struggle between you two is what Life really is.

ADAM: But you've cursed him.

LANDLORD: As I've cursed you! And after all, you owe him something too. If not for him, you wouldn't be here.

ADAM: Oh, on what paradoxes you run your world!

LANDLORD: And you've only discovered the first few. Your descendants will find more—and never solve them.

ADAM: If I were only sure that my descendants weren't going to repeat my mistakes.

LANDLORD: They'll repeat them . . . be sure of that!

ADAM: My breath is getting short. Is this the end?

LANDLORD: The end . . . and the beginning. Like all paradoxes.

ADAM: Give me a pill or something. I feel terribly weak.

LANDLORD: I have something better.

ADAM: What [*Opening his eyes.*]

LANDLORD: I've come to take you back . . . to the Garden!

ADAM [*With a desperate cry*]: No! No! I don't want to!

LANDLORD: You still haven't tasted the fruit of one of the trees there. It's called the tree of Life.

ADAM: Now you're trying to tempt me!

LANDLORD: A last mercy. Your time has come, Adam. Shall we go?

ADAM: No! Leave me here! On earth . . . on earth!

LANDLORD: You came here from the Garden, and to the Garden you return.

ADAM: [*A final groan*]: God! God! To Thee I commend . . .

LANDLORD [*After a pause*]: My soul! [*The lights dim.* LANDLORD *holds* ADAM *by the hand. A sad melody comes from afar, recalling the Garden and its eternal peace.*]

# Difficult People

*by*
YOSEF BAR-YOSEF

One can hardly say that Israeli drama has arrived. Certainly, in terms of energy and willingness to experiment, it is on its way, but no one is quite sure where it is going. However, the stage does seem to me to be a most suitable instrument for the expression of the Israeli ethos. Poetry, which can be the true mirror of the individual heart and soul, especially Hebrew poetry, is essentially untranslatable into English. The Israeli novel is lost in a world flooded with second-rate novels and is not likely to be noted.

In regard to the expression of self, the drama seems to work very well for Israelis in terms of communication with the outside world. The stage is like a mirror, and when the Israeli looks into this particular mirror, he usually sees a double image, in part the *Halutz,* Kingdom Maker, Activist, but behind this image hovers his *Doppelgänger,* the shadow of the Talmudic scholar, the shtetl and all that the pale and the Jewish role in the pale stood for.

One might consider Brenner's novel, *Breakdown and Bereavement,*[1] as a classic case. *Breakdown and Bereavement* is usually considered as the landmark in Israeli literary fiction, rather than part of the Eastern European literary tradition. In some ways *Breakdown and Bereavement* is different from the shtetl novel. However, the characters, themes and sentiments expressed in Brenner's novel find many echoes in the shtetl novel.[2]

Yosef Bar-Yosef in this play seems to follow this pattern. His plays are modern in tone and bristle with psychological insights and aberrations. In addition to these aspects, one might find in his plays and particularly in this play, comments on what Howe considers essentially Yiddish literary themes—exile, return, aspiration, resignation. In context again, one finds echoes of shtetl literary traditions.

In this play at the end of the first act, the major character, Simon, expresses great hope that the idea of Israel will redeem him and his sister, Rachel-Leah:

> We are in exile, Rachel-Leah. We have to be redeemed and we have to accept what the land of Israel sends us, even if it's only last year's oranges.

However, at the end of the play, Simon expresses disillusion with the promise of Israel (as such at present) but has hope for something better:

> You know why the light in Israel is white? It's because of all that sunshine. It's the same snow. . . . The snow in Siberia was hellish. I got out of that hell and I'm still wading in it. I see sunlight and I call it snow. . . . You deserve more, d'you hear? Nothing will help you, you deserve more! What you don't get, you don't get, but I won't let them steal from you what you deserve.

This is the last speech in the play. Stage directions that follow this speech indicate the sound of the horn follows (being played by the eccentric landlord in the next flat). As a result of the stage direction, the play seems to end almost on an abrasive note.

Despite the heavy pattern of Yiddish themes in this play, it calls to mind at times such dramas as Sartre's *No Exit* or a play from the Theatre of the Absurd. The sense of isolation and despair, the eccentricities of character and speech are very Jewish, but not Jewish (in essence) at all. *Difficult People* is like a (Jewish) morality play in which all mankind totters on the brink of the absurd.

Yosef Bar-Yosef is a sixth-generation Jerusalemite. His father was the well-known, somewhat controversial Israeli writer, Yehoshua Bar-Yosef. Yosef Bar-Yosef began publishing in 1952. His publications include several collections of short stories and a novel, *The Life and Death of Yonatan Argaman.* He is best known for his plays, including *Tura* (1963), *The Ewe* (1970), and later plays, *The Wedding* and *The Spot.*

## NOTES

1. Haim Brenner, *Breakdown and Bereavement* (Ithaca, N.Y., and London: Cornell University Press, 1971).
2. For a similar statement regarding the relations between past and present, see Leon Yudkin, *Escape into Siege* (London: Routledge and Kegan Paul, 1974), p. 104.

CHARACTERS

*Rachel-Leah Gold, called Rachel, a forty-four-year-old spinster.*
*Meir-Simon Gold, called Simon, her brother, a forty-seven-year-old bachelor.*
*Eliezer Weingarten, called Leyzer, divorced, a forty-one-year-old Jerusalemite.*
*Benny Alter, an old bachelor, Rachel's landlord.*

*The action is confined to one room of a house in a large English port. It continues uninterruptedly during one evening.*

*Translated by H. Bernard,*
*D. Oklans and Dennis Silk.*



ACT 1

RACHEL *seated.* SIMON *behind her, pacing up and down.*

SIMON: Don't those sirens ever stop?

RACHEL: They're ships. [*Sounds of a shoemaker's hammer from behind the wall.*]

SIMON [*Halts*]: That good-looking landlord of yours, that Benny of yours, hammering away . . .

RACHEL: He likes mending shoes.

SIMON: And eating onions!

RACHEL: He likes onions.

SIMON: Yes! [*Again paces up and down, then stops.*] What a life! All these likes! [*The hammer again.*]

RACHEL [*After a pause*]: What happened to you over there?

SIMON [*Approaches her*]: Why, what do you think happened?

RACHEL: I don't know. You're back, I ask you how it was and you . . .

SIMON: I what?

RACHEL: I don't know. You tramp up and down, you seem angry. You wanted to go so much, you wanted to see what Israel was like after the war. And suddenly it's as if you didn't see anything, didn't bring back anything.

SIMON [*Sits down*]: I brought back a slipped disc, if you must know. And I brought back something else, for you a husband.

RACHEL: I don't understand.

SIMON: I got a slipped disc, you get a husband. You'll understand soon enough. [*Three hard knocks with a hammer from behind the wall.*] He understands. [*Addressing the wall, loud.*] That rotten anarchist, what *he* wants is to marry you, make a respectable woman of you.

RACHEL: I don't understand. [*A knocking at the door, which opens;* BENNY *enters in a shoemaker's apron, holding a shoe.*]

SIMON: Nice of you to come! To what do we owe this honor? Or rather, to what does my sister owe this honor? Her landlord, a notorious anticapitalist, exploits his landlord's rights, bursts into her flat. . . .

BENNY [*Fumes helplessly, speaks in bursts*]: I wouldn't let you have a flat. . . . Not even at twice the rent! Not even if you were starving. You could lie in the gutter for all I care. [*Exits.*]

SIMON: See what you are missing out on?

RACHEL: I still don't understand.

SIMON [*Angrily*]: What don't you understand? I've brought you a husband from Jerusalem. A better one than him [*gestures at the wall*]. His name is Eliezer Weingarten, Leyzer for short. Sixth generation in Jerusalem, a distant relative on our mother's side, divorced, one daughter. But he doesn't have to pay alimony. She gave in on that, just so he'd give her a divorce. [*A pause.*] Cafes . . . [*A pause.*] That's why she divorced him. . . . She wanted him to take her out to cafes, he took her round to his family. He has no friends but lots of family. Now let's hear what you have to say about that.

RACHEL: What do you want me to say?

SIMON: Nothing. . . . He's a shlemazel. Changes jobs all the time. He was a clerk in his last job. Once he wanted to be a plumber. But the family objected. His family's Orthodox. He isn't. He served in the army and he's proud of it. God doesn't interest him, but he's all for truth and justice. And he's a bore. He talks and talks. And to anybody. Only about serious things, mind. Not the weather, or how are you;

straight to the point, down to brass tacks right away. Talks about himself too. And keeps looking for his relatives. He'll look for his relatives here too. Even at Buckingham Palace. And he'll find some if the Queen gives him time enough. Say something before I go on. [*Changes his tone.*] We've talked about this often enough, haven't we? Just before I left we talked about it. You didn't say anything then—and silence is consent, isn't it? You can't change your mind now. It's too late. I've brought him. They showed me all they won in the war, the Wailing Wall, the Jordan and . . . they've won so many things, and I went looking and found you a husband. Answer me? Say something!

RACHEL: Another cup of tea?

SIMON [*Turning to look at her*]: Oh! My back!

RACHEL: You ought to see Dr. Blau.

SIMON: You'll drive me crazy. [*A pause.*] And another thing: he was in a mental home. Only three months, mind you, a long time ago, and he was cured, but you ought to know. What do you have to say to that?

RACHEL: I'll make you another cup of tea.

SIMON [*Turns to her abruptly, in sudden pain*]: Another cup of tea? I haven't drunk the first one yet.

RACHEL: Drink it.

SIMON [*Drinking hastily and in anger*]: There, I have. What did you get out of that? Did *you* drink it? [*RACHEL gets up and takes the empty cups from the table to the kitchenette. Getting up.*] Now look, I suggested the deal to him, he accepted. I didn't advertise in the papers. He just turned up one day. That's all there is to it, so make the most of it. There's no one else around. [*A pause.*] He isn't all that bad. I've made him out worse than he is. I just don't want you to have any illusions, I don't want to see you disappointed again. If you've one more disappointment, I'll go crazy. [*RACHEL brews tea. After a moment.*] He's—well . . . special. He has a special kind of charm, if you look hard, that is. With his last few pounds he took a hotel room. He didn't want to stay at my flat, that'd be at my expense. Coming here from Jerusalem at my expense didn't bother him: it's not his fault you live in England. But once here he wants to pay his own way. [*Looks around the room for her.*] Where are you? [*Finds her. Loudly.*] Get married for once, will you?! Sit down for once! Why are you standing?

RACHEL: I'm making you another cup of tea.

SIMON: Who said I wanted another cup of tea?

RACHEL: I asked you if you wanted one.

SIMON: But I didn't say I wanted one. What do you want to do, drown the world in tea? Sit down, will you. . . .

RACHEL: I want to make you another cup of tea.

SIMON [*After a moment*]: I'd really like a cup of tea. Could you please make me a cup of tea?

RACHEL: All right.

SIMON [*Seated*]: Yes, a certain charm, if you're looking for it. He didn't even want to come to your place with me, he says I'm from your side. Marriage is a meeting between two camps, he says, and he wanted to arrive at the head of his own camp. He's in this city alone, with only a few pounds to his name, yet he's carrying his whole camp around with him. Isn't that marvellous?! . . . And his English—he started learning English from the labels on aspirin bottles his father sent wholesale from America. His family have a lot of headaches; they take a lot of aspirins. They also put potato slices on their foreheads. His mother was wearing a potato bandage when I went to see her. [*RACHEL pours the tea while he speaks.*] Stop crying!

RACHEL: I'm pouring out tea.

SIMON: Where other women cry you pour out tea. Stop it! [*RACHEL carries the cups to the table. SIMON rises, unconsciously blocks her way.*] The one good thing you can say about him is that he wants a wife the way a man ought to want a wife. He's miserable, he's divorced, he's alone, and he wants a wife. He's really quite healthy—a healthy husband with a headache. [*RACHEL tries to reach the table.*] His headache, you know, that's his drive, his energy, it's his . . . his . . . thing. He wants children badly. He said he'd marry you and he'd show her; he'd have lots of children and show her. Show *her!*

RACHEL: That enough, stop it!

SIMON: What's enough?

RACHEL: Let me put the cup down! [*Puts the cup down on the table, sits.*]

SIMON [*Turns to her abruptly, in pain*]: You and he and the slipped disc, you're all ganging up on me. [*Sits.*]

RACHEL [*Moves the cup toward him*]: Here's your tea . . .

SIMON [*Takes the cup, holds it, doesn't drink*]: He may not be to our taste, but then, who is? That's our whole pride, isn't it—our taste, our demands. You deserve something better, of course you do, *we* always deserve something better. And why's that? Because we see everyone else's weak points? Of course, we also see and know our own. H'm! That's quite an achievement, I suppose. And that's why we're entitled to love ourselves. I'm sick of eating myself.

RACHEL [*Bows her head*]: What do you want of me?

SIMON [*The cup trembles in his hand*]: Want?

RACHEL: What do you want of my life?

SIMON [*Grabs the cup, drinks rapidly. The tea goes down the wrong way; he almost chokes*]: I want you to live it!

RACHEL: That's enough, Simon.

SIMON: That's enough of Simon. In Jerusalem I'm not Simon. The name's Meir-Shim'on, Rakhel-Leah. And what's come of all your free love?

RACHEL: Why must you . . . ?

SIMON [*Gets up*]: Seven years you kept Steven here in your flat. Provided for him. You call that free love? You were his drudge! Then he got his degree, packed up and left. So you went and got yourself another first-year medical student, so it'd be another seven years till he too left you. It takes seven years to learn medicine! What do they study there all that time?! And it's been another six years since then.

RACHEL: You don't have to trample all over me just to make your point.

SIMON [*Not hearing her*]: The era of the medical students is over! It's time you got married like everyone else. [*After a moment, quietly*] Why don't you tell me to go to hell? Go on, say it: Go to hell! What do you want of me? What if you are my brother? You'd better worry about yourself first! I can jump from the roof if I feel like it. I've a British passport the same as you. And who said I have to have a husband? Do you have a wife?! Go on, why don't you tell me where I get off?! [*A knocking at the door.* BENNY *enters, holding a pair of women's shoes.*] Again? He just knocks and walks right in! Come to that, why bother to knock?

RACHEL [*To Benny*]: My old shoes, I was looking for them. Thanks a lot, Mr. Alter.

SIMON: I get it, he took them without telling you, so he could fix them. The anarchist dispenses secret charity. Isn't that marvelous? [*BENNY sticks the shoes in Simon's lap and goes out.*] Look, he started mending them, but stopped halfway. He took off the old heels and didn't replace them. He's ruined your shoes.

RACHEL: It doesn't matter. They were old, anyway.

SIMON: No! He has to compensate you. Let him buy you new ones! If you don't tell him, I will.

RACHEL [*Quietly*]: I live here. He's my landlord.

SIMON: And so?

RACHEL: I owe him three months' rent, but he doesn't say a thing. He needs the money, he's got even less than me. I caught cold, I was sick, while you were away. And he brought me in meals. [*A hesitant, stammering horn is heard behind the wall.*]

SIMON [*In a quiet voice*]: How beautiful! The pleasures of the poor. Paradise on earth. Very touching. You know, when something touches me like this, when I smell this paradise on earth . . . [*Loudly, with suppressed fury*]—the blood rushes to my head. And I'll get you a husband, if only because you'll passively accept whatever I get you, whatever this earthly paradise of ours turns up, without complaint! I'm sick of your bowed head, and your moist eyes. And your cups of tea. And your medical journals. Two medical students! Two! A sum total of fourteen years of medicine! And you still subscribe to those medical journals! I've had enough! I'm sick of your clinging to the wall every time you walk down the street. [*Sits.*] You should walk down the middle of the road, like a coach and six. Say something!

RACHEL: I said something before, but you didn't hear.

SIMON: What didn't I hear?

RACHEL: You don't have to trample all over me, just to make your point.

SIMON: Trample all over you?

RACHEL: Let him come. We'll see. I've been trying to tell you that all along.

SIMON: What?

RACHEL: Maybe. [*A brief silence.*]

SIMON [*The bewilderment of blocked anger*]: All right . . . All right. That's enough for me. [*Gets up, puts on his coat.*] *You* receive him. You two'll get along. You'll get along fine. I've done what I can. He ought to be here any minute. [*Goes out.* RACHEL *at first seems to be trying to hold him back. Then takes a mirror, and starts to make herself up. A ring at the door. She hesitates. Another ring. She opens the door.* SIMON *stands in the doorway.*] Ah! That's good. You're making yourself up. I forgot the most important thing: he's forty-one, and you're forty-one too, not a day older. He asked me twice, it sounded too good—such a young bride, only forty-one, on top of a trip here at my expense. He won't ask again, he certainly won't ask you, he suspects everyone's deceiving him. He asks once, maybe twice, and that's it, no more. More would offend. You'll work it out afterwards, somehow. As for children, one can have children when one's fifty. What a world! [*Goes out.* RACHEL *slowly turns to the interior of the room. Again a ring at the door.* SIMON *returns.*] And another thing. This flat—it's yours. That's what I told him. And I'm a wealthy man, a successful agent. We'll work that out afterwards too.

He's honest, he won't walk out on a marriage, it was his wife that walked out on him. I'll be back soon. [*Goes out.* RACHEL *clears the table. A ring at the door. She opens.* BENNY *in the doorway.*]

RACHEL: Mr. Alter. Oh, come in. My brother isn't here. I hope you . . . You know how he . . . But really . . . Come in, would you like some tea?

BENNY [*In the doorway. Embarrassed, agitated*]: I just wanted to explain to you. Those shoes I returned . . . It wasn't directed at you! No! I really do want to mend them, even now. . . . But after what I just heard, I can't. . . . All those lies! It isn't your fault . . . it's me. . . . I'm no good, I'm poison, I . . .! [*Goes out. After a moment* RACHEL *opens the door, as if to say something to Benny. In the doorway stands* LEYZER. *She closes the door in alarm. The doorbell rings. She opens the door. Eliezer Weingarten, or* LEYZER, *stands in the doorway, wet from the rain.*]

LEYZER [*With exaggerated self-confidence, almost gaily*]: Hello.

RACHEL: Hello. Please come in.

LEYZER: First of all you should know whom I am. [*Gives her his hand.*] Eliezer Weingarten.

RACHEL: Yes. Rachel. [*Gives him her hand.*]

LEYZER [*Squeezes her hand overmuch*]: Pleased to meet you.

RACHEL [*It hurts*]: And I'm pleased to meet you. [*After a moment.*] Do come in. [*Closes the door.*] Simon's gone out for a while. [*A pause.*] Please sit down.

LEYZER: First I have to take off my coat, no?

RACHEL: Of course. Sorry. You're completely drenched.

LEYZER: The coat's drenched. [*Starts taking his coat off. Stops.*] Oh. First I have something for you. [*Takes a chocolate box from under his coat, presents it.*] A present for you. Women like chocolates.

RACHEL [*Taking it from him*]: Thank you. [*Places it on the buffet.*]

LEYZER [*His coat off*]: Where should I hang the coat?

RACHEL: Sorry. I'll take it.

LEYZER: It'll be too heavy for you, it's a porter's coat. My father bought it when he was working in the United States of America, in New York. Over there, in the summer everyone sweats and there's soot, and then the winter's cold and frosty.

RACHEL [*Directs him to the coat rack*]: Here.

LEYZER: Thank you. [*Hangs his coat.*] Where do you want me to sit?

RACHEL: Of course. [*Laughs.*] Sorry. Here, by the table, forgive me.

LEZYER [*Sits*]: You apologize too much.

RACHEL: What? . . . I make too many mistakes.

LEYZER [*Looks at her, suddenly says loudly*]: It isn't nice that I'm sitting while you stand.

RACHEL: Of course. [*A pause.*] I forgot myself. [*Sits.*]

LEYZER [*A pause*]: Where are the chocolates?

RACHEL: Pardon?

LEYZER: I brought you chocolates.

RACHEL: Oh, yes, on the sideboard.

LEYZER: Allow me to ask you to bring the box to the table; women like chocolates, but they like their figures better. This is my present, and I don't want you going on a diet with it. Eat now please. I also want to see that I haven't been cheated.

RACHEL [*A pause*]: All right. [*Gets up and places the box of chocolates on the table. A pause.*] I'll eat the chocolates, but you'll have a cup of tea. [*Goes to the kitchenette. Puts on a kettle.*]

LEYZER [*Without looking at her*]: It's not an expensive present.

RACHEL: There was no need for an expensive present.

LEYZER: I don't have enough for an expensive present. [*A pause.*] I also believe that there's no need to bring expensive presents. It's hard to give an expensive present wholeheartedly; whenever you give one you expect something in return. And the person who gets it, takes it greedily.

RACHEL: I never thought of that.

LEYZER: Think of it now. [*A pause.*] I'll give you an example. Leah-Dvora Villmann, my mother's cousin—she's also a relative of yours on your mother's Aunt Malka's side—gave me a big tea service as a wedding gift. [*Stops as if waiting for her response, and then continues.*] She's a poor old widow, with eight children, and they eat bread and oil the way people used to in the Old City. Everyone remembers the Wailing Wall and the synagogues, but they don't remember the poverty in the Old City. They hardly eat any vegetables or fruit, and they are children, they need it. And they pass on shoes from one child to the next. And she gave me a tea service which cost a hundred and seventy-eight pounds. Israeli pounds, not English, but still, it's a lot. It isn't nice to return a gift, but that would have been robbery. I gave it back to her, and she refused to accept it. So I went to Freund's shop and returned it to him—Freund, the son-in-law of Reb Baruch, the Krakover rebbe—and I sent her the money by check.

RACHEL [*A pause*]: She could probably have done a lot with that money. [*Brings the tea to the table.*] I'm pouring yours with milk.

LEYZER: Her husband, Shmuel-Wolf, was killed by Jordanian bullets.

Since then she's had a miserable life. People who don't think enough might think that dying is the hardest part.

RACHEL [*This impresses her*]: That's a true thing you've said.

LEYZER: On top of that, she has a mole on the end of her nose. [*Shows her where.*] Here. It looks like a big drop that's going to drip off any minute. You just have to laugh. [*RACHEL tries hard, and laughs. Sits down.*] It looks like a chocolate drop. And she'd a reason for giving me such an expensive wedding gift. She wanted me to help her get her son Yerukham a job in the Welfare Department. He's her oldest. [*Puts sugar into her tea—a lot of sugar.*] But I wasn't working at the Welfare Department any more. With all her worries she didn't know that, she really doesn't know what goes on in the world. But she remembers the date of every family anniversary, and she always comes to the graveyard. She has reason enough for coming. She cries more than the bereaved.

RACHEL: Take as much sugar as you like.

LEYZER: Rabbi Hassid finally got him a job in a bank. Yerukham, that is. In Jerusalem they do help people, but they laugh at the same time. They might help someone and at the same time they are splitting their sides laughing when they think how they're going to tell someone else about the troubles of the person they helped, that is.

RACHEL: I'll eat your chocolates, you don't have to apologize.

LEYZER [*After a moment*]: What should I have to apologize for?

RACHEL: You don't have to.

LEYZER: I don't have to for what?

RACHEL: For the gift, for . . . oh, it doesn't matter. I just said that.

LEYZER: You didn't just say that, one doesn't just say things.

RACHEL [*After a moment*]: That's true. Anyway, let's forget it. You know exactly what I meant.

LEYZER: Not exactly.

RACHEL: Anyway, let's forget it. Perhaps I'm saying the wrong thing. [*After a moment.*] I'm a bit confused, that's natural, isn't it? [*Opens the box of chocolates, eats, apparently gay.*] They're good, you weren't cheated. Now drink your tea. We made a deal, didn't we? [*LEYZER drinks. She drinks. A brief silence. The light dims. The sound of hammering comes from behind the wall, and stops as the conversation starts up again. Both of them start speaking at once.*]

RACHEL: What do you think of . . .

LEYZER: Do you have something . . .

RACHEL: Go ahead, please . . .

LEYZER: No, you . . .

RACHEL: You're the guest.

LEYZER: That won't do you any good. You first.

RACHEL [*A pause*]: I only wanted to ask you what you thought of the progress of medicine in our time?

LEYZER: Pardon me?

RACHEL: I think medicine's the only sphere where the progress of civilization has brought people true happiness. Not just comfort or power, but real happiness. Only fifty years ago half the babies used to die before they learned to speak. [*LEYZER coughs lightly. Ill-at-ease as she continues.*] Of course, it doesn't make people any better, but it makes them suffer less, and they're happier. [*A pause.*] And it's true doctors aren't better human beings, but medicine helps them to do good.

LEYZER: Do you like to sit in cafes?

RACHEL: What? No. There aren't any cafes here. They have pubs instead. I don't go to pubs much. Sometimes maybe. Why do you ask?

LEYZER: I'll tell you in a minute. [*After a moment.*] Does the plumbing here need fixing?

RACHEL: Pardon?

LEYZER: If there's something wrong with the plumbing, say the toilet, or there's a leaking tap, I can fix it.

RACHEL: Thank you, there's no need, everything works fine.

LEYZER: I wanted to be a plumber. It's a good trade, plumbers are always in demand and the pay's not bad. I'm sick to death of working as a clerk. There are hordes of them, everyone climbing and doing the other down, so they won't climb on their shoulders. I worked for Moshe Cohen, a plumber, but I had to stop. My father and mother said my work disgraced them. I felt ashamed also, without wanting to I felt ashamed. Even when he's alone, a man isn't free to do what would be right for him.

RACHEL [*This impresses her*]: That's true.

LEYZER: They say there's a demon in man.

RACHEL: Oh.

LEYZER: Is your watch all right?

RACHEL: Pardon?

LEYZER: I can fix it if it's not working properly.

RACHEL: Thanks, but there's no need. It's perfectly all right.

LEYZER: After plumbing, I started to learn watchmaking with Yaacov Gingy. But I had to stop. I got such bad headaches, and Dr. Bloch said it was eye strain. I think it was because of the ticking; open clocks on a table are a lovely sight, but even two adjusted clocks don't tick together, it's as if they're chasing each other, they don't rest a minute, they're competing the whole time. And they're just clocks. They're not even people.

RACHEL: I understand.

LEYZER [*A pause*]: They say man is a wolf to man. But a wolf doesn't devour a wolf, not even when he's hungry. [*A pause.*] I haven't been telling you all these stories just to tell you stories. I wanted to introduce myself. I've also given you several hints about the not so pleasant part of my biography, about my marriage. You didn't notice, I liked that. I don't like a nosy woman, one who fastens onto every thing. So I'll present myself to you in a moment in chronological order. [*A pause. A ship's siren is heard.*]

RACHEL: What do you think of this town, if you can form an opinion in such a short time? [*She doesn't feel comfortable about her question.*] This is a gray town, it's like tin. Sometimes I just want to pick up a brush and scrape away all the rust. It's hard for you people to understand why we talk so much about the Israeli sun. You have so much light over there. Simon goes to Israel every two years. I've been there twice, I toured the country a bit, and in the end I found myself in your Post Office building, writing letters back home. The English built your post office, it's very much like the buildings here.

LEYZER: How late do you sleep in the mornings?

RACHEL [*Not astonished this time; she smiles*]: I get up early, too early. That's supposed to point to guilt feelings. I get up early even if I go to bed late. And then I'm tired all day.

LEYZER [*Immediately*]: Do you see my coat?

RACHEL [Without turning her head]: Yes.

LEYZER: You can't see my coat like that—you can only see me.

RACHEL [*Turning her head*]: I see it.

LEZYER: You asked me about this English town. I'll tell you something about the English. Our lavatory was out in the yard—that's how it is in the older quarters of Jerusalem. One day my father had stomach trouble and he had to go out to relieve himself—excuse me—before dawn. The English had imposed a curfew. They were running Palestine and they didn't want to leave. What did he do? He got down on his knees and crawled to the lavatory at the end of the yard, so the soldiers would think he was an animal. On the way he barked like a dog, twice, so they'd be sure it was a dog. Just imagine it: a man . . . a grown man . . . a man who has worked hard . . . All because of politics.

RACHEL [*After a moment*]: You said you'd tell me about the coat.

LEYZER: My father used to cover me with this coat. Our place was small, there wasn't enough room inside for all the kids, so I had to sleep outside, with the rain dripping from the porch roof right onto my bed. I slept pretty well in the wet bed because I was young and tired. But when he got up to pray before dawn, he used to cover me with the coat, and then it was warm and I slept better. [*A brief silence. It becomes almost completely dark. A neon light comes on somewhere in the street.*]

RACHEL: Simon carried me on his shoulders for three days. At the very start of our escape from Russia I got scarlet fever. My father wasn't with us, Simon was the man in the family. I was red as a beetroot.

LEYZER: It's a good thing a woman's had scarlet fever before she gets married.

RACHEL: What? [*Understands.*] Oh. yes. Our mother died in Russia, in Siberia. We loved her very much, we remember her clearly to this day. She died in a snowstorm.

LEYZER: In England they eat a lot of chips.

RACHEL: Oh, not as much as people say, but they do eat chips. It's a cheap food.

LEYZER: It uses up a lot of oil.

RACHEL: I fry the chips in deep oil—the chips come out good and the oil stays pretty clean. Then I put the oil back in a special bottle, and I use it again.

LEYZER: I was testing you. Maybe one shouldn't do that, but I admit I was testing you. [*After a moment.*] I've been married, I'm divorced. I have a daughter. My wife used to throw out the oil she made the chips with. She liked that, throwing out the oil. She liked throwing out everything. We quarreled because of that. Once she said I ought to put the toothpaste back in the tube after brushing my teeth.

RACHEL: Oh. [*Laughs.*]

LEYZER: Why do you laugh?

RACHEL [*After a moment*]: That's funny.

LEYZER: Who?

RACHEL: No one, it's . . . it's funny, to put the toothpaste back in the tube. You have to laugh at a thing like that, don't you? [*Repeats.*] Don't you?

LEYZER [*After a pause, gets up, and in a loud voice, as if angry*]: I've already told you I'm divorced and I've a daughter. I've a few more things to tell you. I want you to know the truth. It was *she* who wanted the divorce. She fled from me as from a monster. She didn't even ask for the money in the marriage agreement, one thousand eight hundred Israeli pounds. I sent that to her after the divorce.

RACHEL: You don't have to . . .

LEYZER: She hid from me as though in a cave. I found out where she was, and I went there, just to bring my daughter a dress. When she saw me at the door, she screamed. As if I was about to slaughter her. I hadn't even said a word, it was just the sight of me—as if I was about to slaughter her. And before that, before I climbed up to her place, while I was standing under the window, I heard her laughing with the child.

RACHEL: You really don't have to . . .

LEYZER: I have to tell you the truth. My daughter's dead, as far as I'm concerned, and all the doctors in the world won't help. I don't know why that is. For me it's a kind of darkness. Ask any questions you like, I'll tell you exactly what happened. Maybe from what I tell you, you can learn something I don't know.

RACHEL: No, I've no questions. You don't have to . . .

LEYZER: Then I'll tell you something else. I must tell you the truth. Maybe you could put on the light.

RACHEL: Yes, of course, sorry. [*Gets up and turns on the light. The lamp hanging above the table casts a strong light on it; all around it is darker.*]

LEYZER: Something happened to me after the divorce. I'll tell you about it, so you'll know everything. I don't want it to happen again: a husband and wife who don't know a thing about each other, and they have a daughter, and they hate each other so much, it's as if that daughter was dead. I'd like us, even before we're married, to be like one family, a brother and a sister, with no secrets or lies between them. That's why I want you to know how bad it was after the divorce. I couldn't grasp anything. It all turned black. I couldn't even do up my buttons.

RACHEL: You don't have to go on . . .

LEYZER: I was put into a madhouse. They cured me, but sometimes, inside, it's still very bad.

RACHEL: You don't have to go through all this. I know about it. It doesn't bother me.

LEYZER [*Quietly*]: What do you know?

RACHEL: Everything you've told me. It makes you miserable all over again, it's not necessary.

LEYZER: How do you know?

RACHEL [*Begins to feel she's spoken out of turn*]: Simon . . .

LEYZER [*A pause*]: He told you . . . everything?

RACHEL [*A pause*]: Yes. [*A pause.*] Maybe you'll have another cup of tea?

LEYZER [*He looks hard at her, as if trying to get a better view of her face, which is in the shade on the other side of the table. He thrusts his head forward, his face lit by the strong light falling on the table. He says quietly.*]: It's not right to say things behind someone's back, to give away secrets. That's two against one. That's . . . That's laughing. That's all against one.

RACHEL [*Loud and nervous*]: He's my brother, isn't he? He's my brother. [*A pause.*] I'll make you another cup of tea. [*The sound of the horn from behind the wall.*]

LEYZER [*Restless, with suppressed anger*]: What's that?

RACHEL: What?

LEYZER: Someone playing. From behind the wall, like a trumpet, but not a trumpet.

RACHEL [*Glad at the apparently relaxed tension*]: Oh, that's my landlord, Benny Alter. He's a bit strange, but he's a good person, he's very genuine. He likes mending shoes. For him it's a kind of religion. He thinks we should learn a craft, and go back to nature. Nice to think like that, isn't it?

LEYZER: He isn't mending shoes now, he's playing.

RACHEL: Yes, he likes playing.

LEYZER: Is he rich?

RACHEL: They say his parents were very rich over there, before the war. But he's not. Most of his tenants are better off.

LEYZER [*Getting to the point*]: You'll forgive me if I put a question to you. I know one isn't supposed to ask such questions. How old are you? [*The playing stops*]

RACHEL: Pardon?

LEYZER: How old are you?

RACHEL [*Laughs in embarrassment*]. Oh. [*A pause.*] Is it all that important to you?

LEYZER: I asked you a question.

RACHEL [*Rises, trying to gain time*]: A woman doesn't have to say how old she is. After a certain age, perhaps she shouldn't. After all, one's age is . . . it's a primitive kind of thing, isn't it? It's really only important on passports. What one feels is what really matters, what one still wants, can still manage. And of course, one's looks matter. [*Laughs.*] How old do I look?

LEYZER: I want you to tell me how old you are. I want to know what I'm being told. I'm not from here, here I've no family.

RACHEL [*After a pause*]: I was born in 1924.

LEYZER: How old does that make you?

RACHEL: Forty-four.

LEZYER: Forty-three. I've just worked it out.

RACHEL: I was born in January. It's almost forty-four.

LEYZER: Now I've been told the truth.

RACHEL: I never told you anything else.

LEYZER: Your brother told me something else.

RACHEL: He wanted to help me. He's used to looking after me. It was he who saved my life. That's . . . [*A pause.*] Maybe you'd like another cup of tea?

LEYZER: Suddenly I have a headache.

RACHEL: Maybe you'd like another cup of tea.

LEYZER: No, thanks, you needn't trouble yourself.

RACHEL: It's no bother. I like making tea.

LEYZER: Perhaps you could put on the light.

RACHEL: I have switched it on, it's on.

LEYZER: Yes. [*A pause.*] When's your brother coming back?

RACHEL: Very soon, I imagine. [*A pause, then, in a loud, nervous voice.*] You don't have a slipped disc, do you?

LEYZER: Pardon?

RACHEL: You turn your head easily. Simon can't do that. He came back from Israel with a slipped disc.

LEYZER: Yes. [*He gets up. They stand facing each other.*] Perhaps you could tell me where the . . . where the toilet is?

RACHEL: In the corridor, first door on the right. [*Turns to go.*] You'll excuse me, I have to make the bed. I can never manage in the mornings. I'm a working woman. [*Exits.* LEYZER *goes to his coat, which hangs near the door, takes some aspirin tablets from it and swallows them. The door opens and* BENNY *comes in. The door hides Leyzer, and Benny doesn't see him. He looks for and finds the shoes he brought back earlier, retrieves them, turns to go out, sees Leyzer.*]

LEYZER: Hello, I'm not from here. But she—the lady of the house—will be back in a minute. Hello.

BENNY: Don't "hello" me. Get back to Jerusalem. Saints, are you? Prophets, are you? Not you! The prophet knew all about Jerusalem. "That join house to house, that lay field to field till there be no place!" Thieves! Now you're thieves and prophets both, eh?

LEYZER: I'm just looking for the lavatory.

BENNY: Lies! All lies!

LEYZER: No . . . I really have to . . . I don't know the . . .

BENNY: I know . . . I heard everything . . . Turning everything over, inspecting it, undoing it like merchandise . . . Shopkeepers! That's all you people are! But she isn't merchandise! [*Turns to go, then turns again towards Leyzer.*] A trumpet?! I don't play a trumpet, it's a horn! That's more than all your Jerusalem! Music! I played and now I'll mend her . . . [*Waving the shoes.*] Now I can . . . And without any lies. Take her if you can! It's nothing, to take. Later you'll throw her away, anyway . . . that's clear! But what'll you take? She'll be walking on my soles, in Jerusalem! Anywhere! But on my soles!

LEYZER: I really have to . . . [*He goes out into the corridor. A ring at the door.* BENNY *opens.* SIMON *comes in. Waves a bottle of wine.* BENNY *waves the shoes and goes out.* RACHEL *comes in.*]

SIMON [*Looks around him*]: Where is he?

RACHEL: In the lavatory.

SIMON: You look down in the mouth. Down in the nose, rather. A bride-to-be's nose should be up in the air. In the lavatory. Mmm . . . [*A pause.*] You don't like him, do you? You don't like any of it? Listen, you'll take him! I bought him a ticket here, and I didn't do it to buy him a ticket back. I don't have enough for that, and you know it. These trips to Israel are ruining me. It's only in Jerusalem I can tell myself and others that I'm Marx and Spencer. Do you follow me?

RACHEL: You mustn't shout, we're not alone in the flat.

SIMON: What!

RACHEL: I didn't say I didn't like him.

SIMON: What?

RACHEL: Or that I liked him.

SIMON: Then what did you say?

RACHEL: I didn't say anything. Can I say anything to you?

SIMON: What did you talk about so much, if I'm allowed to ask?

RACHEL: I didn't say I talked much. But at least he allowed me to answer his questions.

SIMON: What questions?

RACHEL: Whether I sit in cafes.

SIMON: Of course. He would ask that.

RACHEL: I don't.

SIMON: Of course you don't. What else?

RACHEL: If I get up late in the mornings. If I throw out the oil I make chips with. My age.

SIMON: Your age? What did you tell him?

RACHEL: I told him my age.

SIMON: Your age? Your age! Just you dare tell me you told him! How old did you say you were?

RACHEL: Forty-one.

SIMON [*With secret pleasure*]: Of course. [*Laughs.*] You frightened me. These days one can't be sure of anything. [*Suddenly.*] Did you say something?

RACHEL: Do I have anything to say?

SIMON: What do you mean by that?

RACHEL: Am I meant to say something?

SIMON: That's better. [*A pause.*] You lied to him, that's what's depressing you, is it? Well, we've launched a deal, so we'll clinch it. We forget the past too easily. Later on, when you're his legal wife, you can long for your wonderful lost youth. [*The sound of a guitar from the floor above.*]

SIMON [*Listening*]: Our homo! He plays quite well. Not like Benny. A homo but he also runs after skirts. Facing both ways. [*Guitar stops suddenly.*] He never finishes a tune. Nerves! I thought once goyim didn't have nerves. A stream doesn't have nerves. Even that isn't true. Have you ever watched a stream? It's all eddies, restless, it doesn't have a single straight line. Nerves! [*A pause, then, in a tone that could be sincere or ironic.*] We're in exile, Rachel-Leah, we have to be redeemed. And we have to accept what the land of Israel sends us, even if it's only last year's oranges. [*Without a pause.*] Why don't you switch on the light?

RACHEL [*A pause*]: It's on.

SIMON: I'm cold.

RACHEL: The stove's on, too.

SIMON: Maybe it is, but I'm cold. [*A pause.*] Something's happened, something's happened here. I've been standing here a whole five minutes and you still haven't offered me a cup of tea.

## Act 2

*Same room, immediately following.* RACHEL *and* SIMON *are seated. In front of Simon is a cup of tea.*

SIMON: Sit, sit, sit.

RACHEL: What?

SIMON: I sit, you sit, he sits. He's still sitting, on that seat.

RACHEL: Yes.

SIMON: Could be a good sign, you know. He doesn't sit there so long just because he's constipated. No. He's in session. Urgent consultation. He's thinking. Sitting there, he's at home. Whenever I'm in Israel I also sit a lot. But here's the difference: when I sit in a lavatory in Israel, no one ever waits for me, except maybe someone who also wants to go. As far as Israel's concerned, I could stay in that lavatory the rest of my life. Now take him—all a man has to do is to be a prospective husband, as poor a specimen as you like, and he's already got people waiting for him. Look at us: we're doing nothing, we're immobilised. We're just waiting for him to finish. The whole town's waiting, the whole world's waiting, to hear him pull the chain.

RACHEL: Your tea's getting cold.

SIMON: Why *my* tea? Tea belongs to you.

RACHEL: You asked for a cup of tea.

SIMON: What if I did? Do I always get everything I ask for?

RACHEL: It's only a cup of tea. See what you're making of it.

SIMON: What I'm making of it?! Again what I'm making of it?!

RACHEL: I don't know. You never seem to be able to take something simply.

SIMON: Ah! You've learned to speak. What's to take something simply?

RACHEL: I don't know. You want something a lot, you go to a lot of trouble, then you don't want it.

SIMON: I see. But to want something and to get it too, that's greediness, isn't it?

RACHEL: I'm sorry.

SIMON: What're you sorry about?

RACHEL: I don't know. Nothing.

SIMON: You've started pitying me. Next time around you'll bring me back a bride from Jerusalem. [*LEYZER comes in and stands in the passage doorway. SIMON rises, RACHEL only raises her head.*]

LEYZER: I want to go back to Jerusalem. [*RACHEL's head droops.*]

SIMON: What? Oh, I see. But we never talked about that. I thought you two would want to stay here, to get rich first, like us. Quite apart from that, I myself can't go back to Jerusalem right now. And surely the two of you aren't going to leave me all by myself so soon.

LEYZER. You didn't understand.

SIMON: Oh, that's better. You mean that some time in the future you'll go back to Jerusalem. Me too. At the end of time, as they say. That's good. The main thing, as I see it, is that we've agreed on the match. Now all that's needed is for someone to announce it's agreed. Am I right? Someone to bind, that is, to proclaim: Here were two people, a man and a woman, and now they're one. [*Fills up several glasses.*] No point waiting. Tomorrow we'll get married! That is: You will.

LEYZER: You haven't understood me.

SIMON: I still haven't? Well, that shouldn't surprise me. I can hardly understand myself, so how could I possibly understand someone else, and especially . . .

LEYZER: How old is the bride? [*A brief silence.*] How old is the bride?

SIMON [*Very quietly*]: Again, please.

LEYZER: I asked, how old is the bride?

SIMON: The bride is—twenty-two. The bride is seventeen, twelve, the bride is . . . You know what? To clinch the deal . . . The bride is seven. That's my last word—I've already lost on the deal.

LEYZER: You're laughing at me.

SIMON: What do you want me to do?

LEYZER: Give me an answer.

SIMON: Give you an answer! You've asked me the same question twice already, remember? In Jerusalem. You want the answer again. All right. She's forty-one. If you don't believe me, you can saw her open the way they saw trees, and count the rings.

LEYZER: You people aren't telling me the truth.

SIMON: Can you hear what you're saying?

RACHEL [*To Leyzer, quietly*]: I told you. You needn't have asked a second time.

SIMON [*To Rachel*]: What do you mean, "I told you"? [*A pause.*] What did you tell him?

RACHEL: I told him how old I was. He shouldn't have asked you. [*SIMON approaches Rachel. Leyzer is left out in the cold, as it were.*]

SIMON: How old *are* you? What did you tell him?

RACHEL: The truth. I'm forty-four. That's the truth.

SIMON [*Agitated. Produces a snuffbox from his pocket, takes a pinch of snuff. His movements are slow and emphatic. His eyes water, he breathes heavily. He looks at her a long while. Then, quietly.*]: Why? [*A pause.*] Answer me!

RACHEL: I don't know. He asked me.

SIMON: And I . . .? [*A pause.*] Answer me!

RACHEL: I wanted to tell you I'd told him when you came in. You scared me so I couldn't.

SIMON [*Quite restrained*]: And they were one flesh. Already?! In advance?! You've paid up in full before even getting the goods?! Didn't you know you're dealing with the biggest con-man of them all? That's what he is, especially as he doesn't lie! He bought you with his trust, did he? What did it cost him? It's nothing for him. Just truth, that's all. And like a fool, you give him truth, though for you it's everything.

LEYZER: I want to go back to Jerusalem.

SIMON: "Return into Jerusalem Thy City in mercy"? [*Offers him the snuffbox.*] Wouldn't you like a pinch of good snuff? A *shmeck tabik?* A *gezinten shmeck?*

LEYZER: No, thanks, I don't like snuff, it makes me sneeze.

SIMON: I don't like it either, believe me. . . . [*Pushes snuff up his nostrils.*] But I take it. It's said one should always take. What the world gives, take, get rich! [*Draws the snuff deep up his nose.*]

RACHEL: You don't have to take it, you suffer afterwards.

SIMON: What the world gives! Aaa . . . what a pleasure! [*Sneezes into Leyzer's face.*] Sorry.

LEYZER: It's nothing.

SIMON: Why nothing? I sneezed on you, not on nothing. To tell the truth, I feel like repeating that sneeze before you go back . . . for you can go back if you like. [*He almost sneezes.*[ Ahh! It won't come. [*The horn is heard from behind the wall.*]

SIMON: Listen . . . He's happy. He can't play that thing, but he does. He's a part-time cobbler too, sitting and cobbling, and when he gets excited, when he's feeling bad enough, or good enough, he blows that horn like someone else'd suck a cigarette. Isn't there something beautiful in that? Touching, even. Makes you want to pity yourself just a little, doesn't it? And to sleep, to die. [*An irritation in his nose.*] Aaa . . .

[*Sneezes on Leyzer.* ] Simpletons! Truth-seekers? Monsters! [*Pounds furiously at Benny's wall.*] That's enough, shut up! [*The playing stops. To Rachel.*] You lied to him, you and your forty-four years. [*They both turn toward him.* SIMON *laughs.*] Look at you both staring at me. The miracle-worker's here, he who can save and redeem. Without a miracle they'll have to part for always, this miserable pair, the truth will part them. [*The irritation in his nose.*] A . . . a . . . Come on! Sneeze! No, of course not.

RACHEL: That's enough, Simon.

SIMON: Told him the truth, did you? Told him you're forty-four. That's a great truth! An eternal truth, you might say. But in a year's time it won't be true, you'll be forty-five, so it will be a lie! You want him—that's the truth, the only truth. Saying you're forty-four has ruined it, it's as if you told him you didn't want him—and that's the biggest lie of all.

RACHEL [*Gets up*]: I can't.

SIMON: You can't what?

RACHEL. I can't stand this any more.

SIMON [*To Leyzer*]: You . . . You . . . truth-seeker! Your truth's cheated you this time. You're making her suffer, but as for you—you're missing the chance of your life. You . . . you . . . why, it'd be a virtue to deceive you, and you're going to lose the only woman who isn't even capable of deceiving you, you stupid, miserable, cruel idiot.

LEYZER: It isn't because of her age.

SIMON [*Ignoring Leyzer's response*]: We lied to you? Compared to your truth, our lie's a helpless child! . . . What about Rebecca, she stole Esau's birthright for Jacob. Why did *she* lie? And Leah—what a lie that was!—waiting for Jacob in the dark tent, instead of Rachel whom he loved! But then consider Rachel. First she stole those pretty Teraphim from her father, then she lied to Jacob. Nothing there under the pillow, she said, nothing! And do you know what came out of those lies? The whole Jewish people—you, she, me. Sometimes to lie's like praying for help. And knowing how to accept a lie without letting on—that's like anonymous charity. Yes, charity, you champion of truth and justice. You . . . [*The irritation in his nose.*[ A . . . a . . . [*Sneezes into the air.*] What happened to it? I wasted that one. All of it. Whom am I speaking to? Why? Can someone tell me? [*A pause.*]

LEYZER [*A declaration*]: Can you believe I played football in front of my father on Rosh Hashana? To play football on such a sacred day was for him a terrible sin. He would rather die than play himself.

SIMON: What are you getting at?

LEYZER: I asked you a question. Can you believe I did? Can you give me an answer?

SIMON: No, we can't give you an answer.

LEYZER: Then let me tell you I did. I did play. Because of friends. They dragged me into it. I didn't want to, I told them my father might pass the field on his way to synagogue, but they dragged me off with them, they said I was a coward, disloyal, I was needed. So I went off with them, and I played football on Rosh Hashana.

SIMON: I must be going out of my mind.

LEYZER: And my father did pass the field on his way to synagogue, and he did see me. But I didn't know this. You don't notice a thing when you're playing with friends. What do you think he said that night when he got back from synagogue? [*Repeated.*] What do you think he said?

SIMON: We don't think anything.

LEYZER: He didn't say a thing. He . . . [*Takes off his jacket, rolls up his sleeves and turnups, and imitates a goal keeper, catches imaginary balls, jumps with spread-out arms, throws himself to the ground.*[ He played goalkeeper, he did what I'd done out in the field that day, his holy day. That's what he did to me, like this! [*More leaps, then throws himself to the ground.]*

SIMON [*To Rachel*]: Why doesn't he stop it? Where does he think he is?!

RACHEL [*Holding him back*]: Let him be.

LEYZER: And my mother didn't understand what was going on. Here was my father—he was more than sixty then—carrying on like a lunatic. She begged him to stop, cried, tore her hair. The house was smashed to bits. That's what he did, that's what he said to me! Like this! [*Again clutches an imaginary ball to his stomach, bends over and groans.*] Friends dragged me into the game. They forgot about me soon enough—and my father broke down.

SIMON [*Quietly, as if to himself*]: You're crazy.

LEYZER [*After a moment*]: I was crazy. Now I'm not.

SIMON: All right, *I*'m crazy. But what does all this play-acting mean?

LEYZER [*To Rachel*]: I wanted to tell you why I don't want to . . . why I want to go back. I don't want you to think it's because of your age. There's another reason. Friends are like alcohol. You drink and feel happy and warm. You vomit it all up afterwards, and you've an empty skull. Friends are like a drum—noise and nothing inside. Friends are a café—it's pleasant talk but under the table there's a battlefield—

they're putting their hands on your wife's knees. Friends drag you into things for their own reason, smoke you like a cigarette, stub you out, then forget you. Family is something else. Family is a candle flame.

SIMON: What are you getting at?

LEYZER: You two aren't family for me. You don't tell me the truth.

SIMON [*Clutches Rachel*]: This fool here gave you her truth.

LEYZER. That isn't enough. I thought about it a lot. You [*To Simon.*] didn't tell me the truth, and you're brother and sister. I know what a brother and sister are, you can't separate them. You're a family, I'm outside.

SIMON: You moldy, self-righteous saint! You force out of her the truth about herself, then you say that isn't enough for you. [*In his anger he pushes* RACHEL *into* LEYZER'S *arms.*]

LEYZER [*Retreats. To Rachel*]: I wanted to test you. I asked you to know the truth. I'm by myself here, I don't know these streets, I've no relatives, no one to say hello to here. Yes, I was ill, and crazy, as your brother said, and I'm not well yet. I don't want to be crazy again. I don't want that more than anything else in the world. That's why I have to watch out. That's why I can't stay with you now, I have to go back to Jerusalem.

SIMON: Then go! Marry your . . . father! That way, it'll be in the family. [*He approaches Leyzer, pushing* RACHEL *towards him as he does so. To Rachel.*] Let him go back! You've been delivered from Pharaoh's plagues, from boils, cholera, frogs. You've been saved from a clown, an idiot, a kind of . . . a kind of dinosaur! The Messiah's donkey! . . . [*To Leyzer.*] Keep yourself for yourself, you candle flame! Keep to your own family! [*Pushes* RACHEL *back.*] Do you want a family? Then make one! They don't come ready-made. They don't . . . [*The irritation in his nose.*] A . . . a . . . [*Sneezes.*] I think that's enough. Yes, go home, clear off!

LEYZER: I need money for a ticket. [*A pause.*]

SIMON: What did you say?

LEYZER: I need money for a ticket home.

SIMON: I need . . .? You need . . .? What?

LEYZER: I didn't come of my own accord, you fetched me.

SIMON: Oh, my sweet mother! The hell with you! You nebech! Your wife escaped you by the skin of her teeth. I sympathize with her. I'd do the same. I'd leave you my teeth even.

LEYZER: You didn't have to say that, I told you about it myself.

SIMON: What if you did? If someone exhibits his dirty wounds, does it make him clean? You got a trip to England for free, at my expense.

LEYZER: I don't want this England.

SIMON: What luck for England.

LEYZER: You fetched me here by fraud, you'll have to send me back.

SIMON: Now listen to me. I won't give you a penny for the trip back. That's not all. You'll have to pay me back for your ticket here, down to the last penny. And I demand compensation for the misery and shame you've caused my sister and me. You're guilty of breach of promise. Try to tell the court you were deceived, a woman didn't tell you her right age. . . .

LEYZER: She told me the truth. *You* didn't tell me the truth—that's the fraud. Probably there are more lies and more to come.

RACHEL [*From her corner, suddenly*]: It's true, what he's saying. There are more lies, many more, so many he'd do better to clear off now, even if it's only with his bare skin. This flat, for example, isn't mine. And you're not a successful agent. You borrow from me for your trips to Jerusalem, and I borrow from Benny. Some big agent!

SIMON: Be quiet!

RACHEL: And I'm not an old maid of forty-four. That might be all right for someone from Jerusalem. He might even think I'd been saving myself for him. But not me. I'm a forty-four-year-old spinster, with lots of sin behind me. Forty-four.

SIMON: Stop that!

RACHEL [*Brings a wicker basket crammed with laundry to the table, starts folding the laundry*]: I've had men, I've been intimate with them, as they say, and I didn't marry them. And I loved them a lot. And I enjoyed them. But they deceived me and went off, all of them, hundreds of them, two is as good as a hundred, it's more than a hundred. Yes, they walked out on me. In the rain, too. It was raining, and they walked out on me. I didn't get wet, they did, but that's worse, isn't it?

SIMON: You're going out of your mind, he's infected you.

RACHEL: They had very good reasons probably. Men don't just walk out on a woman who's attached to them like a dog. And in the rain, too. Maybe I've bad breath, that's why maybe.

SIMON: Why do you cheapen yourself?

RACHEL: I want him to walk out too. He hasn't lived with me, he hasn't deceived me, so let him at least clear out. He hasn't given me any joy, but he's the last candidate, and a last candidate, even an idiot, drains your emotions. He hasn't just drained them, he's sucked them dry.

There's nothing left. I haven't a single lie left, I've given him them, all of them.

SIMON: Enough, enough, enough!

RACHEL: That's what he came for, to look for lies. So here they are, he can take them and go, I haven't any more. After all, how many lies could I collect? Even I? There's a limit. If I think of any more, I'll send them on to him in Jerusalem, I promise him, but let him go now! He said he wanted to go. [*To Leyzer.*] Why don't you go? [*Approaches him.*] I also sit in cafés. In three at once. And I lie in bed till noon, sometimes till evening. I have lunch in bed. And I throw out the oil from the chips. I fry a few tiny chips in a huge panful of oil, big as this, then I throw it all out, while the oil's still hot. It makes a lovely sound, like this . . . tssss! Tssss! I love that sound. And sometimes I smoke a pipe. [*Goes back to her laundry basket.*]

SIMON [*Holds her back, trying to calm her*]: He isn't worth all this. Stop it. This is Simon talking to you.

RACHEL: He won't go without money. With me it doesn't work without money. I had to pay the others to stay, I'll have to pay this one to go. [*Takes her purse out of the wardrobe, pours its contents onto the table.*] This is all I have. My whole salary! If it doesn't get him as far as Jerusalem, then Gibraltar'll do. So long as he gets out of here.

SIMON [*Puts his hand on the money*]: You're not to give him a penny.

RACHEL [*To Leyzer*]: Take it! Lies and money, that's all I've got. I'm giving it to you.

SIMON: So long as I'm here, you won't give him a penny!

RACHEL: So don't be here! You can go off together. [*Removes his hand from the money.*]

SIMON: You've never spoken to me like this.

RACHEL: Take your hands off my money. And take them out of my life. I slave away at my stupid job, as you call it, for this money. So hands off! You're at a loose end, so you drop in on me day after day, telling me what to love, what not to love, what to do, what not to do, what's stupid . . . I'm sick of it. You needn't come here again. You've no right to tell me how to live my life. I've enjoyed my life, you haven't. Yes, I've enjoyed it.

SIMON: Never . . . !

RACHEL [*Folding laundry*]: Take the money, the two of you can, you're so brilliant. But leave me in peace! I've a room of my own, I've all this laundry to iron, I have to look my best for my job. Really tip top.

BENNY [*Bursts into the room, gives Rachel a roll of banknotes*]: For his ticket! Gibraltar isn't far enough! To Jerusalem! [*Exits.* RACHEL *looks at the money in her hands, and breaks into a quiet but wholehearted weeping. She puts the money on the sideboard, takes up the basket, and, apparently unaware of what she's doing, drags it towards Leyzer. Apparently unaware of what he's doing, he moves towards her. They stop, facing each other.*]

SIMON: I and Benny will give him the money, not you. I was wrong. It was a kind of madness. We'll give him double the amount, just so long as he leaves! He and all Jerusalem aren't worth your little finger! [*Seeing them, he's silenced.*]

RACHEL [*To Leyzer*]: What do you want of me?

LEYZER: If you'll allow me . . . you're carrying this basket . . . [*He picks it up.*]

RACHEL: What don't you like about it?

LEYZER: On the contrary, I like this basket very much. In Jerusalem, they do the laundry in heavy copper basins. Afterwards they place their dry wash in the same copper basins. They're scared of the smallest innovation there. It scares them like a crucifix. You're right to keep the dry wash in a wicker basket.

RACHEL: So what?

LEYZER: There's nothing wrong with it. As I just remarked, you're right. If you'll allow me, I'll help you carry the basket. I want to give you a hand.

RACHEL: Yes, you'll carry the basket for me, and ferret around in it to see if I wash clean enough, the way they do in Jerusalem, and then you'll say you don't want me because it *isn't* clean enough. [*Pulls the basket away from him.*]

LEYZER [*Draws it back towards himself*]: No. I won't ferret around any more. I understood a lot from what you said, and from what you didn't say, and from what you said the opposite of. Now I know you've a clean soul.

RACHEL [*Again pulling the basket toward her*]: Thank you very much. You pick me up, throw me away, pick me up again. Even for a ball there are limits, I'd say.

LEYZER [*Again draws the basket towards him. They seem to be wrestling over it*]: I'm not scared you had lovers. If they tricked you and went off, the shame's theirs. I was scared only of lies. Now you've nothing to lie about, you've made everything clear. It's clear also you're more alone than I knew. I'm also more alone than I know. And I'm sorry for what

I said about wanting to go back. And I'm asking you to agree to our getting married. [*A brief silence. She lets go the basket. The laundry spills out, the basket remains in Leyzer's hands.*]

RACHEL: I'll make a cup of tea. [*A pause.*] Yes, I'll make a cup of tea. [*Goes to the kitchenette.* LEYZER *replaces the laundry in the basket.* SIMON, *dumbstruck, stands facing* RACHEL, *who carries a tray with two cups of tea on it to the table. To Simon.*] I'll make some for you too. [*A pause.*] You didn't ask. [*Simon turns away.* RACHEL *and* LEYZER *sit down. To Lezyer.*] Drink it, it isn't very hot.

LEYZER: You've the chocolates.

RACHEL: I don't want any right now.

LEYZER [*A pause*]: All right, you don't have to. [*Drinks the tea.* SIMON, *confused, slowly circles the table. To Rachel, suddenly, loudly.*] I'll tell you something interesting. In the older parts of Jerusalem they hang out the laundry on ropes stretched over little pulleys between the verandas. On Thursdays you can hardly see the sky for all that laundry. A white wash for the most part. They wear a lot of black and white, the white gets the most laundering.

SIMON [*Hovers over Leyzer and asks a seemingly aimless question*]: You like music?

LEYZER: Excuse me?

SIMON: Do you like music?

LEYZER: Why do you ask?

SIMON: I like to know these things. I collect information in all spheres.

LEYZER: Sometimes.

SIMON: Good. What?

LEYZER: Excuse me?

SIMON: What kind of music do you like?

LEYZER: Marches.

SIMON: Marches?

RACHEL [*To Simon*]: Marches.

LEYZER: Yes.

SIMON: That's interesting, very interesting, that's a special taste. Military or funeral?

LEYZER: I'm no expert. Marches. Why do you ask?

SIMON: Why do I ask? You won't believe this, but that's exactly what she likes. A heaven-sent match! I asked, just like that, like a blind man, and I hit it full on the snout. You see this sideboard? It's full of records—and they're all marches. That's the only kind of music she can listen to. She can't fall asleep even without playing two or three marches. Extraordinary! [*Still standing, slightly removed from Leyzer and Rachel.*]

LEYZER [*To Rachel*]: I'll go on with what I started telling you, if you'd like that?

RACHEL: Yes, of course.

LEYZER: Do you remember Leah-Dvora Villmann?

RACHEL: With the mole on the end of her nose.

LEYZER: That's something everyone remembers.

RACHEL: Yes. [*After a pause.*] What did you want to tell me about her? You began telling me about the laundry on the ropes.

LEYZER: It's connected. As a young girl, she exchanged secret love letters along the ropes with Nakhman Friedman of Friedman and Sons.

SIMON [*Again hovers over Leyzer, and asks, out of the blue*]: Does she buy magazines?

LEYZER: Who?

SIMON: What's her name . . . Leah-Khannah, Khannah-Leah, Zissel-Fissel . . .

LEYZER: Leah-Dvora Villmann.

SIMON: That's it. Khannah-Dvora, how could I have forgotten? Does she buy magazines?

LEYZER: You're making fun of her. She's no money or time for that, moreover she hasn't a head for magazines. She doesn't have the time to lift her head and see if there are stars in the sky. She doesn't need all those things, she has children. [*To Rachel.*] Do you do that?

SIMON: Does she do what?

LEYZER [*To Rachel*]: Do you buy magazines?

SIMON: Not just any magazines. Medical journals! They're seven times more expensive than ordinary magazines. She doesn't understand a thing in them, but she loves them. She also buys expensive tickets to concerts—there are cheap tickets and expensive ones, she buys expensive ones. She'll do without meat and fish, but not that. And another thing, she looks for stars in the sky. She stands by the window and suddenly she'll say: Look, stars! That doesn't cost money, but it is a luxury. It's silly. Not one star there ever says to another star: Look, Rachel!

LEYZER [*To Rachel*]: I asked you.

RACHEL: I always wanted to be a doctor, but it didn't work out. I like medicine.

LEYZER [*Takes a certificate out of his wallet, spreads it out on the table before Rachel*]: Please read this.

SIMON: What's that? [*Reaches for the certificate.*]

LEYZER: I'm talking to her. [*To Rachel.*] You can have it, it's yours.

RACHEL: Tell me what it says, that'll do.

LEYZER: It authorises me to collect donations for the old Jerusalem orphanage. [*SIMON, startled, opens his mouth to say something, doesn't.*]

RACHEL: Why do you show me this?

LEYZER: I want you to know I'll work hard to support you. And if things really work out for me you'll be able to buy all kinds of things you like, those journals for instance, or . . . other things like that. No more than we can afford, though. No debts! Debts are lies.

SIMON [*Partly to Leyzer, partly to himself*]: You collect money for an orphanage?

LEYZER [*To Rachel*]: It won't be my main job. Just for the start. And to keep a family. I'm not a religious Jew, but an orphanage, even if it's a religious one, after all is an orphanage. It needs support. They eat from tin plates there. They've no sheets. They cover themselves with old army blankets that itch. Perhaps they don't feel it. All the same, they're children, orphans.

RACHEL: That's true, it's nice you notice things like that.

LEYZER: They'll give me fifty percent.

SIMON: What?

LEYZER: That's the most you can get. Some give less. But they're poor, it's an old orphanage, so they've no choice, they have to pay more.

SIMON: Did you hear that? Fifty percent of what's donated for those orphans with their tin blankets, sorry: tin plates and army blankets!

LEYZER: It doesn't work out at very much, fifty percent of what's donated for orphans. People don't give you more than their small change for orphans. It's not like a museum. Nobody's looking for this kind of work nowadays. [*A pause.*] Shall I go on?

RACHEL: Pardon?

LEYZER: With what I started telling you.

RACHEL: Yes, of course.

LEYZER: I told you how Nakhman Friedman corresponded with Leah-Dvora Villmann and rejected all the important matches offered him.

That's as far as I got. So I'll finish the story. They finally got the reason out of him. He admitted he wanted her. His family was furious. She came from a poor family, and in any case she wasn't known for any special quality, beautiful embroidery, for instance, or a good heart. There are women known for such things.

SIMON [*Approaches and faces him*]: Go on, go on! How delightful! The groom-to-be's regaling the bride-to-be with stories of time past! Your stories are worth listening to. What stories! And what a headache. Suddenly I've two heads, they've both a headache.

LEYZER: I have some aspirins. [*Takes several from his pocket.*] You can take three.

SIMON: You carry aspirins around with you? [*To Rachel.*] With such a husband your worries are over, you'll always be provided with aspirins. [*To Leyzer.*] Three? But I've only two heads.

LEYZER: Take two aspirins.

SIMON: Thanks anyway. I've just remembered something a lot better for headaches. I'll be right back . . . you two just go on sitting there, bride and groom at the head of the table, eating the instant soup of bliss. Please don't worry yourselves with me. I'll be back. [*Goes to the kitchenette.*]

LEYZER [*To Rachel*]: Shall I go on?

RACHEL: Yes, of course.

LEYZER: But finally his parents agreed—his parents, Moshe-Haim Friedman and Sons.

RACHEL: You said her name was Villmann, didn't you?

LEYZER [*He talks rapidly partly because of his strong feeling for her, partly because of pent-up embarrassment*]: Yes, because in the end nothing came of it. And it was her own doing. They'd agreed to the wedding, they began to prepare for it. Then she said she wouldn't agree to having her braids cut off, before the ceremony, the way they do there. They say she had marvellously braided hair. Her hair would glide behind her on the landing when she came downstairs. All Jerusalem was enraged, but she wouldn't budge. And she came from a poor home, with that mole on the end of her nose. It's said he wrote her a last letter by way of the ropes, saying she loved her hair better than him.

RACHEL: That's terrible.

LEYZER: Nakhman Friedman promptly married Rachel Gvirtzman. And only dumb Shmuel-Wolf would have Leah-Dvora. It wasn't only that he was dumb, he wasn't even young. He didn't even mention cutting off her braids. She decided on it.

RACHEL: A woman shouldn't cling to her long hair because in the end she has neither hair nor anything else. That's what you wanted to say?

LEYZER: No. In fact she had a good life with Shmuel-Wolf. They had eight beautiful children. When he was killed in the shooting from the Tower of David, the youngest, Ephraim, was two months old. She raised them all in good health, and on a tiny pension, on bread, olive-oil and onions.

SIMON [*Returns from the kitchenette, potato slices on his forehead, attached by a wet cloth tied around his head. Pours himself tea, says quietly*]: What a splendid life! Ideal really! Eight children, and, in addition, all those onions! [*RACHEL bursts out laughing. LEYZER doesn't notice she's laughing, he's staring at Simon. To Leyzer, indicating the bandage around his head.*] A wet rag and sliced potato. You recognize the remedy, don't you? The potato slices suck out the headache. It's a Jerusalem remedy. Not inferior to aspirin, and economical, moreover. Afterwards you can use them for chips. Jerusalem's a poor city. Poverty isn't something to be ashamed of. On the contrary, it's something to be proud of. It's a delight.

LEYZER: You're laughing at me, you're laughing at my mother, you're . . . [*Realizes that Rachel is laughing.*] You're laughing . . . [*She laughs uncontrollably.*]

SIMON [*Realizes Rachel is laughing, laughs also*]: Did you hear how he said, "You're laughing"? As if he'd said, "You're dirty, you're . . ."? [*To Leyzer.*] Of course she's laughing. Yes, laughing.

LEYZER [*To Rachel*]: You're laughing with him.

SIMON [*To Rachel. Almost drunk with laughter*]. D'you hear how he says that? Naturally. You touched his heart when you told him how your lovers bluffed and left you. When you cheapened yourself. That's how he'd like you to be always, a hunted creature like himself. It's only then your soul will be clean enough for him. The only luxury he'll allow you—will be a mole at the end of your nose. He's a lunatic puritan! Atonement! Fasts! Marches!

RACHEL [*Tries to stop laughing*]: I can't . . . I can't stop . . .

SIMON: Of course, you can't stop. You and I have to laugh. That's our pleasure, that's what we chose. That's our fate. Laughing, you're ten years younger. It was worth it if only for that.

LEYZER [*To Simon*]: You don't want me. [*RACHEL stops laughing.*]

SIMON [*To Leyzer*]: I don't want you? [*To Rachel, with something resembling a laugh.*] He does have charm, if you're looking for it, doesn't he?

LEYZER: Nothing'll help. The two of you really don't want me. The two of you really don't need me. I can't be family for you, ever. [*Gets up, takes his coat.* RACHEL, *astonished, gets up also.* SIMON *takes a step toward him, then stops.* LEYZER *puts on his coat, his hat.*] But you've helped me reach an important decision. I remembered my daughter. I'll start saving up for a flat for her. Her mother won't let her see me, it will probably take years before she even realizes I'm alive. But when she grows up, finds someone suitable, begins to think about a family, she'll find a home prepared for her, one I've built for her. She'll need me in the end. Goodbye. [*Goes out.* RACHEL *sinks down into her chair, weeps soundlessly.*]

SIMON [*Forced laugh*]: Well, what do you think of that? He throws himself out! And without a ticket. That represents a clear profit! How airy this room is, suddenly. And we've learned a lesson also. Education is an important thing, isn't it? [*He stops, he has a sad, tired look. A ring at the door. A pause. Another ring.* RACHEL *gets up, opens the door.*]

BENNY [*Stands in the doorway. Returns Rachel the shoes he has mended*]: Your shoes . . . I took them . . . They're better than new now. I'll always mend them for you. Be as sick as you like—I'll fetch you anything you need. You deserve it! [*Sees Simon, stares at his potato bandage.*]

SIMON [*To Benny*]: What are you staring at? [*To Rachel.*] He's staring at me! [*Puts his hand to his forehead.*] Potatoes. Why not? You should know. You're an anarchist, mend shoes, blow the horn—why shouldn't I walk around with potato slices on my head? Surely you won't complain. I'm not much, but I have a sister, a treasure. Yes, I have a little sister, that's why I have potato slices on my forehead. Why not? They feel good there. Juicy, soft. They suck up all the poison. You can hear it. Mts-mts. [*Into Benny's face.*] Mts-mts . . .

BENNY: You think yourself clever! . . . You big fool. [*Exits.*]

SIMON [*After him*]: Mts . . . mts . . . .! [*The sound of the horn, louder and stronger than before.* RACHEL *pours tea. To Rachel.*] He has charm too, hasn't he? If you look hard enough. But if you don't, what then? All the charmers, me too, all of us, come to you. Yes, difficult people. [*A pause.*] It's all because of Israel. When I was there I was sure it'd work. Over there he seemed a real find. In fact, it all seemed like milk and honey—trees, stones, people. They tell me they get up in the morning happy. What's there to be happy about early in the morning? That white light of theirs, like snow. So I decided I'd bring you, no, for me too, I'd bring us back a piece of that light, a piece of cake from that celebration. Him! There you are! [*Laughs, removes the potato slices from his forehead, lays them out before her, continues laughing.*] You know why

the light in Israel is white? It's because of all that sunshine. It's the same snow . . . [*Stops laughing, breaks down.*] No, it's me, not the snow. . . . The snow in Siberia was hellish. I got out of that hell and I'm still wading in it. I see sunlight and I call it snow. [*A pause. Then suddenly firm, almost angry.*] You deserve more, d'you hear? Nothing will help you, you deserve more! What you don't get you don't get, but I won't let them steal from you what you deserve! [*He sags but continues standing there;* RACHEL *gets up and slowly takes the empty cups from the table to the kitchenette. The sound of the horn.*]
Curtain

# The Night of the Twentieth

*by*
YEHOSHUA SOBOL

This play is a recreation of an important historic moment in Israeli history. This recreation is not entirely accurate except in general outline. In this sense it might be compared to a Scott novel. Sobol has put together "a credible, suspenseful situation out of diaries, fragmented memoirs and literary descriptions of the period."[1] The action of the play is set at a mountain camp above the Sea of Galilee at the beginning of the Third Aliyah (1910–1920.)

The play focuses on a group of young Zionists who are preparing to move out the next morning to settle Mansurin—"Nobody knows what awaits us there." These young Zionists engage in a night-long discussion about the kind of life they are going to live and the kind of settlement they are going to create. During this discussion, a great deal of self-examination takes place (and incidentally an examination of the question of Jewish identity as well). The whole scope of the play's activity is encompassed by this night-long discussion.

In the morning the settlers leave. Nothing is really settled, except perhaps that the various persons involved who were strangers at the beginning of the play are more in accord with one another at the end. During the discussion, two major philosophies developed. One of the major characters, Ephraim, indicates that he considers the motivation for concerted action in the future should spring from God, country, and traditional Jewish values. The other major character, Moshe, indicates that he considers these traditions are all dead and have failed in the past, and that "we will all start everything like automatons and put off really important things . . . because of rotten myths."

Moshe indicates that the only wellspring to action must come from a certain type of intimacy whereby each of the settlers must know one another "as a woman knows her husband . . . otherwise where will you find the strength to send me out to kill or be killed in fights with Arab tenant farmers!"

Sobol has created a very intense play centered around discussion. The play shows us a critical moment in history and it also gives us a portrait of the pioneer, not as the eagle-eyed, strong-muscled monolith, but self-doubting, in many ways fearful and uncertain of what he is doing and essentially all too human.[2]

The plays written by Jehoshua Sobol, a young and popular Israeli playwright, include documentaries, satire, and serious drama. In 1971 he wrote *The Days That Come,* a documentary about old people. In 1972 he wrote a play entitled *New Year's Eve,* concerning the conflict between generations in Israel. In 1975 he wrote *The Joker,* about the war, reflected in an apartment complex. In the past few years he has been adapting and updating a Greek trilogy for the modern Israeli stage. In this trilogy, Sobol turns the House of Atreus into the House of Kaplan. The first part of the trilogy begins during the War for Independence, 1948.

## NOTES

1. Edith Zertal, "Two Directors, Boulevard Approach, Social Documentation," *Theatrom 75/76* (Tel Aviv: The Israeli Center of the International Theatre Institute, 1975–76), p. 41.

2. For other interpretations in regard to this drama, see Gideon Ofrat, "Introduction to the *Night of the Twentieth*" (Tel Aviv: Institute for the Translation of Hebrew Literature, Ltd., 1978), p. 6.

See also Mendel Kohansky, "Unraveling the Myth," *Jerusalem Post,* International Edition, April 20–28, 1980, p. 15.

CHARACTERS

*Ephraim, of middle-class Viennese origin. (male)*
*Moshe, a tailor's son, from Galicia, served in the Austrian Army during the First World War.*
*Nehama, a student, of good family, from Vienna. (female)*
*Naphtali, eighteen-year-old high-school student, of good family. (male)*
*Miriam, twenty-year-old, flirty, "mischievous." (female)*
*Akiva, budding artist, wood-carver. (male)*
*Shifra, of good family, from Baden. (female)*
*Time: night of the 20th October, 1920.*
*Place: a tent on a mountain in Galilee.*

*Translated by: Michael Salkind.*



All are busy packing bundles in preparation for their departure for permanent settlement in Mansurin.
Movement on stage—action and reaction.

PROLOGUE OF SORTS:

ACTOR OF THE PART OF MOSHE:
When the first World War ended, the *yishuv* in Eretz Israel was in bad shape. Yossef Haim Brenner wrote: "The little community which is still here, is of one mind: the salvation of the Jewish People and of Eretz Israel will come from neither prophets nor High Politics, but from new groups of laboring men and women. The main problem is that of the human element."

And indeed, in the year 1920 the firstcomers of the third Aliya, the first graduates of the Hashomer Hatzair Movement from Vienna, Innsbruck, Lvov and other cities and towns throughout the former Austrian Empire, begin to arrive. They live in temporary work-camps during their first months in Eretz and absolutely refuse to join any of the existing political parties. Very soon the rumor spreads through the remnants of the Second Aliya that the new wave of immigration is bringing in new young people of a kind unknown in the land till then.

[*Lights fade. Darkness in auditorium and on stage. Background music:anthem of the Poale Zion Movement. Music fades. Stage lights. All are busy packing bundles. Working in silence. Silence lasts about half a minute.*]

AKIVA: They're all so quiet roundabouts. Why you too, Naphtali?

NAPHTALI: I'm ashamed of what I'm thinking.

AKIVA: Scared of what will happen tomorrow at Mansurin?

NAPHTALI: I wish I were . . . I dreamt about you. You're dressed in scale armor like a medieval knight. You're riding a fine charger and are galloping toward the lands of Mansurin. The savages come out of their huts to oppose you. They shoot arrows at you and hurtle stones, but you don't fall back a single step. You brandish a heavy mace. . . .

AKIVA [*Interrupting*]: How cruel and bloodthirsty—you should be ashamed of yourself!

NEHAMA: The two of you should be ashamed of yourselves.

AKIVA: Where's your sense of humour, Nehama? "Amid blood and fire Judaea fell, in blood and fire Judaea shall rise"!

NEHAMA: That's not funny; it's cynical. Naphtali doesn't count, he's not capable of getting two consecutive serious words out of his mouth, but you, Akiva, I'm surprised at you. Ever since you were taken by Naphtali's charm you've lost all individuality.

AKIVA: We'll settle on the land and over us will fly a flag engraved with the word "Blood."

EPHRAIM: That's an argument that belongs in the past.

AKIVA: In the future, Ephraim, the future.

EPHRAIM: The matter was settled before we even came here.

AKIVA: We're not responsible for what happened two generations ago. But tomorrow we'll settle on our land and our first act will be a bloody fight with Arab serfs.

EPHRAIM: The land was fully paid for.

AKIVA: A full price was paid for Umm Junni too.

EPHRAIM: There was no fight at Umm Junni.

AKIVA: There was.

EPHRAIM: Were you there that you're so sure?

AKIVA: I heard all about it from Dvorin.

EPHRAIM: Dvorin! He was a black pessimist, a professional slanderer, completely embittered. Before leaving Eretz he tried to run down those who stuck it out and stayed. It's a good thing that such offal leaves the country. At least there'll be some sort of natural selection and only the strong and the pure will remain.

AKIVA: And if we have to fight?

EPHRAIM: We won't have to.

AKIVA: And if we *do* have to?

EPHRAIM: If they attack us we'll defend ourselves. And we'll count each blow so that, God forbid, there won't be any loss of life among them. As far as it depends on us there'll be no bloodshed between us and the serfs.

NAPHTALI: Why not stay here? Where's the great rush to get down off the mountain?

EPHRAIM: This is no place for farming.

AKIVA: We don't even know yet what we want our society to be like. We haven't had time. They should give us more time.

EPHRAIM: There's a policy of settlement. Our turn came up, the luxury of squatting here on the mountain is over.

AKIVA: Policy! . . . Barely thirty miserable settlements and some sixty thousand Jews in all of the towns and villages. I sat down yesterday and turned the leaves of the calendar . . . a fortnight to the 2nd of November. The date grinned at me with a sort of fatefulness, rejoicing at our misfortune: the Balfour Declaration . . . what hopes arose. Jewish youth would immediately rise, and come in multitudes. Jewish youth, however, continues to live the good life in Vienna, in Berlin, in Lemberg, in Chernowitz.

EPHRAIM: A very good life indeed! They're living in a fool's paradise. They don't feel the ground burning beneath their feet.

AKIVA: We're hiding the truth from ourselves. I raised my head today and looked around: empty and barren mountains right up to the horizon and we're slung on top of one of them. . . . Great things are happening in Europe, the world's being turned upside down, and we've wrenched ourselves out of the centre of the cosmic drama and somehow now find ourselves in an empty and barren corner of it. The most God-forsaken corner of the universe.

EPHRAIM: Right. Do you prefer a more comfortable life? I prefer to live dangerously.

AKIVA: We ought to get up tomorrow morning and, instead of loading the baggage onto the automobiles and going off to Mansurin to scrap with some flea-ridden serfs over a plot of stony ground, we should rise as one man, cross Syria, cross the Caucasus on foot and go to Russia. The great event awaits us *there.*

EPHRAIM: Go to Russia! We've left Europe, we've slammed the front door in her face and now you want us to return by the servants' entrance. . . . Europe is cruel and barbaric, capable of creating only sentimental culture. European culture doesn't tolerate the singular, the exceptional.

MOSHE: Do we?

EPHRAIM: Do we what?

MOSHE: Do *we* tolerate the exceptional? What are *we* doing here at all?

EPHRAIM: In our hands we hold the messianic hope of a whole nation, of all mankind. What do we intend to build here? One more place for Jews to live in? Neither better nor worse than the Jewish community in Vienna? Which doesn't solve the problem any more than the Jewish ghetto of Berdichev?

AKIVA: Well all right. What's happening now all over the country? Most of the immigration camps are sunk in sadness, dejection, apathy, emigration, emptiness.

EPHRAIM: Is that *all?* And what about the talks and debates? What about the singing and dancing halfway through the night, the dreadful transition to a life of labor and getting the better of an entirely new language. . . . Social revolution deriving from the individual, we are waging a cultural war against the whole *yishuv* of Eretz as it is today.

AKIVA: Feeble signs of any sort of social integration. People leave the immigration camps daily and move to the towns. To the private building contractor, to the lack of taste and silliness of town-dwellers' tea parties. To the city! They're looking for the light—they're becoming bourgeois, Ephraim! The soul goes out to become bourgeois and the Levantinism of the country speeds the process, and they look it . . . !

NEHAMA: Nevertheless, there's one bright spot: Deganiya. . . .

AKIVA: Deganiya, Deganiya, Deganiya! Deganiya is an exotic blossom. One goes to Deganiya and returns from her, but the spirit of Deganiya doesn't give breath to the generation.

EPHRAIM: Why look to Deganiya? Take us; take our common meal after a backbreaking day road-making. . . . Take the most trivial things: a plate, a spoon, a slice of bread—these are the channels through which the world's eroticism flows to us. We have created anew something that European culture lost long ago: the offering table of the commune . . . the love feast. . . . I know: all these are mere beginnings, experiments. But, our work will stop being a mere experiment only when it stands in the midst of reality of nationhood. We shall redeem ourselves and this land only if we become the passion of our generation.

NAPHTALI: Aren't you asking too much? How'll I manage the passion of a whole generation when I can't even come to terms with my own private little passion. . . . [*Rebukes from all sides:* "Naphtali!" "Really!" etc.] No really: what do you want? The Lord takes a whole people, scatters them all over the world, without any reason, and destroys a few tens of thousands here and there. . . . No way to go, no way out. . . . Then suddenly he takes a handful of young fellows and girls, shakes 'em out back into the Land of their Fathers and tells 'em to begin all over again: I don't understand! Where does he expect us to find the strength for it?

EPHRAIM: In necessity! If you'd been speaking seriously I'd try to answer you.

NAPHTALI: I'm the most serious of the lot here! I'm a funny fellow. When I sing—I'm funny, when I try to dance—I'm even funnier, and when I get up the courage to say a couple of words to a girl—woe's me what I look like! But I'm serious *now!* They told us all about regenerating our lives and what not! But life in Eretz is so much harder than we thought.

EPHRAIM: Then it seems, we didn't think seriously enough.

NAPHTALI: Right! Hard and bitter. . . . Where'll we find the exaltation of the Spirit?

EPHRAIM: In your wailing! You *Weltschmerzer,* you!

NAPHTALI: During two months I had my meals in the Workers' Canteens: the Russian Jew seats himself on one side, the Galician on another, there's no social contact, people curse and whoever can—packs his bag and leaves! To Russia, to Poland, to Germany. . . . We'll change that? We're the clowns of the Jewish people. The clever ones stayed over there . . . and they continue to do business as usual: commerce, studies, career . . . and that's the size of it.

EPHRAIM: What do you suggest we do about it? Give up?

NAPHTALI: Well go ahead and show me something different!

EPHRAIM: I should show you something different? Why? I can dive deeper into despair than you. If I were to cry out what's inside my soul you'd all flee to the ends of the earth.

NAPHTALI: Go ahead, get it out.

EPHRAIM: Yes? Well, no one will have the privilege of hearing it. Me.

I'm a Don Quixote! A sort of holy madman . . . why must we cling to weakness, of all things? We should say to weakness: *"Noli me tangere"!* Just as Jesus said to Mary Magdalene: "Don't touch me"!

MOSHE: That's the most dangerous kind of weakness, Ephraim!

EPHRAIM: What?

MOSHE: The need to stay clean at all cost. . . .

EPHRAIM [*Regarding Moshe, amused*]: For the first time I've caught on who you remind me of: you remind me of my father!

MOSHE: I remind you of your father?

EPHRAIM: Exactly! He too, all his life, knew only to ridicule, to wound, to strike only from ambush. But to fight face-to-face—fair fight, that—never! He always knew when to attack you in moments of weakness. From behind. That's how he ruled the house. When I used to return at night from the clubhouse he would welcome me with: "Nu? Preparing the Zionist Revolution in Vienna?" I didn't even answer him. I bided my time. I was waiting for when I could tell him: "Father, I'm emigrating to Eretz." When the great day came he became sweeter than honey. [*Chuckling.*] The newspaper fell from his hands, his mouth trembled. It took him a long moment to recover from the blow. His talented son, the pride of the family, throwing over the University, the career in the Firm, throwing away all the Kultur that this Polish-Jewish immigrant, Yank'l Joachim Schneider, admired so much . . .*his* son throwing it all in his face and emigrating to Eretz-Israel? I thought he'd have a fit!

SHIFRA: And then what happened?

EPHRAIM: . . . "Adventures are all right for young men with financial backing. Don't worry, you can go to Palestine. I'll open a bank account for you here in Vienna and when you're sick of your Zionist experiment don't be ashamed to come home."—"you won't see the day," I told him. Says he: "Don't say things now that will make you return with your tail between your legs. It's much pleasanter to come back with your tail held high, like a real thoroughbred tomcat which always falls on its feet." Mother couldn't stand any more of this and said: "Warum bist Du so Zynisch, Joachim?"—"I know my boy through and through," he told her. [*Tapping his palm.*] "When hair grows here, that's when he'll be a true idealist!" [*Pointing to Moshe's cheek.*] When grass grows there, I answered him, that's when you'll see me again in Vienna! That was my parting from him. [*The group bursts into song: "Between Three o'clock and Four."*] I want one thing only: to free myself of inner conflict. To go forth. To *do* things. You all want some ready-made substantiality. It'll be a bad day for us in Eretz when our lives will be based on "substance." We must live in a condition of constant formation, in the tension of constant becoming.

NAPHTALI: What do we do about the gloom all around?

EPHRAIM: I wouldn't give up even if we were in total, merciless darkness. The things in Eretz that will be built up out of strife and suffering will not be in vain.

NAPHTALI: But where do we stand now?

EPHRAIM: On the way!

NAPHTALI: Yes! Always on the way!

EPHRAIM: Yes, *always* on the way. [*The group joins the singing. The singing ends. Quiet falls. All sit around, dreaming.*] Who were the prophets? A handful of crazy intellectuals, persecuted by priests and kings. And they dispensed mental food for generation after generation. Who created Christianity? An odd community of despairing people who cut themselves off from the rest.

SHIFRA: What kind of society shall we form? A Selma Lagerlof community? The Tolstoian Village?

MOSHE: Why not the Hassidic group, something like the Hassidic gathering. . . .

NEHAMA: Everything's open to us, all we have to do is choose. To reach out and choose. It's frightening. . . .

SHIFRA: We must become children again. A child doesn't use names for things. A child touches a table. For it, it's not a table, it's wood. Not wood—naked material. Reality. It touches its mother. Neither mother nor flesh. Touch. Sensation. Warmth streaming from flesh to flesh, the kiss flowing from lip to lip. The union when one body inseminates another; one darkness, the other . . . We must give up using words. . . .

EPHRAIM: We'll have land. Fields. A village like the villages in Styria. With green pastures, and cows. Apple orchards, and pears. And we'll tend them.

NAPHTALI: In the mornings we'll yoke the oxen to the plough. At midday we'll gather in the shade of a tree. The girls will bring sauerkraut and sausages, chops, red wine and cheese. We'll plant a *vineyard.* The grapes will be black and they'll taste of sunshine and limestone. Merchants from Jaffa and Jerusalem will come to purchase Mansurin wine. . . .

EPHRAIM: In the evenings, after work, we'll wash, put on simple clothes and stand about watching the sunset. Our table spread with jugs of water and bread and we'll sit around it and be silent.

MOSHE: Why're you so keen on our shutting up all the time?

NAPHTALI: Words are only a means of communication. True communication is by looks.

MIRIAM: Exactly.

MOSHE: Then you two look at each other! [*MIRIAM and NAPHTALI look at Moshe as though they do not understand.*] Nu, what are you staring at *me* for? [*To Miriam.*] Are you afraid to look Naphtali in the eye?

MIRIAM: Afraid? What have I got to be afraid of?

EPHRAIM: Naphtali's private little passion.

MOSHE: If you're not hiding anything by your silence, then you've nothing to be afraid of.

NAPHTALI: D'you mean we should do it now?

MOSHE: Do you want to wait for Judgment Day? Until Meshiach comes?

AKIVA: But here? In front of everybody?

MOSHE: Is there anything immoral about it?

NAPHTALI: No! On the contrary. . . .

AKIVA: It would be different if the wish to do it had come from him. But like this, with you egging him on and pushing him into it. . . .

NAPHTALI: He's right! Akiva's right: if it had been on *my* initiative . . .

MIRIAM: You don't want to, Naphtali?

NAPHTALI: I do want to!

MIRIAM: Then do it, come on!

NAPHTALI: Do what?

AKIVA: They've managed to get you all mixed up, you don't know what you want any more.

NEHAMA: Why are you defending him so hard?

MIRIAM: Oh, come on! [*She gets up, stands opposite Naphtali. He raises his eyes to hers, hesitantly. They gaze into each other's eyes.*]

NAPHTALI [*Unable to contain his emotions*]: It's . . . It's so strange. . . .

MIRIAM [*Puts her finger to her lips*]: Sh . . . don't speak.

NAPHTALI: I don't know what's happening to me. I'm trembling all over.

MIRIAM [*Stretches out her two hands and takes Naphtali's*]: Come, I'll hold you.

NAPHTALI: Wait. [*Snatches back his hands and wipes them on his trousers, hard.*] My palms are wet.

MIRIAM: Never mind.

NAPHTALI: My palms are always sweaty. It's not that that I'm worked up about.

MIRIAM: I like warm and moist skin. Gimmee. . . . [*He reaches out his hands without coming closer and she takes them in hers.*] D'you feel it? My hands are moist too.

NAPHTALI: I've always been shy of shaking hands with anyone, because the sweat breaks out immediately.

MIRIAM: Doesn't this feel good?

NAPHTALI: Yes, it's nice . . . how I'm trembling. . . . I'm telling myself all along that I'm holding a tree, to try and stop trembling. But it doesn't help. . . .

MIRIAM: Stop thinking so much and try to feel *me* trembling.

NAPHTALI: What, you're trembling too?

MIRIAM: Don't you feel it?

NAPHTALI: Now that you've told me, I *do* feel it. Are you scared, too?

MIRIAM: No. I'm trembling because I feel good. Don't you?

NAPHTALI: Yes. Very good. . . .

MIRIAM: Don't be so tense.

NAPHTALI: I'm *not* tense.

MIRIAM: You're wound up like a spring. Relax the body. You're shaking with the strain.

NAPHTALI: Well, you're shaking too.

MIRIAM: I'm trembling because my whole body is beginning to sing. Don't hold yourself off so. Stop being so on guard. Let things happen to you.

NAPHTALI: I can't. . . . [*He tries to withdraw his hands, but she holds them.*]

MIRIAM: You can.

NAPHTALI: I'm no good at this. I don't know what to do about it. In a minute I'll lose control . . . leave me alone! [*Frees himself.*] I'm a failure. I knew it from the beginning. I shouldn't have got into this. Why did I? You all saw. . . .

SHIFRA: You started it. Show us how . . . You're the bravest of the lot of us.

NAPHTALI: I'm neither brave nor strong. I'm unable really to love. You all saw what happened. Miriam, you can only be my big sister—I can't start up anything with you. Nehama, too, demands from me more than I'm capable of giving. When you look at me, I know exactly what I am—not even a corner of me remains private—and I need you to mother me.

NEHAMA: I can't do that. Why have I always got to be the strong one? Nobody's going to give me of himself what I need. You're always wondering why I fight so hard that we should have a social framework with clear ideals, with principles and laws. If this is not to be, then I'll have to start thinking about myself and I'll certainly do it. But was it for this that I ran away from Vienna? I sometimes feel we haven't got the strength to even start making something of our lives, the way we want to, and I feel like getting up and getting out.

EPHRAIM: Comrades. Let's not lose our heads. We're losing control of ourselves. Come, let's try to get back to . . .

NAPHTALI: Ephraim . . . no, it's better I shut up.

MOSHE: No, speak out!

NAPHTALI: Ephraim . . . I sometimes have wicked thoughts about you. Sometimes I actually hate you.

EPHRAIM: O.K. I don't have to be loved all the time, to be caressed and petted. I hate you too sometimes! Big deal. . . .

NAPHTALI: Sometimes Akiva and me . . .

AKIVA: Naphtali!

NAPHTALI: Sorry. I'm sorry I spoke.

MOSHE: What's about Akiva and you?

NAPHTALI: Nothing. When I really get started talking, I don't know what I'm saying. I'm a bag full of holes. I'm sentimental and I play the clown to hide it. Here, at this moment I'm off on a penitential confession, complete with flagellation and all, only in order to hide some truth from myself.

MOSHE: What do you and Akiva talk about?

AKIVA: I thought we'd finished with this buffoonery.

MOSHE: Naphtali, you haven't answered me.

NAPHTALI: Should I tell them, Akiva?

AKIVA: Am I lord of your lips?

NAPHTALI: In truth, not!

EPHRAIM: Enough of this clowning. You can keep your secrets to yourselves.

NEHAMA: Fine! Everybody'll go around with all kinds of secrets and that'll be called living together!

SHIFRA: Maybe we've got to learn how to live with our secrets.

NEHAMA: If we'd wanted to keep our secrets properly we should have stayed in Vienna.

MIRIAM: When I see you, you Naphtali, sitting there in your corner, hiding some little secret of your very own. . . .

NEHAMA: Not just Naphtali: both of them!

MIRIAM [*Continuing, to Naphtali*]: and smiling to yourself sort of secretly. . . .

NEHAMA: You get a most unpleasant feeling.

SHIFRA: Why are you attacking them like this?

NEHAMA: Because I don't understand what's going on!

SHIFRA: Why are you shouting?

NEHAMA: They're either with the Group or out.

MIRIAM: There's also a sort of feeling of festiveness about 'em. . . .

NEHAMA: Sure! And it's because of us that they feel like that. . . . We make them special. . . .

SHIFRA: What's all of a sudden . . . I don't catch on . . . do we point them out?

MIRIAM: Oh, Shifra.

NEHAMA: There's whispers going round the Group and not since yesterday.

SHIFRA: What do they whisper in the Group?

NEHAMA: Want me to get up on a soap box and yell it out?

SHIFRA: I haven't heard any whispers.

NEHAMA: Well, of course. You're deep in your Ibsen. Do you pay any attention at all to what's going on around you? Have you noticed yet that we're not in Vienna? That we've already reached Eretz Israel?

SHIFRA: Why are you talking to me like that, Nehama? Don't I work on the road like you? Don't I break stone just like you? Aren't my hands just as blistered as yours?

NEHAMA: Oh! One can't say anything to you, Shifra. At every second word you burst into tears.

NAPHTALI [*To Nehama*]: And are *you* insulated against tears?

MIRIAM: No one ever saw Nehama crying. She's as tough as the boys.

MOSHE: Where were you when she spoke before? People just don't listen to what's being said around here.

MIRIAM: There are some girls, who from a psychological point of view . . .

NEHAMA: You'd better let psychology alone.

MIRIAM: Why? On the contrary, I too sometimes feel it's a pity I'm not more masculine, like you. . . .

NEHAMA: What nonsense!

AKIVA: And frightful lack of tact.

MIRIAM: Why? [*Coquettishly.*] If I were a boy, I'd master all the women around. Women have such desires . . . such strong ones . . . from the psychological point of view it's so simple. . . .

NEHAMA: Starting up on psychology again!

MIRIAM: Maybe I don't know so much . . . I'm not so learned as you. . . .

NEHAMA: Then that's enough! [*Pause.*]

MOSHE: Good! Then if it's not to be Naphtali, perhaps Akiva will tell us. Straight from the horse's mouth.

EPHRAIM: Nu, Akiva, do us all a favor: scratch up some awful secret, and let's have done with it all.

AKIVA: I've nothing to tell you.

MOSHE: You give us all the feeling that you have.

AKIVA: That's the feeling that you get, not that I give.

NEHAMA: I too think we can't stop now. We've crossed the Rubicon, and we've got to talk the whole affair out, openly.

EPHRAIM: I don't want to discuss the whole murky affair!

MOSHE: You're a minority of one, Ephraim. The Group wants to.

EPHRAIM: Since when do you speak for the Group?

MOSHE: Why don't you want to discuss the matter? [*Silence.*] Afraid? [*Silence.*] As long as we haven't cracked the shell of the swollen ego, we've achieved nothing! With your permission: we've reached a crisis.

EPHRAIM: Right! At least someone's said something that makes sense. We've reached a crisis. It's quite natural. The hard work, the unclear future. It's alarming. Everything depends on us alone, on what we'll do and on if we'll be able to take on the responsibility for what we'll do . . . to overcome our weaknesses . . . to silence poisonous whispers in the soul, to crush underfoot the worms eating away at the will, to overcome, with an iron hand, all doubts. . . . [*Outburst.*] In a few hours the automobiles will arrive. We'll load the baggage on them and go out to Mansurin. . . . Nobody knows what awaits us there with the serfs . . . what will happen at midday . . . if all of us will be alive in the evening, or if some of us won't see nightfall . . . and suddenly we divert ourselves to side issues . . . and give ourselves up to sickly soul searching. We should simply go to sleep and gather strength for tomorrow!

MIRIAM: I want to say somthing. Akiva, Naphtali, I personally don't care especially, but . . . haven't you felt that people are talking about you in the Group? You're always together. At work. After work.

EPHRAIM: You too, Miriam? Do you too have to play Moshe's game?

MIRIAM: You . . . all of you make all kinds of jokes, make fun of all kinds of things which other people take seriously . . .

AKIVA: Does that bother anyone? Whom should it bother?

MIRIAM: Not me, but . . . the Group. . . .

NEHAMA: You two are drifting away from the Group.

AKIVA: Me, maybe, but not Naphtali.

MIRIAM: The two of you together.

MOSHE: We've got to face the facts.

NEHAMA: I must say it: after I've spoken openly here and everyone here has talked about the most intimate personal things, and then we go off in the dark and see you two together whispering secrets to each other, then I say to myself: Oho! now they're saying all the things they didn't say at the discussion . . . now they're talking about me. . . .

MIRIAM: Now do you understand why it's upsetting?

EPHRAIM: Let's not regard it as disturbing. It may be just the thing to bring about spiritual awakening by means of sublimation. . . . [*Silence.*]

MOSHE: Akiva, Naphtali . . . what's between you two?

AKIVA: Nothing!

EPHRAIM: Air . . . don't you see? What else could there be between them?

MOSHE: But you have something special. A closer relationship.

AKIVA: Perhaps. . .

EPHRAIM: There's a Vestal flame between them!

MOSHE: There's a feeling that something special is happening between you which excludes everyone else in the Group.

AKIVA: I don't understand: what do you all want of us?

SHIFRA: I don't understand either!

MIRIAM: Don't you remember when I tried to explain it to you, and you didn't catch on to what I was talking about?

MOSHE: Naphtali, what's between you two?

SHIFRA: No! We've got to stop this! It's torture! Torture . . . why should we even touch the matter? By what right do we meddle with such brutality? It's something beautiful, pure. Two friends who find it good to be together . . . we mustn't discuss such things! It's something live. Like a chick. Like a kitten. Why do you need such glaring light?

Let there be dusk, twilight. Are you afraid of the dark? [*Silence.*] Oh! I want to kill.

MOSHE: Kill who?

SHIFRA: All living creatures! All life. . . .

MOSHE: Start with one person. I volunteer as the first in your grand slaughter. [*Pause.*] Words, words. . . .

SHIFRA: I simply don't know how to love.

MOSHE: Love who?

SHIFRA: Anybody. I don't love anybody.

MOSHE: Say you don't love me.

SHIFRA: Oh, go away.

MOSHE: Say it. Scared to?

SHIFRA: I don't love you.

MOSHE: Why don't you love me?

EPHRAIM: You're tormenting yourself, and her too.

MOSHE: Am I ugly?

SHIFRA: Leave me alone, leave me in peace.

MOSHE: Ugly in the deeper meaning of the word. An ugly spirit in an ugly body. An egoist who's only interested in others as a source of stimulation. . . . This, of course, makes me different from the rest of humanity, above all from you? Not so?

SHIFRA: You are in need of much compassion.

MOSHE: Don't be so merciful. Express your hate in words. Say how much you hate.

SHIFRA: I know what I'm atoning for.

MOSHE: She invited me up to her parents' villa in Baden, once. Last summer. Before we came here. How they laughed! At the Hassid boy from Galicia . . . made fun of the plebeian Zionist, the tailor's son.

SHIFRA: I never even mentioned your origins once.

MOSHE: Did you have to? Every gesture of mine gave me away. [*Laughs an evil laugh.*] I used the inner fork for the first courses and when the maid cleared away the small plates she also took away the other two. [*Laughs.*] When they brought the main course, the Galician Zionist was left without a single fork to aid him. Shifra called the maid and whispered something in her ear . . . not aloud, God forbid!

EPHRAIM: Moshe, I think that'll do, for all of us.

MOSHE [*To Shifra*]: You don't love Ephraim either? Tell him that you don't love him.

SHIFRA: I hate you!

MOSHE: Tell Ephraim, Ephraim.

SHIFRA: You want to ruin everything. Everything that's beautiful, that's pure, you want to destroy.

MOSHE: Oho! What a short memory! Already forgotten what you said before? You said you didn't love anyone, so tell him!

SHIFRA: I see you now. You're quite transparent. You're playing Brand's part: all or nothing! You thought: just let me get there and I'll take control of the Group. You arrived a couple of months after we did and found us managing without a leader.

MOSHE: What group do you mean?

SHIFRA: And in harmony. You can't accommodate yourself to that, can you? You're ready to ruin everything in order to get control.

MOSHE: Is the Group without a leader?

SHIFRA: You're trying to crumble and destroy everything that has grown up amongst us, so that we'll all be dependent on you . . . you're not capable of living among us as equal among equals. You're not capable of weaving a modest personal poem into our web, you've got to demand all the attention, loudmouthed and hoarse. You have to force yourself on others. Can't you see what you're doing to yourself?

MOSHE [*Stubborn, mulish*]: You said you didn't love anyone. Then say it to Ephraim. What, is it so difficult? Look—you don't love him, then tell him so.

EPHRAIM: Moshe, nobody's asking you to strip yourself.

MOSHE: No? Well, anyway, I'm enjoying this.

MIRIAM: Not every nude is aesthetic.

MOSHE: Certainly not mine. [*Grins.*] I came here out of shame. Shame brought me to this country. I saw the Zionist functionaries abroad and I was filled with shame at the thought that I might become one of them. If I hadn't been so ashamed, I wouldn't have come here.

EPHRAIM: You came to Eretz because of such a petty matter? Shame of becoming an aging Zionist in the Golah? Isn't it possible to stop being a Zionist?

MOSHE: We're living half-lives, that's what we're doing. We're already talking of the Offering-table of the Commune, the Sacred Meal, about the Great Silence! We came here to show all the West, once and for all, how free Jewish people can do things! Let the whole damned West look at us and be ashamed of itself. Let them see how a community of human beings, liberated from decayed superstitions, simply live together, man with fellowman! But how is this possible when the Galuth is right here with us! And here! [*Points at each member of the group.*] And here! [*Points at Shifra.*]

EPHRAIM: Galuth? Are you afraid of saying the truth? Do you know what's here, and here, and here? Pandora's boxes! Weak fathers begat us and hysterical mothers reared us. The inner rot is this: fear of facing the world and lack of conviction. But we've got rid of all that. We burned the bridges behind us and came here. We've given ourselves new birth. And you're doing your best to revive a corpse. You don't know what you're doing!

SHIFRA: Moshe . . . forgive me . . . I apologize for everything I said.

MOSHE: Forgive! Apologize! You don't love me. How could it ever have been possible? I'm someone who is shamed to the very roots of his soul, and that's how I think and feel, and that's what I look like. A man who is shamed has little erotic attractiveness. But Ephraim: whee! He came here because of ideals, symbols! Not because of some small and miserable shame-even-to-exist. Because of Ibsen's Brand! A genuine walking legend, blown up to the bursting point! The very tremor of eroticism.

SHIFRA: I too ran away from Vienna out of shame. After you'd gone, they were all silent at first—so embarrassed. Then they exchanged glances. At breakfast Papa slipped a word, Mama smiled wrily . . . and then they all burst out laughing . . . they laughed at lunchtime . . . they laughed over *Kaffee-mit-Kuchen* . . . they laughed at Shifra's Zionist gallant until the perspiration dripped into the *Schlagsahne*. . . .

EPHRAIM: Shifra, leave off. . . .

SHIFRA: I really saw them for the first time. I *saw* them: Mama with her smothering goodness. She had only one serious care in life: to balance our diet between constipation and diarrhea. There were never any periods of beauty in her life, even such as when the family functioned smoothly. She never ever really lived. Her whole life passed in fear of the outside world. Her hands were always filled with sweets and goodies and whenever a mouth opened to say something—she immediately pushed her goodies in. Papa used to call her "*dumme Kuh,*" dumb cow, stupid cow, he used to say to her: "One eats for pleasure, dumb cow." And she would laugh in a way that made one squirm . . . "dumb cow." And Papa, a spoiled, petty tyrant, even when he was with *his* mother. . . . Everything was his due and he granted all of us the privilege of serving him. I'm talking of them as though they were already dead.

NEHAMA: You're describing *my* parents.

NAPHTALI: Mine too.

SHIFRA: Grandmas used to call him "*mein Kind*"—he with his double chin and paunch and hairs growing out of his ears. . , . "*Was ist los, mein Kind?*" [*Visualizes a picture.*] His spoiled little mouth pursed and Mama brushing off the shoulders of his suit. . . . [*Mimics her father.*] "Nu, stupid cow, finished?" And at night the dialogue in their room: "Nu, dumbbell of a cow, finished your toilette, already? Well, come on, stupid cow." . . . [*Childish and simple.*] I want those days back when I didn't understand or know about things. . . . When I didn't understand a single word.

MIRIAM: Come, Shifra.

SHIFRA: As a child and as a girl all I heard was words. . . . I need you all around me. I need your love.

MIRIAM: We do all love you.

SHIFRA: How can you? You don't really know me. You know some imaginary Shifra who doesn't exist at all. You know a comedienne of a Shifra who shows you exactly what you want to see. You don't know what thoughts pass through my head. What dreams fill me. When I wash myself all over, I stand naked and look at my body . . . what a splendid body . . . I want people to see it. The whole world to pass in front of me and see. [*Takes off her dress.*] There's a certain part of the body which contains woman's true beauty. Not the face. Nor the breasts. The belly. Not exactly the belly: a part of the belly. There's no word for it in Hebrew. The Old Masters knew this. I visited Italy with my parents once, as a little girl. Michelangelo's David in the Accademia in Florence . . . One could see the column of air rising from the loins . . . my arms reached up. . . . "Shifra, what are you doing?"—"I want to touch it" . . . My father was alarmed: "Shifra, what's the matter with you? Put your hands down immediately!" When I came ashore at Jaffa it was a warm night, fragrant with orange groves . . . it didn't get me by the nose or by the heart, but by the belly. It penetrated my belly. I suddenly had butterflies in my tummy and they rose from my belly and spread all over my body right down to my fingertips. My whole body disintegrated, my flesh evaporated, only the belly remained, and it shook. It sort of blossomed inside. That part of me is beautiful. Like a harp. [*Outburst.*] *That's* what occupies my mind now, while we sit here, thinking of what will happen tomorrow, and if there'll be a clash with the Arab serfs, and who of us here will pay for it with his life. [*Buries her face in a blanket, weeping.*]

NAPHTALI: I couldn't close an eye last night. I got up and wandered around the camp. The wadi was pitch black. Jackals howling—black, shadowy jackals everywhere. One almost brushed against me. I picked up a stone and threw it and the devil ran off into the night, laughing: hee-hee-hee! A mendicant from Europe came to seek the Blue Bird in the Orient. . . . Suddenly I became a jackal in the night . . . rubbing against the tents, slipping by, peeping . . . a livid face sitting holding his head in his hands while the sounds from the next tent cut his flesh: a fellow and a girl there, panting, gasping feverishly . . . gradually stronger, faster . . . but this isn't like in Salzburg . . . suddenly—crescendo, holds for a moment—diminuendo . . . quiet . . . "Fair are the nights in Canaan." . . . A sigh, rustling, grinding of teeth . . . stifled sobs and a deep voice mumbling drearily. And from another tent, a monotonous duet: two voices stirring a pudding of self-analysis according to a recipe by Rebbe Sigmund Freud, *ad multos annos,* amen. To educate, or not to educate. . . . They'll all get up in the morning, wipe the cobwebs from their eyes and go off to crack rocks with crowbars. And the New Society, New Man, can look out for themselves. . . . For the life of me, I can't see the difference between all this and what goes on between some Inga and Franz in a fourth-class Viennese hotel, except that *they*'re drunk on beer and fiery kirsch . . . while we here . . .

EPHRAIM: So what, Naphtali? What's the big discovery? That we're not monks and nuns? We're young, twenty-year-olds and we've all got sexual impulses. Isn't that normal? It's all quite simple. Young fellows and girls. Backbreaking work. Daily life full of tension. People wander about at night, among the tents, looking for a little warmth, a little love. What's so terrible about that? I know, we've not yet reached the point were we'll be able to raise the erotic force within us to sexual potentiality which will set an entirely new relationship with woman . . . but we're seeking.

NEHAMA: The main thing is that in the meantime some of us find themselves temporary solutions. This one hides in his tent, his soul in tears, those two have already found themselves something else to do. And as to the rest of the Group. . . . Let's pretend that we're continuing seriously to enquire: Free Love or not Free Love and what do we do about the erotic force within us. . . .

AKIVA [*Ironically*]: What d'you want? People aren't born equal: some are born to seek and some to find.

MIRIAM: And some to peek. . . .

NAPHTALI: To eavesdrop, to eavesdrop!

NEHAMA: And what's wrong with peeping? Perhaps those two are showing us the right way . . . or at least the most convenient and ready-to-hand. . . . We're seeking, aren't we?

MIRIAM: Why do you hint all the time? Are you afraid to speak out?

EPHRAIM: The institution of the couple scares you, doesn't it? Scares and repels you, doesn't it? The becoming attached, the farewell to childhood, the gravity of fatherhood . . . the unborn child peers out at you from the womb, and he's a harder judge than God Himself. . . . Tomorrow, or the day after, each one of us will have to make the terrible choice: to accept responsibility for the sexual force driving him towards woman, or to become the most despicable creatures on earth: senile children. . . . Perhaps our problem is the Problem of the Rejuvenation of the Family. What erotic power there was in the Jewish family!

NEHAMA: You are suggesting that we leave off from all attempts to give new meaning to the relationship of the sexes: you are proposing that we set up couples.

EPHRAIM: Possibly, I say: possibly.

NEHAMA: To find me a husband, I should have stayed in Vienna. Really, potential husbands was all I lacked in the University!

EPHRAIM: I'm not suggesting that we stick to the rags we brought with us from Europe. We've always condemned the bourgeois marriage bond, the egotistical couple. I'm talking about giving the passions of our generation a new form.

MOSHE: I rather think that those passions will be giving *us* new forms.

EPHRAIM: It's easy to make fun! Ever asked yourselves what makes the couple so strong? Social systems have arisen and fallen, one set of morals replaces another, religions have vanished, empires have become clay, whole human societies become dust, and the couple endures. Tribal society no longer exists but Jacob and Rachel are with us today.

NAPHTALI: To call up all of history, even wake up God from his nap, just to justify the formation of a single couple. . . .

MOSHE: Nonsense! Do you know where the strength of the couple lies? In revelation. Two human beings reveal one to another every kind of deformity. Narrow shoulders, fallen breasts, flabby belly, flat backside, bony hips, scabby legs, miserable maleness, sunken and rundown nakedness . . . frigidity, premature ejaculation, impotence . . . the couple have no secrets from each other. Two human beings stand facing one another like two utterly disclosed infamies. That's why all of history, all the religions—even God Himself shatters against them, like piss against flint. There's nothing in the world stronger than a man who reveals his real self. That's why the couple survive war and pestilence, stand the test of the birth and death of children. Form a couple? Certainly! We'll redeem this land only if all of us become one big couple, if we'll have the strength to reveal our deepest shames to one another. To reveal and expose everything, here and now, before all.

SHIFRA: How?

MIRIAM: We should all get undressed?

EPHRAIM: He means spiritually, I hope.

AKIVA: He means literally, in the physical sense. He's suggesting that we all take our clothes off.

MOSHE [*To Shifra*]: Do you really think there's no place for you in the Group? You are mistaken. The Group can contain the naked individual and will only be strengthened for it. The couple, outwardly dressed and inwardly naked, the Group cannot contain. Couples will form, children belong to specific couples will appear and that will end the Group. A bunch of egoistical couples. What is the egoism of the individual compared to the fierce egoism of the couple! The solitary individual is open to all things, the couple excommunicates the whole world.

EPHRAIM: It won't happen to us. We'll find the synthesis of couple and group.

NAPHTALI [*Laughing*]: We've already made that wonderful synthesis . . . we've got to get used to the idea that four persons are involved in every sexual act. . . .

MIRIAM [*Ironically*]: Are you so sure? . . .

NAPHTALI [*Regarding Miriam*]: I wish I could say.

MIRIAM: You speak with such certainty! [*Ironically.*] On what grounds? On the grounds of vast experience?

NEHAMA: Miriam, leave off.

MIRIAM: When I hear such speechifying I get the yen to ask: have you ever slept with a woman?

NAPHTALI: No

MIRIAM: Aha. Listening to you I thought you'd already had a score of mistresses. Let me disclose a secret, Naphtali: in the sexual act only two take part, and sometimes not even that.

AKIVA: Bodies or souls?

MIRIAM [*Turns to him, surprised*]: What?

AKIVA: Don't lower your eyes, Miriam. Come, let's look each other in the eye, honestly. Without fear. Without shame.

MIRIAM: I'm not ashamed of anything. Maybe you are.

AKIVA: I didn't mean to speak out tonight. I have things to tell you which perhaps should not be said in everyone's hearing.

EPHRAIM: Then shut up.

AKIVA: We've all gone too far tonight, now there really isn't anywhere to go back to. When I was with you, I wasn't really with you, and you weren't with me. We both knew it very well and yet we did what we did.

MIRIAM: That's not much to be proud of.

AKIVA: I have no pride at all.

MIRIAM: And I have no rancour toward you.

AKIVA: Do you forgive me?

MIRIAM: D'you want me to forgive you? You're welcome. I'm ready to forgive, if that's what you need. . . .

AKIVA: No! I don't need it at all. It was something without any significance, really. You see, the main protagonists had no part in the whole affair. . . .

MIRIAM: I didn't say *that.* To be precise, you came to me all storm-tossed: "Miriam," I was aware that I asked myself: Akiva? Why should he come to me? What does he want of *me?* Why, he never ever really looked into my eyes. And I knew what you thought of me. I knew you didn't think me very important. That you despised me. That you saw me as no more than an empty, silly creature, without great thoughts, without an awakened soul. I waited for you to look deep into my eyes, but you didn't. I saw that you felt bad. That you were suffering. So I said to myself: if he'll be with me, maybe he'll feel a little better. So I gave myself to you without thought. That's how I am: I give myself easily . . . and you weren't such a bad lover! The embraces and the caresses and the kisses, real works of art: precise and subtle. . . . if you'd been able at that moment to bestow a little warmth, I would really have opened out, and you would have known incomparable happiness. But it was an imitation of love, you're not capable of more than that.

AKIVA: When a man wanders around in the night, looking for somewhere to go he knocks on many doors. And it sometimes happens that kind people open to him and invite him in. That's what's known as "hospitality" and it is a virtue. but it's not exactly love. In spite of our efforts that everyone should love us, it may be that love has only one address. Then why tell me I'm not capable of more than what happened? Perhaps you weren't that address?

SHIFRA: How cruel! Why are you tormenting her? Because she was kind to you? You men, you great sufferers! Don't you know that a girl has a soul, that she too can suffer? [*To Akiva.*] You deserve that someone should do to you what you're doing to her. I pray that someone will be found to do it to you.

AKIVA: That someone's already here. Do you want to know her name?

SHIFRA: I don't want to know anything.

AKIVA: It's you, Shifra. [*Silence.*] Pure, hard and shining like the rocks on these mountains on winter nights.

SHIFRA: I don't want to hear.

AKIVA: You all came down on us, on Naphtali and me: what is the secret of the relationship growing up between us? One day, without our knowing how it happened, Naphtali, and I revealed to each other our love for you. Each of us loves you and wants to gain your love. We used to talk about you for days on end. Each would run to share a stolen crumb of happiness with the other: "Today at midday rest, Shifra looked my way, and there was something tender in her glance . . . yesterday, I looked at Shifra, but she didn't notice . . . just sat there banging at stones with her hammer. . . . Suddenly she raised her head to relax a moment and our eyes met, and she smiled" . . . and me trying to persuade Naphtali that your love goes his way, and he—proving to me by miracles and marvels that the happiness will be mine. . . . [*Turns to Moshe.*] I hate you, Moshe. I'll not forgive you what you did tonight. Your pedantic picking, your need for absolute definitions for everything. Now I know what I didn't want to know: Shifra doesn't love anyone here.

MOSHE: Not Ephraim either. Shifra's love is unengaged.

SHIFRA: I love you all. Why do you demand that I should choose one person and give *him* everything leaving remnants and crumbs to the rest. . . . How can I? I'd like to choose, but I can't. I want each one of you to be my lover and I'll be his or hers. . . .

NAPHTALI: The girls too?

MIRIAM: Shifra is better than I. She's pure and I'm corrupt. Compared with her, all of us. . . .

SHIFRA: You're wrong, Miriam. You're good, I'm much worse than you. You're always giving. It's so beautiful, how you give, without reckoning. And all I know is how to take.

MIRIAM: No, Shifra. We're all too full of suspicions about each other.

SHIFRA: Let's stop talking. Let's take our clothes off and be close together. [*All begin to undress as one, in an attack of hysteria.*]

EPHRAIM: One moment! Before you all begin to strip, I have an announcement to make. We hadn't especially intended to announce it tonight, but there's no purpose in keeping it secret any longer: in Mansurin, Miriam and I will live together, in a separate tent. [*Silence. Undressing stops.*]

NAPHTALI: The two of you together in a tent?

EPHRAIM: Yes, we two together in a tent.

NAPHTALI: In a tent of your own?

EPHRAIM: In a tent of our own. We're going to raise a family.

NEHAMA: And you want the Group to sit down and discuss the matter now?

EPHRAIM: No, I'm simply informing you.

NAPHTALI: Interesting!

AKIVA: That's what I call a surprise.

NEHEMA: I hope that Miriam, at least, isn't surprised by the announcement.

MIRIAM: You'll be amazed, Nehama, but I'm not surprised at all.

NEHAMA: I'm truly amazed. Ephraim managed to hide the matter from the Group so beautifully, that I thought he also managed to hide it from you.

MIRIAM: We thought that things would come to a head anyway, and that the Group would reach this stage of things on its own. We didn't want to hurt anybody. We'd like everyone to be happy. [*Turns to Ephraim.*] That's right, isn't it?

NEHAMA: I too don't want to cause you and Ephraim any trouble, but I don't want to suffer either. It's that I thought that the value of living communally meant that every one lived for the other and not just for himself alone. But I seem to have been mistaken. Suddenly, Miriam and Ephraim have made their breach and tomorrow somebody'll say he wants to eat apart, that he finds the way I eat unpleasant . . . and someone will say that he has found some other, more interesting work, so I prefer to break the whole thing up completely.

MIRIAM: Why break up? . . .

NEHAMA: Because suddenly I'm beginning to feel like a leper. . . . O.K. That's how it seems to be: some people don't have to lift a finger and everyone loves them and some are destined to spend their lives in toil and struggle that a little room should be allowed them in this world and that at best they'll be given a little appreciation, perhaps, perhaps! Appreciation, you underdstand? But love? . . .

SHIFRA: Why do you say that?

NEHAMA: Because suddenly I saw my life in the Group over the years, years and years! I'm destined to be some sort of beast of burden who, in the end, will be given a little appreciation. I don't want that! I, too, can be their kind of egoist and look for, and find me, some man who'll "love" me! Why not? I, too, just like any other woman, can let loose the chicken that's locked up cackling in my soul, cluck-cluck-cluck-cluck! And catch me a cockerel, feather me a nest and lay eggs! And the whole world can go to hell with its burden of suffering, at any rate outside the limits of my snug and secure nest, *there* it can croak!

SHIFRA: I'd like to run away to a desert island and die there.

MIRIAM: You're not to blame that they love you the way they do. And I'm not to blame either! I loved every one of them, almost . . . and they loved me each in his own way. It was easy to have me . . . what I gave of myself I gave easily! I was drawn to it and I don't regret a single thing. I am as I am, that's how I was made! Do you think I didn't know that not one of you would go the whole way with me? I knew it all along! And now I know that it can only happen with two people who devote themselves entirely one to the other.

NEHAMA: Then wall up your nest all 'round, plaster up every crack . . . so that no other bird may enter nor any sound penetrate. . . .

MIRIAM: Why should I? I don't at all think that it should put an end to all the other relationships. What, after all, are relationships, how deep do they go? If I live with Ephraim and feel good with him . . . if he loves me and is good to me, I'll be good to you too, within my limitations because I care about such things. I'm not indifferent towards you.

MOSHE: Are you willing even to give up a part of Ephraim?

MIRIAM: What do you mean, what part?

MOSHE: If Shifra were to ask Ephraim to spend a night with her . . .

MIRIAM: What's all of a sudden?

NAPHTALI: . . . Or a week. Like Jacob with Leah and Rachel: "Fulfill her week." . . .

NEHAMA: Or conversely: if you should suddenly get the desire to spend a night with Moshe. . . .

EPHRAIM: Even if Miriam were to agree, I would not.

NEHAMA: But Miriam is a free human being, isn't she? D'you think you have complete possession of her heart?

EPHRAIM: We're all free human beings, but there's a limit to freedom too.

MOSHE: He doesn't want to possess her heart, all he wants to possess are her ovaries.

EPHRAIM: Allow me to ask you a question, Moshe: how do you dare to speak in public of what's between me and Miriam? How do you dare to use your not too healthy imagination, and speak of things you've neither seen nor heard nor are able to have any idea about? How dare you stick your sting into the most sensitive and delicate places of other people's lives and squirt your poison there? Where do you get the cheek to burrow and pick in the inner sanctums of other people's lives? How d'you dare?

MOSHE: How? There's no inner sanctum in my life, my life is secular, absolutely secular, from beginning to end. And what's not in my psyche, I'll not let you erect between us. Neither you nor anyone else who wants to live in partnership with me. If anybody will try to surround himself with walls of sanctity, I'll destroy them gladly and without regrets.

EPHRAIM: Very well. Then let's get undressed! It's exciting! It's pleasant, it's even suitable in this climate. Who needs to think of what will happen in Mansurin in ten hours time. Why think of anything at all? At long last we've found our vocation here: to get undressed. In Vienna we couldn't work such wonders, could we? Back there, getting undressed in company would have landed us in the loony bin next morning, but in Eretz Israel everything goes! Here's the aim and end of Zionism in one short lesson: to get undressed! The news will spread throughout the Galuth and tens of thousands of our young fellows and girls, craving to get undressed will come to Eretz! Come to undress in Zion . . . it's hard to imagine a more rousing slogan . . . anywhere! I suggest we go naked to settle on Mansurin—the serfs will run away to the ends of the earth for fear at the sight! What have we come to! You simply don't want to think seriously about what's before us. You don't want to think of how far we've come and where we are right now.

MOSHE: It's you that don't want to see. Tomorrow we have to go out into danger. Possibly, death. And one day the Group will say to your son, Miriam—up and onto one of them there mountains and stand guard. Will you have the strength to go on living in the Group if he doesn't come back? Knowing that the Group never even opened itself out to him, or to you, either? That the people who sent your son out to die hid their real selves from you? Or perhaps we'll send him out in the name of the Agricultural Center, which is sending us to Mansurin? What kind of life will that be? The moment the first person's son falls, people will go around here with iron in the soul, death in their hearts!

EPHRAIM: Wait till the first children are born, grow up, till we actually need to send them out. . . . You're putting the cart before the horse! Sufficient unto the day. . . !

MOSHE: We're going there to take the place of people who were there before us, to evict them—from *our* heritage. If we'll be content to swap their right for ours, *we*'ll disgust even ourselves. We may do what we're going to do on one condition only: that we'll found a society there based on supreme values.

AKIVA: What's a society based on supreme values?

MOSHE: It's a society whose motivating power stand above all judgment. Beyond any religion. Beyond any idea, custom or tradition. It's a society in which every person gives everything to every other person, everything—without reservation or accounting, and demands the same of every one else. It's a society about which I don't know a thing, because it doesn't exist, neither here nor anywhere else in the world, and we must up and create it! Or else—do nothing but stuff ourselves and guzzle and grow fat and pile up possessions and become dull and stupid and disintegrate and die. What am I asking all-in-all? I'm asking that you speak to me—me, Moshe Goldberg! I, Moshe Goldberg, am not Hercules! I'm Jewish and weak, with a neurotic soul in a sick body . . . a man who fought in foreign wars and nearly got killed for a process of history which was not related to him in any way. A man who doesn't want any connection with history any more! Neither Austrian nor Russian nor Jewish. A man who wants only contact with his fellow human beings . . . a man who cries out to you: look at me eye to eye . . . know me as a woman knows her husband, a father his son . . . how else will you be able to send me tomorrow to kill or be killed in the fight with the Arab serfs, and what for at all? Indeed, what for? Lowering your eyes, you'll say—for the Agricultural Center? Or squinting upwards to the empty heavens, whisper: Homeland, People, History? Well?! . . .

EPHRAIM: Why do you make light of homeland, people, history? Who are you to be contemptuous? Whoever loves the land deeply, understands its ways and is aware of its secrets. . . .

MOSHE: Land doesn't have ways or secrets! It doesn't need to be loved. Land is material—raw material. It has no life, nor soul nor spirit. Only man has. I look into *my* soul and see neither homeland, nor people, nor history. Only a terrible yearning to live like a human being, together with other human beings. That's something that people have simply never done anywhere in the world to this very day. Let's start by telling the truth. Without people and without Homeland and without the Passion of our Times. Nothing can stand against truth when it starts gushing out. Can't you feel the power ready to burst out? What are you afraid of? What have you got to lose? A swollen ego living off petty lies? Well?

EPHRAIM: And by stripping we'll redeem ourself of all these perils?

MOSHE: What stripping all of a sudden?

MIRIAM: Ah! Now you're backing out! You're scared of your own ideas.

MOSHE: It wasn't I who suggested getting undressed.

MIRIAM: I heard you.

MOSHE: You always hear what you want to hear.

NAPHTALI: Then what do you want us to do?

MOSHE: I want us to cast off our outer shells. To stop chattering and begin getting to know one another. So, that we'll know why we're going out to this, or any other, action. Why just Akiva, and Nehama, and me, and Naphtali, and Shifra, and Ephraim, and Miriam. What each one of us wants from the other, what I expect from you and you expect from me.

NAPHTALI: You begin: show us how.

MOSHE: I'm not sure that it ought to be done by words.

MIRIAM: Then how? What does knowing one another mean?

MOSHE: Possibly by silence.

AKIVA: Before, you suggested we undress, and then you went back on yourself. Before, when Ephraim spoke in favour of silence, you made fun of him. Now you suddenly raise the banner of silence. Pardon me, Moshe, you don't know what you want.

NEHAMA: I too have a bad feeling. You did something terrible that night. You shook us up and pushed us into matters about which you yourself know nothing.

EPHRAIM: Don't take him at his word. He wants to withdraw, so allow him to withdraw with dignity.

MOSHE: Dignified withdrawals belong in your psychologics, Ephraim!

EPHRAIM: Another expert on my psychological theories!

MOSHE: You always put yourself so bravely to do things! Suddenly, you're all alone, with no papa to watch over you and immediately: Quick! Let's have a symbol instead! Let's have a Myth! Let's have the significance of the action before we do anything, otherwise we may wet our pants! Country, People and History are whispering at your ears? Psychologics of a spoiled, nice boy.

EPHRAIM: Allow me not discuss *your* psychologics.

MOSHE: On the contrary! Discuss them all you want!

EPHRAIM: They don't interest me.

MOSHE: Do they scare you?

EPHRAIM: They repel me. You're just one big inferiority complex. I've nothing more to say to you.

MOSHE: Outer Shells. *Klippoth.* One shell on top of another. Stifling! What makes you be like that? What are you so afraid of?

EPHRAIM: What do you want of us? By what right do you look down on us? Why do you rebuke us and scold us and preach us morals all the time? Why d'you want us to be ashamed of ourselves whenever you're around? To be ashamed of our beliefs and their outer expression? Of our dreams? Why do you undermine and pick at us and try to weaken us just when we need every inch of physical and moral strength? And we must not fail! The king is hemmed in a corner, the position is at checkmate and instead of concentrating all forces for the struggle he gets up and asks why play at all? If we lose this game there'll be nowhere to go! If we're checkmated, the whole Zionist project will collapse!

MOSHE: The Group must not get off this mountain before we begin to understand our own selves and each other, otherwise we'll end in disaster.

MIRIAM: But what do you mean by "understand each other"? I don't understand!

EPHRAIM: Masturbation.

MOSHE: There are already enough countries living by Hottentot moralities. There's no need to set up one more. We want to create a New Man. To do this we must expose everything, destroy everything, to start out clean. *Tabula rasa.*

NAPHTALI: What'll we tell the Agricultural Center?

MOSHE: To leave us alone, and let us try to prepare ourselves for the ordeal.

NAPHTALI: He's quite right. I haven't had a chance to talk about *my* complexes.

AKIVA: Naphtali, this isn't the time for it.

NAPHTALI: I, *too,* have complexes!

NEHAMA: Stop your joking, Naphtali, nobody's laughing.

SHIFRA: Undressing.

NAPHTALI: No! [*Goes to her and catches hold of her hand.*] Don't do it.

SHIFRA: Why not?

NAPHTALI: If you get undressed, we'll all have to get undressed too.

SHIFRA: That's right, we all have to get undressed.

NAPHTALI: I can't. I live in a stranger's body.

SHIFRA: Don't be afraid, Naphtali. We all love you.

NAPHTALI: All . . . because I'm a joker. You all regard me as a sort of pleasant joke. [*Undresses slowly.*] My whole existence among you is based on my hiding my real self, so sometimes someone gets the thought: what's with Naphtali that we don't understand? And Naphtali nourishes himself on these scraps of attention and sucks a little existence out of them . . . not a very important existence, but all the same . . . Naphtali manages to live on it. And he says to himself that if it's not much, it's still something. As you see, he's still around. Sometimes, thanks to this drop of mysteriousness, it even appears as if this here Naphtali has some sort of secret, all of his own. . . . Because what else is Naphtali? Nothing! An illusion . . . a pretense of a human being. Naphtali is someone who has to rant and rave so that even he himself should know that he's angry. Has to sigh and sob to know he's sad; to laugh and sing to know he's happy. Naphtali is the sort of person who only when he dies will know that he ever lived. It's some time now that I think I'm not quite right in the head, because I compare myself with you and I see that you're all people with important thoughts and lots of emotions, whereas I . . . that's why I wanted so much to come to Eretz Israel. I said to myself: Naphtali, if you'll take such thoughts and History and moral values . . . And now here I am in Eretz and it hasn't happened: I remain the same old Naphtali. So now I say to myself: Mansurin! Seize the land! Forward, it'll put some stuffing in you! and I await the great event. And I'm quite prepared for the great moment when some serf will swing his club and I'll crack his skull with a rock. . . . Crunch! And I'm aware of myself and watching for the wonderful moment when Naphtali, the shapeless, lukewarm milk-pudding will turn into a hero, of whom tales will be told to step up the heartbeat of coming generations! They'll say: Ahh! Those were real men, in those days . . . and in the meantime, if you like, one can always get undressed. [*Runs away, singing, chased by* AKIVA. *Starts singing: tune of "Here we go gathering nuts in May."*]



EPHRAIM: What'll we look like if tomorrow we'll send the trucks back empty, and suddenly announce that we've discovered ourselves to be not ready yet! What'll we say? That we're sitting here analysing each other? They'll laugh at us! The Hapoel Hatzair and Achduth Ha'avodah people will treat us like children! They'll say: What did we tell you? Bewildered intelligentsia from Austria! Impotents! Berl will come out with a lovely sardonic article.

MOSHE: If Berl is afraid of facing his own complexes and traumas, that's his business! Their Machiavellianism doesn't interest me. We didn't come here to dance to the fiddles of political parties with programs. The world's full of the calamities that these madmen bring about. But not here and not with us.

NAPHTALI: I agree with Moshe! I feel that if we go out like this, something bad will happen! I'm full of destructive impulses! I've got a very strong death wish! Maybe I came to Eretz Israel because of a death wish!

NEHAMA: Enough, Naphtali! Stop your joking for once!

NAPHTALI: No, I won't stop! I won't stop! Moshe, show us what you mean. You be first, we'll follow you.

MOSHE: Me? . . . [*Silence.*] I would begin if I knew how. A man can't do it all by himself. Not as a confession. There are some things that when you merely say them they become lies. You've got to help me in this. Help me.

SHIFRA: But how? I, too, want you to do this for me, but how?

NEHAMA: I, too. . . . I go around all the time with the feeling that I'm all wrong, and I feel also, that the answer can't come from me myself alone.

MOSHE: Perhaps, we've got to stop all this speechifying first. Maybe we should just stay quiet for a couple of days or three, or perhaps a week. Stay put, silent, and look at one another . . . and discover each other for the first time. [*Silence.*] Maybe to feel each other, maybe to stop running around, to stop *doing* . . . then perhaps something will happen.

AKIVA: To look and look and look! To look a whole week! What'll you all discover after looking at each other for a week?

EPHRAIM: They'll discover that a nose has two nostrils and that there's an ear on each side of the head. [MIRIAM *bursts out laughing.*]

AKIVA: Maybe we'll discover that there's no difference between the fellows and the girls.

NAPHTALI: That'll prove Weiniger wrong.

AKIVA: What are you talking about? Shut up and pay attention! Moshe's already clipped your tail feathers! [*MIRIAM bursts into noisy laughter.*]

AKIVA: You very nearly *have* turned into a girl.

NEHAMA [*Mimicking Miriam's laughter*]: What are you laughing at? What's so funny? Laugh, laugh at the anti-feminist jokes these men are making!

MIRIAM: I didn't laugh at *that.* I suddenly imagined Naphtali peeking. . . . [*Laughs.*] How do you peek: like this . . . or like this? [*Laughs.*]

AKIVA: Shhh. . . . To look at each other . . . to look at each other. . . .

MOSHE: Go ahead and laugh. [*Outburst.*] Laugh! One day you'll lie dying and then you'll suddenly realize that all your lives no one ever really looked at you or cared for you!

AKIVA: Woe! Woe!

MOSHE: When you're dying you'll understand that all your lives you've done useless things! You scuttered around! Carted yourselves from one place to another, read newspapers, publications, brochures, reports, novels. . . .

AKIVA: Frightful!

MOSHE: Dying you'll understand that all your lives you chattered and prattled and philosophized. . . . You'll die one day and then you'll realize that you've wasted your lives on nonsense! That you didn't touch what was within your reach, didn't say what could have been said and didn't do what could have been done! You'll die realizing that you had one chance only and that you wasted it thoughtlessly! I've seen war, I saw dying men's eyes. I *saw!* With these hands I held the head of a man dying of a bullet in his liver, in a frenzy on the stretcher and grunting like an animal: "*Eine Schweinerel! Eine unverstandliche Schweinerel!*" He went pea-green, frothed at the mouth and died! Died! You're children, you! Children! Hapoel Hatzair! Achduth Ha'avoda! Berl! Shmerl! Mama! Papa! People! Country! Children crammed with complexes! You'll die like animals not knowing why you've lived!

NEHAMA: Moshe! Moshe! Maybe we really should do what you want! But we simply must go down from here tomorrow! We can do all you said over there, too! We'll do it there! In Mansurin.

MOSHE: There won't be time there.

EPHRAIM: Our great moment has come! People expect of us! The eyes of the whole Movement are turned toward us!



MOSHE: You're waving flags again!

AKIVA: And you're tearing them down. We want to believe! We must believe!

MOSHE: Today, here, is our last chance. Tomorrow we'll go down there and start our war, and we'll have time for nothing else.

EPHRAIM: But we'll do something! We'll raise a settlement! And yet another!

MOSHE: I'll not let any one make a manifesto out of me! Such a chance, to start everything anew, one gets only once in a lifetime! So, instead, we start off everything like automatons? And put off the really important things for when we have time for them! Because of rotten myths? I'm not going down to Mansurin tomorrow!

NEHAMA: You can't do this to us! You're destroying the Group.

MOSHE: Do what you want, I'm not going down.

EPHRAIM: Comrades: I respect Moshe's decision. But even if I'm the only one left, I'll go down. I'll go to Mansurin. The time has come, the alarm has sounded, that's all there is to it.

AKIVA: Me, too. What about you, Naphtali?

MIRIAM: I'm going too.

SHIFRA [*To Moshe*]: You'll remain here all alone, when we go?

MOSHE: You can go without me. The need to do things is pressing you. To prove something to yourselves, and to the whole world. I didn't leave a father with a bank account in Vienna. I left a poverty-stricken tailor of a father, weak, numbed by hardship and bewildered. I don't have to prove anything to anybody.

NEHAMA: You're not right, what you're telling us! D'you know why I came? D'you know why I'm going down there? I saw the pogrom in Lvov from *near.* The pogrom with which the Polish lumpenproletariat celebrated the annexation to Poland. I saw a young Jewish mother run down the street with her pram, her eyes like a hunted animal's, not knowing which way to turn, right or left, forwards or back! That's why I'm here, that's why I'll go down tomorrow, because for me Europe is finished! And not to prove anything to anyone.

NAPHTALI: We won't let you stay behind. We'll take you with us by force. We'll take you along like a bundle where ever we go. And if you resist, we'll force-feed you a bottle of alcohol, put you in a straitjacket and take you with us to Mansurin, or where ever in hell *we* go! We'll carry you with us like a curse on our heads! We can't leave you behind, we just can't. [*SHIFRA gets up and begins to unbutton her blouse.*]

NAPHTALI: What are you doing?

Don't believe a word I say,
Don't believe, it's all in play,
Don't believe, 'cause all I have
Is my dead half
For sale today!

AKIVA: Enough!

NAPHTALI [*To Moshe*]: You asked what *are* we doing here? We're a sort of last gesture made with failing strength, a sort of geste of defiance to annihilation, that's what we are. Defiance in chaos . . . because chaos is here . . . [*points at the group*] amongst us . . . in each one of us and we don't want to *see* that.

EPHRAIM: Naphtali, come here: we're all scared, you're not alone. Our youth is shuddering and dying—changing into a dreadful growing up—and they're trying to draw us into a barren, empty desert. Remember the moments of silence and illumination in that damp and dark cellar in Vienna. There was mythic power there. The fog outside; inside, dimness and pure desire to create. There, in that dark cellar in Vienna, the truth about life was revealed to us. We were naïve boys and girls and we dreamed a beautiful dream. We felt ourselves destined for great, proud lives. That we were setting forth on an historic mission to revive the destinies of a People. Never, even in our vilest nightmares, could we have believed that a year later we'd come to this—treading the finest sentiments of our youth underfoot, with all those cold, hard words. Neither Past, nor History, not Destiny: a new idol is being set up for us—naked man.

AKIVA: You know all too well what we shouldn't do. The question's what we should.

EPHRAIM: It's quite simple: pick and burrow into each other's soul and everyone wallow in his own vomit and his neighbor's. That's the way of it, isn't it?

AKIVA: I'd like to explain it to him in other words. He doesn't like the word "mythos." Use something like "the essential core of the People."

EPHRAIM: On the contrary, let's have the word up for discussion. I'm not afraid of mythos.

MOSHE: Quite the contrary! You love myths.

EPHRAIM: Right! What else pushes me to belong to this country?

MOSHE: Just the mythos.

EPHRAIM: Right!

MOSHE: And what makes a bond between you and *me?*

EPHRAIM: What?

AKIVA: The common belief in the same mythos.

MOSHE: Does he want to hear of my beliefs at all?

NEHAMA: And what attaches him to Miriam?

NAPHTALI: Myths, myths.

AKIVA: The myth gives the direction: we're trying to reach the essential core. We came here in the belief that this is the way to it.

MIRIAM: Naphtali, at least, has a good reason to be a woman hater: he's never tasted a woman.

NEHAMA: Yes? Well, if you want to know, you're strengthening their anti-feminism.

MIRIAM: Really? How?

NEHAMA: It would be worth your while to read up on your Weininger, then you'd understand.

MIRIAM: You live only by books.

NEHAMA: D'you know why we came here at all?

NAPHTALI: *Das ewige Weibliches* is draeing us aloft!

MIRIAM: Perhaps you'll tell me.

NEHAMA: I wanted to tell you something last Friday, but I held back. I thought it would be just too cruel.

EPHRAIM: I have only one reply: our fate in eternity was revealed to us in the form of a certain ancient people and a certain small country.

MOSHE: What is fate? What's eternity?

EPHRAIM: Our people and our land.

MOSHE: "People!" "Land!"

EPHRAIM: We must be humble before them and accept whatever time sets upon us.

MOSHE: And where do *we* come into the picture?

EPHRAIM: We didn't start this job and we're not obliged to complete it, but we're not excused setting our hands to it!

MOSHE: He'll soon begin reciting the Ethics of the Fathers.

EPHRAIM: That's right. We carry in us the unknown destiny of a whole nation. It may be that only through fatherhood will we get to know what we're doing here at all.

AKIVA: We must strike fear. Even among ourselves, otherwise we won't have the strength to do anything. We must jut out of the ground like a rock, so that everyone will step aside in dismay. In respect. Be like a tribe in ancient times. Every act of ours must be symbolic. We must make our lives hard and silent as stone. Proud. And fierce. And sure of our right. That's how we have to descend upon Mansurin.

MOSHE: The only thing missing now is an altar, and an unblemished calf. Pity we threw away the blood of the goat we slaughtered yesterday evening.

MIRIAM: One moment, Nehama: what did you want to tell me on Friday, and didn't?

NAPHTALI [*Separate speech*]: One thing's clear: if we were all men here we'd manage somehow, but with women . . . How in hell can one come to any sort of arrangement with women? Suffer for 'em, sweat for 'em . . . [*Imitates Ephraim.*] "*Noli me tangere!*"—easy to say, but how d'you go about it? A painful thought! . . .

NEHAMA: You see, Shifra? We can thank Miriam for this.

MIRIAM: What did you want to tell me on Friday and didn't?

NEHAMA: You're beginning to allow yourself too much lately. Shifra and I are fighting tooth and nail to prove that we girls are not less than them in any way. That we can work with crowbars and pickaxes just like them. D'you think we find it easy? D'you think I find it easy to dig ditches and break stone? Or Shifra? What d'you think?! That while we're killing ourselves fighting to maintain the status of the girls in the Group, you'll go and nonchalantly justify all the nonsense that Akiva and Naphtali spout from Weininger against the weaker sex!

MIRIAM: What? . . .

NEHAMA: Precisely that!

SHIFRA: Leave her alone.

NEHAMA: Why should I leave her alone? Has she the least consideration for us? When she returns from her adventures at four o'clock in the morning and we have to tear ourselves away from our lumpy mattresses at half-past five, with cut hands and aching bodies, Madame here has mysterious headaches, mysterious faintnesses, a mysterious tiredness, sort of sickness! What d'you think?! D'you think you can allow yourself to invent all kinds of excuses to shirk getting up early in the morning? And dodge work? And that's not all: when we bring her food, to the tent, for this princess with her mysterious indispositions, food we deny ourselves, what does she do? Gives the cheese and eggs to Mephisto! To the cat! And then has the cheek to explain with her charming smile: "I don't feel like the menu today"!

What would she like? A peach, for instance! She does rather feel like having something to eat, a peach, now! Bring her a peach . . . or sauerkraut and frankfurters! . . . You're quite without any sense of responsibility! D'you think you're living in a doll's house or something?

MIRIAM [*Hysterical outburst*]: Suffragette! Suffragette! You suffragette virgin! [*Throws around rags and odds and ends out of an open bundle.*] Dried up suffragette virgin! [*Ephraim tries to restrain her, she shakes him off.*] Leave me alone! Maiden suffragette! Got a womb in your belly? No, a museum! An academic library, not a womb, that's what you've got there! An arsenal of great thoughts, not a womb! That's what you've got! [*AKIVA tries to restrain her.*] Don't touch me! Iceberg! Have you got a cunt? Got a vagina? A university corridor, that's what you've got!

NEHAMA: You're mourning over yourself!

MIRIAM: You're not a woman at all! Not a woman!

NEHAMA: I'm sorry for you!

MIRIAM: But you're a woman, too, just like me, and not a man! You're not a man! She's not a man! She's a woman just like me! You've got to find yourself a man, you must! A man who'll sleep with you and give you pleasure! A man who'll put a prick into that university corridor and turn it into a vagina, and chuck all the big ideas out of your womb! That's what you need!

NAPHTALI [*Tries to hold her*]: Miriam . . .

MIRIAM [*Pushes him away*]: Get away from me, you unborn babe! He'll toss all the books and big ideas out of there and replace 'em with an embryo! A baby! A child, a child! That's what you need . . . you poor thing . . . poor thing . . . poor thing. . . . [*Collapses into Nehama's arms.*] Forgive me, forgive me . . . really I love you, I do. . . .

EPHRAIM [*To Moshe*]: Well, are you satisfied? We really revealed ourselves, didn't we? Got what you wanted? Here you have the human being in all its nakedness: take it and form it! I don't know how we'll get along with one another anymore. It'll be very hard.

MOSHE: It'll be hard for all of us.

SHIFRA: Don't answer them, Moshe, they don't understand you. [*To Ephraim.*] I can live with him, if he wants. . . .

NAPHTALI: Just a minute! Before you decide for good what's going to happen here and to whom, I too have news for you: in Mansurin, Naphtali is going to live with Naphtali, all alone in a tent. And no one is to expect from him either happiness, or honor, or stability, or security, and it may be that no one will be able to love himself through Naphtali, but that's how it is! Naphtali's love is for the having! Anyone who wants can come and help himself. . . . [*Calling like an auctioneer.*] Naphtali's heart—going for the first time, for the second time, for the third and last time! . . . There it is. . . . You don't want, I don't care. [*Gets down on the ground to gather up the scattered odds and ends.*]

MOSHE [*To Ephraim*]: Y'know, I've seen people murdering each other for a scrap of bread. I swore then that if I could find a place where people live and share their bread and clothes and don't exploit or cheat or murder each other for them, then I wouldn't ask for anything more. . . .

EPHRAIM: What words destroy can't be mended by words. We've got to leave it to the future. [*The cast freezes in their places in midaction.* MOSHE *to footlights, aged by fifty years, and addresses audience.*]

MOSHE: It'll soon be daybreak. We'll load ourselves onto the automobiles and get down off this mountain. And in the name of all sorts of big words which have no connection at all to what's happening and has happened to us, under compulsion and in haste, constrained by confused and shapeless remnants in the soul, we'll go out to fight other human beings, as bewildered and dazed as ourselves, to kill and be killed, and all those not present this night of the Twentieth of October will, in years to come, tell children legends about the things we believed in and in whose name we went out to dispossess other fellowmen. And to take Possession of the Land. And time. Time, like a child which knows not what it does, will make a play of us.

# Cherli Ka Cherli

*by*
DAN HOROWITZ

One of the most interesting aspects of modern Israeli drama is the willingness of both the author and the director to experiment with dramatic form and methods of staging. Many native authors will abandon standard form to create ingenious effects. Those involved in the actual production of plays seem to have a flair for the visual. This flair for the visual seems to be characteristic of production in Israel on all levels.

*Cherli Ka Cherli* is a good example of this kind of experimentation. The author, Dan Horowitz, and the director, Ilan Ronen, indicate that the stage setting for this play should be that of a "class picture" with certain modifications.[1] The central figure in this play is the chorus representing "both the individual and the audience." The front part of the stage is to be a mirror for the audience (that is, a "mirror image" in which the members of the audience might see themselves). The individual characters within the class picture are alternately human and life-sized doll-like representations. The dolls represent the following: a fighting man, 1948, wearing a duffel coat, holding a home-made gun; a kibbutznik, blue shirt and "tembel" hat; a parachutist with his helmet and weapons; a Nazi soldier with his various insignia, trappings and boots; an Arab with a scimitar between his teeth and finally a Diaspora Jew with his prayer shawl and phylacteries. Also on the stage are live characters and musicians.

The front of the stage serves as a staging area where confessional monologues take place. The costumes are simple. The dolls are all dressed to represent stereotypes. The human characters are all dressed in dark blue trousers or skirts and white shirts. The choreography is strict and supposedly unrealistic. The musicians included stand to the rear of the class picture and the music is used to clarify the material and underline the various monologues.

The play attacks the age-old Jewish question, that of Jewish identity. Each speaker is to represent "the abstraction of one trait or of a single desire for Jewish-Israeli identity."[2] These monologues are at times narrated by the whole chorus, one individual or one part of the group. The many identities taken together are to represent the development of the sabra in Israel. The sabra is seen as "at times beautiful and at times ridiculous," but his attempt to build a new way of life is essentially Jewish.

*Cherli Ka Cherli* is an Israeli folk song which is quite old (fifty years). The lyrics in this song resemble in part the American folk song, "Oh Susanah"—"It rained all night the day I left/ The weather it was dry." An eight-year-old Israeli expert, Ofer Tur Sinai of Jerusalem, rendered the first two verses as follows:

> The Boy Scouts and the Girl Scouts, Cherli Ka Cherli
> They went away by train
> They drove to Jerusalem, Cherli Ka Cherli
> It took them two hours.
>
> When they arrived in Yemen, Cherli Ka Cherli
> There they saw Haman
> And Haman was sitting on the potty, Cherli Ka Cherli
> And he ate like a pig.

Dan Horowitz is a prominent young playwright who is very active in the Israeli Theatre. In addition to *Cherli Ka Cherli,* he adapted *Breakdown and Bereavement* by Y. H. Brenner for the stage in 1973. He has also written two new plays, *Yosele Golem,* 1981, which is a re-write of the traditional play, *The Golem.* In addition, he has written a play called *Uncle Arthur,* which features one actor and four puppets. He is currently a Lecturer at Tel Aviv University, Department of Theatre Arts. He has been chosen Festival Director of the First International Conference and Festival of the Jewish Theatre, held in Tel Aviv in July, 1982.

## NOTES

1. All material and quotations regarding the play have been taken from Dan Horowitz, *Cherli Ka Cherli,* trans. Karen Alkalay and Hannah Gut (Tel Aviv: Israeli Centre of the International Theatre Institute: 1978).
2. Ibid.

### CHARACTERS

*5 Characters*
*2 Musicians*
*6 Dummies*

*Translated by Karen Alkalay and Hannah Gut.*



### PICTURE 1:

I'd like to point out a few facts calmly, without hysteria. You may consider them the way you do a questionnaire. Simply answer true/false.

It's true that millions of people were killed in World War II. It's terrible. It's true that the Russian prisoners suffered more than all the others. But no child was thrown into the gas chambers just because his peenie was cut.

True or false?

O.K. Denmark. There are a few righteous gentiles. But you can check this yourself. It's all listed by memorial forests. Just compare the forest planted in memory of those who died with the trees planted in honor of some righteous gentiles. I'm talking about facts. No head doctor is going to tell me I'm paranoid. No one would dare tell me that we're not forsaken. Or that the world's suddenly better. I'm talking about facts. This cut peenie is a fact. No need for more proof.

### PICTURE 2

Then onto the chest of Hanina ben Taradion they placed wet sponges so that his soul would depart slowly from him. Hanina ben Taradion—everything burning around him, the fire blazing, the organs carbonizing one by one, but on the chest wool sponges, special ones. Soaked in water, so that he'd die slowly, slowly. Get the picture? Now turn it upside down. If you're going to fall asleep, or rest, or grab some nirvana or forget, because of the pleasant aroma, because of the hay, because of the dinghies, or because of sclerotic attacks—then I say no! It won't do! There'll be no narcosis here. Here there will be awakening sponges on the chest. But this time, of fire. Of burning. Of boiling alcohol. No sleeping. No nirvana.

We haven't gotten anywhere yet. Otherwise this would be your last sleep. Sponges soaked wakefully on the chest, clear? Move it!

## PICTURE 3

They told me a story about three presents. Y. L. Peretz. Three presents. I want to talk about this business of the first present. What is the weight of a bag of dust, where is the dust from exactly, from the Negev or the coastal plain or really, truly Jerusalem? What is this, to cling so to a bag of dust? After a breakin, when the burglars are in the house, to lean on it. That's not earth, that's dust. Let them take the dust! That's the way you go after dust?

That's the way they go to work—"*Arbeit macht frei*"—and clench a bag of dust to their hearts. That way they join choruses on the way to the purifying showers with a bag of dust. Have any signs of dust remained between the fingers, after death? And that's a present. For ascension. I wet the dust—it's mud. It's also made to harden in the sun later. That's stupid. It's nothing but grains, food for worms. I piss on it—I scatter it.

Dust. If gazing in the dust pulls my eyes downward so that I don't see anything, just hang on to the bags, I don't give or take presents like that.

## PICTURE 4

Ladies and Gentlemen, Exhibit #28 Museum Photograph. Size seventy-five by sixty. In the upper section a row of S.S. officers rejoicing in the morning. In the bottom center they're cutting off the beard of a Jew. What does the beard say to you: "Silently he came up to me and before the eyes of all the mocking faces, he cut. Those who cut, cut and those who mock, mock. What young faces the mockers have. And I, a remnant of honor falling in the morning roll call. How long did the fall take? And who are the guardian angels guarding that camera as I fall down? And the sky is above. And the face laughs. All before and behind me my rag remnant and I fall and try to hang on, maybe forever in the frozen picture but I'm surely on my way. And if I don't lose my balance, and there is always right and left in the world, and the eyes are in place over the mouth. And if the direction is down and the sky above and the faces around me laugh and nothing in the world not even a still small voice can keep me from my way down. Maybe when I grow up and flourish I'll become a mattress one of these days. And be rejuvenated at the end of time. Monument for a morning. I heard a click."

Exhibit #28 gentlemen. Seventy-five by sixty. Let's continue.

### PICTURE 5: "German picture"

MOTHER [*Singing to child*]:

> Hanschen Klein, ging allein
> in die weite Welt hinein
> Stock und Hut, steht ihm gut
> Hans ist wohlgemut—

BOY: [*Repeating after her*]:

> Hanschen Klein, ging allein
> in die wel-te Welt-hi-nein

MAN A: Aussteigen!
MOTHER [*Singing*]:

> Und die Mutter weinet sehr, tam, tam, tam. . . .
> [*A sound is heard on the drum,*]

MAN A: Rechts, Links, Rechts, Links.
MOTHER [*Singing*]:

> Stock und Hut, steht ihm gut, Hans. . . .
> MAN A: Rechts?
> MOTHER: Steht ihm gut, Hans . . . Hans?
> MAN A: Ich sagte rechts!!
> MAN B [*Directions in an exercise class*]: Links, rechts, und links rechts, rauf und runter, links und rechts sehr schon, sehr schon, nicht aufhören, rechts, links, weiter,

gut, Los, los, weiter machen. Na, was ist mit Ihnen? Weiter, weiter

OLD MAN: Ich kann nicht mehr, Bitte, glauben Sie mir, kann nicht mehr!

MOTHER: Hans?

MAN A: Nicht schuldig!

MAN B: In neunzehn-hundert-neun-und-dreissig schreibt Brecht

BOY: Beethoven, Beethoven. . . .

OLD MAN: Also lass uns alle beten an Jesus—Maria und die drei Engels . . . [*The boy laughs.*]

MAN B: Na, schon, Brecht schreibt also Mutter Courage, eine art Tragodie.

MOTHER [*singing*]:

Und die Mutter weinet sehr. . . .

MAN A: Sh . . .

MAN B: Na, sei schon ruhig du . . . eine art Tragödie, ein Stück Scheisse.

MAN A: Stück Dreck, das seit Ihr doch alle, Stück Scheisse . . . Stück Dreck, das seit Ihr doch alle! Nicht wahr? Was? Nein! Nicht schuldig. Ja, ich bin Adolf. . . .

MAN B: Sh . . . sh . . . Beethoven . . . Beethoven.

TOGETHER: Beethoven . . . Beethoven . . . Beethoven . . . offen . . . offen . . . Bach . . . Offenbach . . . Offenbach . . . offen bach . . . gas ofen . . . gasofen . . . gas . . . gas. . . .

MAN A: Im Sinn der Anklage—Nicht Schuldig.

MAN B: Na schon . . . Was regen Sie sich auf? Heide, nehmen Sie sich ein bischen Schlagsahne! Wunderbar, was sagen Sie?

MOTHER: Hans?

MAN A: Ich bin Adolf.

MAN B: Macht doch nichts aus! Macht doch nichts. . . .

MAN A: Ich bin nicht schuldig.

MAN B: Aussteigen!!

MOTHER [*singing*]:

Und die Mutter weinet sehr, denn Sie hat kein Hänschen . . . mehr. . . . [*Fade out.*]

### PICTURE 6: "A HOMESPUN LULLABY"

My baby, my little child,
Lay your head on my belly
My belly like a fiddle
With a hole in its middle
I will protect you
No one will hurt you
Lie on my belly, My Wunderkind
Be my sweet, my own.

Strings like bars
Will scare off intruders
Here you'll be safe
Lay your head
Come back to your place
Home, my baby
Safe back where you belong.

### PICTURE 7

I have a great coat. I have round black eyes. I have a cap. I raise my hands. I am the boy whose hands are raised in the picture.

### PICTURE 8

What will you do, kid in the grey coat?
What will you do, kid in a cap—
When you raise your hands
Facing the shooting monsters,
Get out of the picture,
Get out of the picture!
Play some trick, Run! Draw your gun.
Roll out of the picture and threaten
Everyone so they'll never find you again
In the picture. Inside the grey coat
Hands up, on your head a cap.
Get out of the picture.

### PICTURE 9: "BOY WITH CAP"

I have this cap on my head that is woven.
Not cotton nor blue-white nor khaki,
Not silk, maybe a bit greasy from my father's sweaty hands.
At night I didn't play storm the castle. Or field games.

I've got a cap on my head.
And when I take account of my dress.
Maybe I'll have *schlaikes** when I grow up, not for sure *gatkes,***
And what will my mother in the homeland say
When I grow up, after I drop my hands, what will she say
—when I pack my knapsack on Saturday night—to my father:
That they'll keep me warm. In good health. Gatkes keep you
warm.
You can tie up the sleeves and fill them with dust, for sandbags.
You can fly them on a post to know which way the wind blows
and around the neck in times of flu,
With alcohol to keep you warm. You can strain putrid water
from holes in the desert and tie them like a rope
on the cliff side, for climbing.
Sometimes in times of need in dreams, maybe they can be
contraceptives for my rising manhood, but primarily
it is best to hide them so they don't peek out from the
cuffs of the trousers. Altogether, the best thing is to
tear them in a tug of war, but now we'll give them to mother
to dream of yeast cakes and everything about the new homeland.
I'm just a punctuation mark until I lower my hands.
Maybe I'll leave them on my cap when I get tired.
No doubt. I'll leave them on my woven hat in the future.
In the meantime I am up front and my mother's dreams are
behind.

### PICTURE 10: "I'M FROM HERE, DAD'S FROM THERE"

My father was born between double walls. The first ray of light that lit his room in his infancy penetrated through double walls. They hid gold in them. When my grandfather built his house he certainly recalled that there were pogroms. So a cellar was needed to hide the gold and jewelry when there were pogroms. Me, I was lying in the cradle, when my first ray of sun burst at me from outside. No partition, not even a curtain. From the azure heights, free falling, right to me, on my muscles, a ray of light—while outside a horse ploughed, the shesek fruit tree blooming in the beginning of summer, cinderblock walls and the window open. That's the way my first ray of light hit my bosom.

I had uncles. I'm sure that my uncle had gold teeth; otherwise what were the Germans looking for in the pogroms? Certainly not the source of the Jewish tongue—that is Yiddish, that is spices, that is Tzitses, the four corners of the Talis.

*Suspenders.
**Long underwear.

PICTURE 11

I remember myself so I say: Me, I'm barefoot, sometimes a burr sticks in me and I squeeze. And when it's out, a drop of red blood comes out too. Burning sometimes on the street, sometimes in the grass. Sometimes on a small soccer court, its floor red clay. There the children bring fruit offerings on the Feast of Weeks. My bare feet in sandals, sometimes sand between my toes. Sometimes a burdock gets caught between the sole and my bare foot. Sometimes I cut my big toe nail with my teeth, and I smell earth.

PICTURE 12

I'm from the flute of the shepherd, wandering among the trees, among black goats reaching up on two feet. From the flute of the shepherd, I—a sound, floating. Tongue crushing leaves from the trees and teeth munching green from the trees, and I from the flutes to the trees, to the ears of the goats between the branches like rays of sunlight, easy and willing in the pleasant warmth. I'm from the flute of the shepherd.

PICTURE 13

I'm a salad.

Anointed oil. I'm the salt of the earth. I'm a peeled cucumber grown in the garden. Aside a reddened tomato. From the salted Dead Sea, divided, sectioned. Kissed by a row of pearl onions like white teeth. And peppers lubricated in refined olive oil.

Take carrots mashed! Heaped like the bower of the bride and groom. Turned turnip, thinning of the cornstalks. Bare feet. Lemon. What devotion: of the carrot spine, of the pepper pips, of the tomato seeds, and lettuce too. I who come from the level of the earth, and from its sides and underneath kohlrabi. . . . In any casc I'm really really close to the land. A virtual acquaintance. A knife couldn't come between us.

PICTURE 14

I'm the Open. Nice to meet you. Everything should be well and open. I'm the very sandal on my foot, by the bonfire, in summer nights. The distant light that ties crowns on the flower of the fire. All will be well. Here are the hands. Stretched out to take from the sea. Roast fish. Why not? I'm even the certain smell of the baked potatoes. The permitted breast, southward ho, the wilderness. Desert trips arranged in me one by one inside my knapsack. Two wide straps and air. How much air do I contain? How many distances in my sweet lungs? The certain week of I-know-the-score: Ten-four. Give me a light. Everything's all right. We've got the might. I'm assured—water restriction. Straight, strong, strained. Water on all sides. Surfing on the waves, wafting horizons. Even my armpit is full of horizons. What am I if not hands-in-pockets? Eating ice cream on Allenby Street, ice cream, ice cream.

## PICTURE 15

I'm Handspan. Handspan. Handspan. From the belt from under the waist up to the fold over my pocket. I'm all handspan. Here from the distance between the thumbs to the tip of my pinky. I'm alive, a kind of handspan. What's in me and what isn't in me? I'm sensitive. That isn't a question. Who isn't sensitive? The shudder coming from the Bedouin, coming from the boors, the healthy, barefoot on earth, fill the earth.

The shudder comes from the flute, from the baa of the sheep, from the acorns, so, so deep inside me. I'm the handspan. I'm the forwarding thrust. Whole neighborhood thrusting forward in the pants. From where?

From the impulse, the pressure. Maybe movies. Maybe mongols. Ginger is ginger. And Gengis Khan thrusts forward. Stop looking down your nose. What's with you, aren't you a man? From the *debka,** from the debka. You're a healthy Circassian. You split targets. You flood the area. You don't let your spirits fall. You are the forward thrust at the head of all nations, at the head of all nations. An arrow thrust forward, buddy.

## PICTURE 16

I'm Ho-ho of the open shirt
I'm Ho-ho of the up-up shirt
Of the foot going up up up.

I'm the haystack Ho-ho going up in fire
I'm the Ho-ho an OK of fire

*Arab dance for men.

I'm the rising up until the midnight hour
And who ever leaves is a spoilsport.

I'm on my way up
Above all the treasures I arise
Up up in the milky way
Anti-crematorium, nice

Sweat-wet-barefoot-rising-open
Almost a Hassid—Ho-ho rising! Wheeeeee
Hai-de-de-dai, dai-da-me
Clean, I'm clean, I'm clean, cleaner than a golden spot.
I'm strong up up in the milky way Ho Ho Ho.

## PICTURE 17

I'm Cherli Ka Cherli the first
King of the boy scouts and the girls
Always prepared
To protect
The weak.

The distinct impressions are that Cherli Ka
Cherli jumps over the bonfires
And he makes the coffee rise and fall seven times
Before the seventh rising he adds eucalyptus leaves.

I'm Cherli Ka Cherli the first
King of the boy scouts and the girls
Love to crunch flowers
Chrysanthemums in one hand
In the other Anemones
And when I clap my hands
The aroma is wonderful

Cherli Ka Cherli loves to swim in the pool especially the breast stroke He curses old ladies and keeps the ten scout commandments.

Cherli Ka Cherli laughs a crazy laugh and sends everything to hell
He's in charge of first class (tam tam)
He's one of the doers (tam tam)
Hands in pockets
Thumbs out.

I'm Cherli Ka Cherli the first
Dreaming of seas and pools
And birds of the wing. I love clams
Roast fish, dinghies floating,
Sometimes I think I was born from the sea.

Cherli Ka Cherli
Is tied with a double clove hitch to night games,

He counts off.
He's the pathfinder.
He licks the pebbles.
He skips a stone four times over the water.
I repeat, hands in pockets, thumbs out.
In his day, Cherli Ka Cherli was the orgasmic dream of the movement.

I'm Cherli Ka Cherli the first
King of dreaming and doing.
In the end of days, after the Wars
I want to be a seagull shepherd.
I see myself standing, my arms crossed on my breast,

In my hand-colored strips tied to the seagulls' necks—like light harnesses
With a flick of the hand I free them
To the sound of my whistle they come.
In the end of days, after the Wars
I want to be a shepherd of seagulls.

## PICTURE 18

BRIDES: Come, my beloved, come, my beloved. Let us descend to the vineyards

GROOMS: We can't hear you, We can't hear you.

BRIDES: Come, my beloved, let us descend to the vineyards.

GROOMS: Which vineyards, my sister, which vineyards?

BRIDES: We shall eat grapes, we will lie on the ground, we'll lie on the ground.

GROOMS: We lie on the ground, we lie on the ground.

BRIDES: Waiting in the crevices of the rocks, Waiting under each blooming tree.

GROOMS: Waiting under each blooming tree in the foxholes. Waiting for orders in the excavations.

BRIDES: In the excavations you are clean.

GROOMS: Didn't we swear that the sewer pipes would never again be a hiding place?

BRIDES: Come, my beloved, put thy hand in mine.

GROOMS: Our hands are clean, our hands are clean. Only our mouths are full of dust.

BRIDES: Beloved, Beloved, come to the vineyards. Come to the gardens. Between the mountains and the rocks.

GROOMS: Between the mountains and the rocks in the valleys our bodies are scattered. Can you hear us, sister? Can you hear us?

## PICTURE 19

When we say "with the finger on the trigger," I am the finger on the trigger. It's not a question of the rules for target shooting. How many times is the trigger pulled? Is it with two pulls and a squeeze? Because I'm not a finger on the trigger—I'm *the* finger on the trigger. Shameless. I'm another finger, the middle one, bigger and longer. The way it should be—certainly not closed while squeezing.

And when I squeeze the trigger, I want the shell long and the bullet short and wounding and exploding. Explosives stuffed in crazy to kill. I said lots of throats. To slit, I said. Lots of ribs broken. No guilt. So there'll be a little balance and harmony in nature. Isn't there a better law than the law of equilibrium?

Behind the gun handle—there's no shoulder. Behind the gun handle stands Bat Ami—daughter of my nation! And for all those slaughtered Bat Ami stands behind the handle and I'll squeeze, without mercy. Isn't there a price? Even infants they put into closed rooms and turned on the gas.

You think there's something sick about the desire for revenge? I desire. Quietly. Surely. I deserve it. All the way. I'm a finger single and unique. Long. And I'll feel in heat, shuddering. A real finger stretching over the trigger. To keep me warm, so the double bullet will hit the road and destroy. All this taking into account who's behind me, beside me, and in front.

I open my eyes and I say that if there isn't a rule of equilibrium here—what *is* there here? Only me—the only possible finger on the trigger. Take only me.

## PICTURE 20: "DISCUSSION"

O: This is a point. Awaiting additional orders. Stop.

A: So hang on. The little train that says I think I can, I think I can.

O: Which train?

A: Does the rattle of the trains mean anything to you? O.K. So squeeze, from the hip. Take off, my friend. By your armpits you are picked up by a mother with a baby. They point a gun at them. Remember. Albums.

B: From the hip, friend. I suggest you squeeze.

A: Stripped pajamas. Remember. Your mother. Didn't she tell you?

B: If you ever turn your back to him he'll shove a knife into you and then—the balls. Either it hurts or it doesn't. If you shoot, it won't hurt, because if they hurt, it means you didn't shoot.

9: This is a point. Awaiting additional orders. Stop.

A: You, sir, don't know what the Arabian desert is—so now you'll know. You, sir, don't know what curfew is—so now you'll know. You, sir, don't know anything, anything. So forward—press, overcome, get, chase, divide the loot. Come on press the trigger.

C: I'm pressing.

°: This is a point. Awaiting additional orders. Stop.

C: If you take the village, you'll have the city too.

B: What are you? A vegetarian? You should want to kill and kill. Because if you don't kill, you're dead.

°: This is a point. Awaiting additional orders. Stop.

A: Just like 1 plus 1 are 2, so it's one house and another and another. So it's face to face combat. So it's nest obliteration. So it's extermination. So it's a purge.

B: This is a purge, Mister. A purge. Remove all the shit from your head. Give yourself an infusion, if you want to live. All your blood is full of disease. Transfuse the blood!

C: Why not learn to throw stones?

A: Do you want to dream of angels going up and down the ladder? Great. Go take a shower, open the gas!

B: Hesitations, my ass, sir.

A: This is no time for angels.

B: Angels are in the next world.

A: Over, do you hear this?

B: Stick out your chest.

A: It's better than turning your back! So straight from the hip. Think about the first harvest.

B: The Festival of the Harvest! The festival of the first harvest.

C: First harvest.

A: Reap, buddy, reap. If you don't reap you'll be reaped.

B: That's your problem!

A: Do exercises.

B: Rechts, links.

C: Run.

B: Get ready.

A: Climb up the rope ladders. Forget the angels, understand? From the hip. Not from the head. Forget the head.

C: I said forget the head. Pass! For God's sake. For God's sake, pass, pass, pass!

°: Therefore I'm just passing by—pass. Pass!

PICTURE 21

QUESTION: Are you the writer S. Yizhar?

YIZHAR: Yes.

QUESTION: S. Yizhar is Yizhar Smilanski.

YIZHAR: Yes.

QUESTION: Are you the one who wrote about the banishment of the Arabs?

YIZHAR: Yes.

QUESTION: Did you find out something?

YIZHAR: Pardon?

QUESTION: Quote: "We'll clear something up for you like lightning. All at once. This is the Diaspora. That's what Diaspora is."

YIZHAR: I wrote that.

QUESTION: You wrote that, quote: "It is impossible to be satisfied with anything as long as tears shine in the eyes of a child walking with his mother into the Diaspora."

YIZHAR: Yes, I . . .

QUESTION: You wrote, quote: "Never did the machine guns bestow any claim . . ."

YIZHAR: Yes.

QUESTION: But you also wrote, quote: "We live in a generation of war. Thus stood the stars when we were born. In death we are equal and this is the era of death."

YIZHAR: Yes, I wrote that.

QUESTION: Are you trying to be righteous?

YIZHAR: No.

QUESTION: You trying to back down?

YIZHAR: No.

QUESTION: But you love to be out in the open?

YIZHAR: Yes.

QUESTION: A horse escaping out to the open?

YIZHAR: Yes.

QUESTION: Are we the abolishers of the Diaspora to you?

YIZHAR: I don't know.

QUESTION: But the echoes of the footsteps, quote: "In your ears reminded you of Jeremiah, the grouchy mourner of Anatot*"?

YIZHAR: Rolling like thunder.

QUESTION: And many read you?

YIZHAR: Yes.

QUESTION: Many youths?

YIZHAR: Yes.

QUESTION: Like mother's milk?

YIZHAR: Like calories, vitamins, bananas and sour cream.

QUESTION: Certainly, like calories, vitamins, bananas and sour cream. Are you S. Yizhar?

YIZHAR: I am S. Yizhar.

QUESTION: Is it such a big deal to ask questions?

YIZHAR: No.

QUESTION: You just wanna ask and write stories and poems?

YIZHAR: No.

QUESTION: A man's life is worth more or less than a dunam of land, S. Yizhar?

YIZHAR: What did you say?

## PICTURE 22: CHORAL CHANT

Don't dream of ladders
Don't dream of angels
Life isn't wings
Life is earth

*Refrain:* Open ears open eyes
At attention march
He who will not guard to-night
Tomorrow will not rise

*Birthplace of the prophet Jeremiah.

Don't dream of clouds
Don't dream of balloons
Life isn't heaven
Life is earth

*Refrain:* Open ears open eyes
At attention march
He who will not guard to-
night
Tomorrow will not rise

Don't dream of birds
Don't dream of stars
Life isn't a dream
Life is earth

*Refrain:* Open ears open eyes
At attention march
He who will not guard to-
night
Tomorrow will not rise

Don't dream of legends
Don't dream of dreams
Life isn't poetry
Life is earth

*Refrain:* Open ears open eyes
At attention march
He who will not guard to-
night
Tomorrow will not rise

## PICTURE 23

I'm a coffin.

I'm the brother to lots of coffins here in the land. In me there lies a young man. His hair is combed and arranged. My boy—straightened out—lies in me, with a deadly explosive in him. Pale, quiet and cold. His toes are yellow. I am a coffin.

I'm the brother of lots of coffins here. Some of them have anyway been eaten away—the earth flames them. Carrying me and my boy's corpse at a snail's pace, rocking in a baby buggy. Here he lies on his last journey like his first journey to earth. I'm the coffin, made of pine, in whose thighs resin flowed.

Now I'm dry. I'm made of ribs, ribs. Dreary. In me there's a boy. His toenails are yellow.

### PICTURE 24

That's it. I want to be a horse taken out to freedom. Back to the wilderness. I want to cross borders, to run. To *neigh* like a horse about the days of the Messiah. A horse like a horse. No borders. These are the days of the Messiah. Everywhere is abroad. Even here is abroad. Imagine. Free to run! No borders! What do I want to be? I said it. I already said it. No "Border ahead! Stop!" I'm international. Has anyone ever seen a horse with a passport? I take a knapsack on my back and cross rivers. A Tigris, a Tiber, a Sienna—triplet. Triplet after triplet. What do I care? As long as I cross borders with a knapsack on my back. And I eat here and there like a sparrow. Seeds here and there, chestnuts here and there, mushrooms. I feel the wind on my back—I walk forward. Always forward. Looking at the view, castles, forests, sailboats, no borders. No passports. No stamps. Open. Just a knapsack, going forward and everything open ahead. Open. Open! Like open. O-P-E-N. Wide. Open. And I have just a knapsack on my back. Where don't I get to? Everywhere. Everywhere bullseye. Triple bullseye. You can rest your head and dream till morning. And then go on walking. What, walk? Gallop! A horse doesn't get calluses. Right—O.K.! Left, O.K. too! Why not? My map is nights . . . wheels, carts, mandolins!! As long as we go? Go!

And I go. I have air in my lungs. I'm healthy. How long do I gallop? I gallop! I have no camp, I have no village. I walk. I go into an easy gallop and again I walk, I don't have to run. No one's after me. I walk, I trot. I drop into one country after another with a knapsack on my back. I wander like the Wandering Jew. I don't know where I'm going. I have no camp. I have no village. I have a knapsack on my back and I walk. And that's the way I walk from country to country. Is that what I wanted?

### PICTURE 25

I want to be a little kangaroo in Australia.
Is that taboo to be a kangaroo in Australia?
I want! And I'm a little kangaroo in Israel.
And I want my mommy. I want.
To go into mommy's pocket. I'm scared.
I've got two long legs and two short ones: that's me.
That's the way I was born.
I want to be a little kangaroo in Australia.

### PICTURE 26

I want to be a Brazilian. A Brazilian. A Brazilian from the Branch Forest. Tanned. Sipping warm Coke on the east bank of the river, and I don't care about anything, only, only, that my wife lets me have it nightly, nightly, cuz I don't have any enemies. What do I care if you're here? I don't have to hold the ladder. I've got dark skin. I smile. I run away from alligators and speak Portuguese. Here we die with a kiss, spitting poisoned arrows out of a reed from under the moustache. Fou, fou. When I sweat I feel good. I have such big drops on my shoulders. Regular dew drops. Dew drops, dew drops for me, for me. And I break the burning air. I have a sweatband on my forehead, what do I care? My hair falls into my eyes. I don't have to hold up a ladder. You know what a prick I've got? When I lie on my wife I roll sand in my hands, I live by the beach, in the Branch Forest. Here, here.

### PICTURE 27

Iceland, Iceland, beauteous fishlets with eye shadowed eyes.
Loads of eiderdowns. Rinse me and curl me
In your virgin fronds, Iceland. Ah!
There one can lie outstretched
On holiday, sighing in bliss.
All white, clean, winking to pleasing warmth
And sweetness of popsicles, fudgicles,
Maybe furs. All there in Iceland.
Softness, purity, bluing and the sweetness
Of sucking, and sometimes red ears
From nice warm frostbite. All there in Iceland, far north.
There is also Iceland.

### PICTURE 28

I'm Cherli Ka Cherli the second.
Springy king alert to every place and valley.
I'm Cherli Ka Cherli the second
Know each and every weapon and caliber
Every cairn harbors a memory

I'm Cherli Ka Cherli the second, king
of Raids in the sea, air, or mud
No dirty tricks
I was raised here on calories, I have memories of vitamins
Don't be righteous. I hate vegetarians.

I'm Cherli Ka Cherli king
of the convoy crossing the desert and
swooping down on my enemies from the sky
Don't be righteous.
I eat like a horse and drink like a camel
I'm healthy
So whatja want?
That they shouldn't give us weapons?
Don't be righteous.
I'm Cherli Ka Cherli the second
alert to every place and valley
Ya-be-yeh what yokels! Decided
to be vegetarians, white cheese, soap.

I'm Cherli Ka Cherli the second king of
Air, sea, valley
If I don't reign here
Who'll reign here, vegetarians?
Don't be righteous!
Up yours!
In the sea on air and in bed!

I'm Cherli Ka Cherli the second, king
For ever and ever
I'm not "Vonce there was a vizard"*
I'm *the* Vizard!

## PICTURE 29

We're talking about facts. No shrink can tell me that I'm paranoid. No one would dare tell me. We're not forsaken. This cut peenie is a fact.

## PICTURE 30

Jumping Jack! Jumping Jack! Jumping Jack's my name, I'm Jumping Jack. I'm like an atomic clock. Is there anything more definite, more genuine and more accurate than an atomic clock? I'm Jumping Jack. The fear! The fear they engraved in me, "Jumping Jack."

I'm fed on mother's milk. I'm fed on father's worms. On my father's worms' worms. On my father's worms, worms, worms. They drowned all my world in milk. Can somebody vouch for me? Really

*"Once there was a wizard—Elementary English Language text.

and truly? So I eat and drink milk. To be more accurate, and very reliable, and very definite. Is anyone else ready to vouch for me Jumping Jack? That's how I am. I don't laugh. But I'm scared.

## PICTURE 31

Sleep my boy sleep
They're not behind you
Sleep like a baby
Sleep we're guarding you

You've got muscles
And you're already strong
You'll be a bully
You can rest long

You breathe air
You breathe health
That's no fraud my boy
Sleep my sweet boy

Sleep my boy sleep
They're not behind you
Sleep like a baby
Sleep we're guarding you

## PICTURE 32

We're talking about facts. And no shrink can talk to me about paranoia. Because if they find us one day with our pants down they'll shoot right away at whoever has a cut peenie.

## PICTURE 33: "BETWEEN SCENES DIALOGUE"

WRINKLED MAN: Who are you?

PINCH: Pinch Parsley.

WRINKLED MAN: Pardon?

PINCH: Pinch Parsley.

WRINKLED MAN: What are you doing here?

PINCH: I'm here.

WRINKLED MAN: And that's it?

PINCH: Of course that's it. I have no meaning. I'm the beaming tomatoes, fruit of the land, vegetables all year round. I don't build strong muscles, I'm not muscles, I'm not a muscle. I am pinch by itself. Existing for itself. Scattered with no questions. If I don't come—there's still a salad. Nothing special. No qualities. Something you add if it's there. Not the center, not the most significant, not on the crests.

WRINKLED MAN: You will pardon me.

PINCH: Yes.

WRINKLED MAN: You're not insulted?

PINCH: I'm not insulted.

WRINKLED MAN: You mean without a backbone?

PINCH: I'm a pinch of parsley. That's it. What's so hard about that? Fans little palm leaves. A bit of aroma wrapped in a rubber band.

WRINKLED MAN: Bunches, bunches

PINCH: Bunches, bunches

WRINKLED MAN: You've got no complaints?

PINCH: I've got no complaints. Of course not. I was a pinch and remained. And remained. And remained. No more nor less.

### PICTURE 34: "OG, KING OF BASHAN"

What do I want to be? I want to be like a planted tree with calves stretching over rills of water, transporting people from bank to bank. A muscleman. With my fist I could smash heads but I'd never do it.

What do I want to be? Mighty, Great. Big. Black probably. To be planted. Enormous, deep in the black earth. Moving gates of cities in my dream. Muscles all around. A Poet. In one hand flying butterflies high above. I want to be Og, King of Bashan—taller, bigger skipping long distances. A Hassidic dancer. Don't want to beat anybody up. What do I want to be? Massive as a trunk. Weighing an enormous forest. Conquering storms even. I'm sure I'll have a beard. And a large hat rises from my forehead like a ladder. But I'm bright and clear. I wouldn't hurt anyone. Just embrace me, my eyes. And if there is someone who doesn't see that in my eyes? Who doesn't see it in my eyes? And I don't want to go up in smoke. I have to be Og, King of Bashan.

It's only muscles. In my life I have to. And I say to myself Og, Og, what else do I want to be?

### PICTURE 35

I'm Cherli Ka Cherli the third, king of history. Without bullshit. No fooling around. I want to live, and well.

As a university graduate, I know what Hobbs told us, and as a graduate of the Technion, I'm an engineer. In short, gentlemen, I'm a power engineer. The source of power, gentlemen, in the past, present and future, was and is (for us) gold. Any comment?

Gold is energy. How many kings did we buy with gold? How many children did we raise thanks to gold? What kept us going in the past, and what's keeping us in the present? Gold, gentlemen, yellow cash. Hard and certain.

Even guided missiles can be deviated from their course, but not gold. That's certain and therefore the mission is gold.

Have I already said that it's worthwhile learning Jewish history?

I, Cherli Ka Cherli the third, say: I have to be strong. I don't have a choice. They won't catch me again with my pants down, because I have strong hooves—gold hooves. Therefore, gentlemen, I, as Cherli Ka Cherli the third, tell you. I chose to be a travel agent in all airlines. I have safety deposit boxes all over the world. That's my way. But each of you gentlemen will find his own way when the target is gold. In order to survive everywhere. Without dropping a dangerous anchor. There is a gold artery hidden in our body. It must be exploited.

My sweets! If I have to choose solid, a base which doesn't rust, while considering my university diploma and my technical engineering and any credit in the constant unit, let me tell you that I choose gold. For Pete's sake, take it easy.

### PICTURE 36

A: It means that I don't have a choice. I have to ask the question that I ask all the time. That means I *must.* I have to. I don't have a choice.

*: Do you want to ask if you're beautiful?

A: Certainly.

B: So you're asking.

A: Yes, I want to know if I'm beautiful.

B: Undress and we'll see.

*: Here they won't tell him to undress.

B: Let him be photographed.

**: Smooth. Without sandals. From tip to toe—barefoot.

B: You've been told to undress.

**: Adopt a disaster.

B: Suffer, then you'll be beautiful.

A: Am I beautiful?

***: The question is if you're clean.

A: What do you mean by clean?

B: Cleaner than a golden spot.

***: Sure he's clean. Then others do the dirty work and he stays clean.

A: I'm asking if I'm beautiful.

B: Undress and we'll see.

A: So am I beautiful?

**: If you're in the air all the time—there's air pollution in the air. Haven't you heard—ecology—shmuckology.

***: Because of prophets like you we become bent over.

A: I have to know if I'm beautiful.

B: Undress and we'll see.

*: If you walk around without a hat, do you at least go to the synagogue on holidays?

**: Put a nylon stocking on your head.

B: Take X rays and we'll see.

***: An open shirt in the next world.

**: Shlaikes the day after tomorrow—Go to Australia.

B: Undress.

**: Here they won't tell you to undress.

***: He who undresses endangers his life. I repeat: he who undresses endangers his life.

A: I must know if I'm beautiful.

B: Then listen. If they X-ray you, you'll get a blank picture. Nothing. They won't see anything. It's all empty inside.

A: What do you mean?

*: X ray is dangerous. I repeat: X ray is dangerous.

## PICTURE 37

If they ask, so what? What then, all in all, do I say? What do I answer? Maybe like a mannekin I prepare for many winters. That's why I've got so many hats. For instance:

I have pants with shoulder straps. Gabardine.
Down to the knees. Pants.
Hair out straight along the forehead. Sometimes a top
Hat on head.
On the holidays, once,
I wore a cap. Once I had wings—4.
But I also wear sooty overalls.
Since from tip to toe they look for marks of identification on me.
Then I say: I had simple cloth.
Cotton. On Saturday, white cotton.
Reeking of motherland odors, what?
But the skinnybones, I say mainly from the skinny knees,
Is prepared for many winters.
Open shirt, Big deal! From underneath,
From the left shoulder to the right hip
An ammunition belt.
So what do I say: Tricks!
Kaleidoscope! Somebody writes a history. Clothing.
Doesn't fit into the category of folklore? Gatkes
For instance. Shlaikes for instance.
I didn't mention yet the coat of many colors.
What's expected of me?
Then why do they ask "So what" all in all?
I say, I had many winters;
That's why I have a wardrobe.
All mine. Not half mine. All mine.

### PICTURE 38

If they ask "so what," I say—musicals. With all the knowledge of the situation as it is, I passed the age and health. I go for a stroll. If only I knew how to play an instrument. To sail, to eat oily salads, to study Shelley and Byron even though I was cut when I was only eight days old.

I want to spread cream on my lips to protect them from chapping and dryness. I will tour Greece in spite of the weight of the responsibility of Bat Ami, the daughter of my people. I'm tired. And I'll pop a lot of bottle caps. I eat grapes. That's what I want.

I know there are many dead. I know there are many clothes and many buttons. And in the night a man approaches a woman and unbuttons her button. I will lie in bed, and in bed will be feather cushions and eiderdowns in the winter and we'll love. In spite of all the weight of responsibility of Bat Ami, let her get in under my bed please like slippers. I'm going to sleep now for a few years please. For God's sake. Yes. Iceland, and I'll fly to Australia, why not? Near New Zealand.

My Hanania ben Teradion, I will remove you like a bowtie on the toilette table and leave you shut away all night. I'm going home.

### PICTURE 39: "SONG"

If they ask me so what, so what do I say.
I walk the streets at night sometimes counting
headlamps on my way,
And hear people singing in the shower at night.
I read the ads, What will be, who won't be and I
Hear slowly, slowly hearing from which
hidden corner, voices calling me: Hey
Come home, stop hiding, everything will be O.K.

### PICTURE 40

I'm a simple boy. I'm a simple boy lying
Under the bushes next to the house.
Even hammer sprinklers won't wake me up
And footsteps of a dog in the street, won't
wake me. No screams will wake me
Because I'm not asleep. I'm awake, I hear them calling me.
Cherli Ka Cherli! And I don't wake up
Let them shout, and they're shouting and looking for me.
How nice for me.
Maybe I'm lost.

# NAÏM
# Based on the novel, *The Lover* by A. B. Yehoshua Adapted for the stage by Nola Chilton

This play was adapted from the novel, *The Lover,* by A. B. Yehoshua.[1] A. B. Yehoshua is a gifted young Israeli novelist who is just beginning to attain the international reputation he deserves. Yehoshua's work is always complex in terms of both technique and content and this novel is no exception.

In the novel Yehoshua uses internal monologue to great advantage. Each of the characters in the novel indicates his state of mind in turn, reacting to events happening around him. This gives the author leeway in the novel to deal with the subject matter on several different levels. Repetition is not so elaborate as one might find in Faulkner's *Absalom, Absalom!* but the use of overlapping as a narrative device is part of the novelist's approach to his materials.

Yehoshua's vision in regard to character is never simple and this is particularly true of his major male characters. As an example, one might refer to any of the protagonists in his series of short novels found in the volume *Three Days and a Child.*[2] The motivation of the major male character in most of these novelettes springs from a complex set of circumstances and the reader is made to feel at times (when

Yehoshua is most intense) that the protagonist is moving in a world that is suspended and almost Kafkaesque in nature.

The novel, *The Lover,* does not quite reach this level, but these elements are present. The novel opens with a rather startling statement. The protagonist, Adam, states: "In the last war we lost a lover. We used to have a lover, and since the war he is gone."[3]

The action of the novel is played out against the background of the October War in Israel as Adam, the protagonist, searches for his wife's lover, Gabriel Arditi, who has disappeared since the first day of hostilities. This sense of quest is background to most of the action of the novel. In his search, Adam enlists the aid of a fifteen-year-old Arab boy, Naïm, who is employed by Adam in his garage as part-time mechanic and errand boy. Adam brings Naïm home—casually at first. He and his wife, Asya, are attracted to Naïm because Naïm resembles their much-beloved first son, Igal, a partially deaf child who was killed in an automobile accident. The accident involving this child is used as a focal point in the novel to indicate the breakdown in marital relations between Adam and his wife. Adam's daughter, fifteen-year-old Dafna, is attracted to Naïm in a different way for different reasons.

As I have indicated, the novel works out its statements at a leisurely pace on several levels and it might well be nearly impossible to reproduce it satisfactorily in several hours' traffic on the stage. Nola Chilton has done an admirable job in preserving the mood and sense of this work.

The play concentrates mainly on Naïm's relationship to the family as surrogate son to Adam and Asya and as lover to Dafna. The play also concentrates on what the novel has to say about Arab-Jewish relationships. The play emphasizes the progression in feeling between these two groups toward the essential humanity of the individual (rather than seeing an individual as a member of a hostile racial group).

The novel closes with the same events that close the play except that Gabriel Arditi returns to the family fold. It might be noted here that there are a number of reasons indicated in the novel in regard to Adam's not playing the outraged father when he catches his daughter with Naïm. In particular, the novel emphasizes Adam's state of mind at that time. He has had sexual intercourse a short time earlier with Dafna's fifteen-year-old girlfriend.

Nola Chilton has been directing plays for the Haifa Theatre for many years. She is best known for her interest in the documentary theatre. She has directed *Co-Existence* by Yahoshua Sobol, which featured monologues by Israeli Arabs. She also directed *Days to Come* by Sobol, in which young people were used to create old peoples' way of speaking and behaving. She has also gathered the material for another documentary, *Women in War.* This play featured five actresses portraying five women discussing the war.

## NOTES

1. A. B. Yehoshua, *The Lover* (New York: Doubleday and Company, 1978).
2. A. B. Yehoshua, *Three Days and a Child* (New York: Doubleday and Company, 1970).
3. *The Lover,* p. 3.

CHARACTERS

*Asya, the wife*
*Adam, the husband*
*Daky, the young daughter*
*Naïm, young Arab boy*
*Vaducha, old woman*

*Translated from the Hebrew by John Auerbuch.*



*Backstage, save for ten cubes arranged upstage to form seat and foot-stool arrangements for the five characters. These same cubes are carried downstage by the characters to form tables, chairs, bathtub, tow truck, etc., as needed for later moments on stage.*

*When stage lights go up, actors are seated upstage where they remain in character, each on his own cube, to move into shifting scene areas which movement and lighting demark fluidly with no break until fades into darkness at end of play.*

NAÏM: The Jews don't spot me as an Arab any more. Nobody does these days. Only the Arabs still aren't sure. Has something in me changed? Am I in some way no longer me?

DAFY: People just don't realize how depressing it is to be an only child. Most depressing is the silence. The terrible quiet.

VADUCHA: I am a second-generation Jerusalemite. A fruitful family. At the end of the century almost every Sephardi walking the streets of the Old City had a little of my blood in his veins. And now, at the end of my days, nobody alongside me . . . except the Arab.

ASYA: The word revolution haunts me. I want desperately to teach . . . to find my class. Such a pain in my chest for wanting to be with my pupils. But what revolution are they talking about? I ask myself what sort of a revolution? It's a war. It's only a war.

ADAM: My tiredness grows deeper in me. Till when I ask myself. Starting to live in total isolation. The family is falling apart.

NAÏM [*Crossing into spot (dsl)*]: They're getting killed again and when they're getting killed we have to make ourselves small. To lower our voices. To be careful not to laugh out loud even at a joke that's not about them. To know always where to draw the line. That's the main thing. And whoever doesn't . . . better stay in his village and laugh alone in his fields . . . or curse the Jews as much as he wants . . . but in his own vineyard. Those of us who move among them must be careful. No, they don't hate us. Whoever thinks they hate us is all wrong. We're outside their hatred. We're like shadows for them. "Take, bring, catch, lift, sweep, carry, unload . . . move!"—that's how they think of us.

In the beginning, when I first came to work in the city, it was very interesting in the big garage. New faces all around me . . . coming and going . . . Jews of all kinds bringing their cars, laughing and shouting . . . some of the mechanics Jew bastards . . . some local Arabs . . . real crazy with all their weird jokes. On the walls . . . [*The three girls move from their stools into calendar poses.*] pictures of girls in their naked skins . . . wild . . . so beautiful you almost stop breathing . . . Jewish and non-Jewish . . . blondes, black-haired . . . Negroes and redheads. Something out of this world. Lying with closed eyes on new tires. Opening the doors of classy cars. Tits, asses and legs . . . long ones . . . on engines or a set of new spark plugs. They drew the whole year's calendar on the ass of one girl. It was big enough. These pictures made me crazy. Afraid to look and doing nothing but. The small one hurt me . . . he'd get so hard. A couple of times my underwear got wet. At night I was squeezed with wanting. I came like a fountain. I would jump from one to the other, unable to give up any one of them, kiss, get hot, come . . . and he's hard again. [*Girls return to stools in slow motion.*] Then little by little I got used to the pictures and after a month I could look at them . . . just the same as the pictures of the two presidents, the live and the dead one and the old lady . . . their prime minister. [*ADAM crosses to him with broom and then moves (dsr) with back to audience.*] After a week they gave me a broom and I spent my time sweeping the floor, picking up old screws, spreading sawdust on oil patches . . . in charge of keeping the garage clean. Some job . . . both impossible and boring at the same time. Everybody gave me orders . . . Jews and Arabs . . . whoever wished. Even strangers passing through. Fetch . . . boy . . . grab hold, boy . . . clean up, boy. Anybody who felt like giving orders would find where I was. They called me boy, on purpose, to bug me. But I kept a hold on myself. I didn't want to start anything. Then it began to get me down. I lost interest in the whole bit. Even the cars . . . until I get to be a mechanic . . . and what for? And who's the master here? It took a long time for me to figure out who was the boss of the garage . . . the one who owns it all . . . they call him Adam. [*Starts sweeping in a straight line across stage to Adam.*] One day just before I finished work . . . sweeping the second time around . . . I got to the place he was standing talking to somebody. I waited for him to move. He didn't feel me standing there with the broom. I'm sure he didn't know who I was or that I'd been working in his garage for more than a month already.

ADAM: I've always refrained from visiting their villages . . . being a guest in their homes . . . as some of the other men who employ them do. It always ends in trouble. Altogether I've kept my distance the last few years. The business does very well without me. There are already workers I don't know because of the big turnover. During the last few years the place became filled with boys . . . some of them really children. [*Turning to Naïm.*] What do you want?

NAÏM: That you move a little. I have to sweep under you.

ADAM: I look down. A little Arab boy with a big broom. Looking straight at me with dark wise eyes. Something pinched my heart. A memory of Igal, my dead son. I don't know why. Who brought you here?

NAÏM: My cousin, Hamid.

ADAM: How old are you, boy?

NAÏM: Him too . . . boy. *Yamah shmo.* Fourteen years and three months.

ADAM: How's that? Didn't you want to finish school?

NAÏM: The truth . . . yes. But my father didn't want me to. Father decided to make me a master mechanic like Hamid. Two sons studying in the family were enough for him. I'm the youngest so I must work. Faïz will soon finish medicine in England and Adnan also wanted to be a doctor. None of the universities here accepted him. He began to think he wasn't doctor material. . . . He thought maybe he had a talent for something else. At night he did research on the gaps in the border fences. One day he cut out. Someone saw him in Beirut. We thought maybe it would help for him to be away from the Jews who bothered him so bad. Who would have thought he'd come back so soon?

ADAM [*Putting hand on Naïm's head*]: What do they call you?

NAÏM: Naïm. No Jew ever put his hand on me before. I could have recited a poem for him . . . if he had asked me to. He really hypnotized me. Since then he smiles every time he sees me. As though he remembers who I am. [*ADAM returns broom to (us) cube.*] A week later they took me off sweeping and taught me to tighten brakes. Not hard.

I started to tighten their brakes for them. One day they pulled me out from under a car.

ADAM [*Crossing (ds)*]: What do they call you?

NAÏM: Naïm.

ADAM: Take this key. Go to my house. On the little cabinet in the hallway you'll find a briefcase. Bring it to me . . . where are you running? Do you know the Carmel?

NAÏM: I know.

ADAM: Take ten pounds and bus 22. It's Habikurim St. 20. [*Crosses over to cube.*]

NAÏM [*To spot*]: I found his house on my own. A three-storey house in a quiet neighborhood full of trees and gardens. Wherever you look you see the sea . . . a patch of blue between the houses. Really beautiful. Just a few people in the streets. Some old women with carriages feeding the fat babies. Those Jews spoil their children terribly and then send them off to war. The apartment was dark but I liked it. Lots of pictures on the walls. On the radio was a picture of a boy about 5 in a black frame. You could tell right away it was his son. I found the case and I should have left. But suddenly I wanted to see what goes on in their kitchen. I never looked inside a Jewish fridge. Suddenly a key in the door. A girl of my own age wearing a school uniform. [DAFY *moves into the spot.*] You could see right away she was his daughter. Pretty, but his daughter. A bit thin, but pretty. A bit short, but very pretty. . . .

Your father sent me for a briefcase he forgot. He gave me the key.

A pity that I saw her because now I won't forget her. I just had to see her to know I loved her even before I saw her.

DAFY: Would you like to drink something?

NAÏM: No. [*She crosses over to her cube.*] In half an hour I was downtown on my way to the garage. [*Crosses over to (dsc).*] Suddenly I got an idea. I went into a hardware store and had a copy made of the key. I went back to the garage and gave him the case and the key and the change from 10 pounds. I could feel the duplicate key slipping around inside my shoe. From then on I was always on the lookout for him. I could sense when he was in the garage. I smelled him . . . just like a dog. I carried his house key with me . . . moving it from pocket to pocket. Sleeping with it under my pillow. Carrying the key was like toting a small gun without a license. Whenever I want I can get in there again. Open the door . . . pass through the rooms . . . eat some chocolate . . . take something to remember them by . . . even money, or a book of poems . . . and if she opens the door again . . . [*All the girls take poses of provocative Lolitas and tease him.*] I'll say in a quiet voice . . . your father sent me to bring you to him . . . [DAFY *to him physicalizing his fantasy until they end in a sommersault at Adam's feet.*] and she'll follow me down the stairs and see that I'm not just a dumb worker and we'll go straight to her father and I take out my key and give it to him: YOU SEE, I COULD HAVE RAPED HER BUT I TOOK PITY ON YOU! [*He stands up and returns with Dafy to (us) area.*]

ADAM: This little Arab, my worker, what goes on in his mind? What are his interests? Where does he come from? How does he feel here? I'll never know.

Rainy days. A heavy winter. I wake as always at 5 A.M. Pillows and blankets on the floor and chairs. Dafy's night wars. [ASYA *moves her cube (dsc) and sits.*] Asya curled up beside me like a fetus. How to describe her? Where to begin? I look at my wife all the time with a stranger's eyes, hearing the bitter, challenging tone in her voice. . . . Seems to me that she's moving further and further from reality. Could someone, seeing her as she is, fall in love with her for me? Dreaming again. Always dreaming.

ASYA: Here he is. Igal. I mustn't lose him again. Riding a bicycle back and forth outside the house. He's alive. What happiness! Thin cables leading from the brakes to his ears . . . as if he must listen to the brakes. No, it's not Igal. . . . It's a replacement Adam brought me. I don't care. It's wonderful that Adam could find a substitute. Igal, come here a moment. He doesn't look. He doesn't hear. Maybe he's deaf. Maybe he, too, is deaf. . . .

ADAM: On that Saturday Igal went to visit a friend of his who lived on the same block. His friend wasn't at home so he came back. It seems, I can't be sure, that he switched off his hearing aid on the way back. I had devised a little cutoff switch to wear next to his heart under his shirt. [*The three seated actors start moving slowly forward to stand aligned with* ASYA, *who rose during her dream.*] Then he saw his friend on the other side of the street . . . waving to him . . . and he started crossing the street . . . in total silence . . . the car coming toward him not very fast, honked its horn, but Igal went on walking in that silence of his . . . a slow walk straight into the car. [*They all walk slowly (ds) into the path of collision.*] It all happened very slowly and in total silence.

ASYA: I started walking the streets searching for a replacement. Then I saw the bicycle crushed with the cables coiling out of the brakes . . . still quivering . . . Somebody said . . . she has come . . . [*They all stand, stopped by collision.*]

ADAM: She has come to life. [ASYA *returns (cs) to her cube. The others to theirs (us) leaving Adam alone in the spot.*] Asya, I whisper to her, trying to enter her dream. But she turns her back to me. . . . I brought my wife a lover. Yes, it was I who found Gabriel. I've noticed before that people give themselves to me . . . as though saying "take me," and sometimes I do. Gabriel, our lover, a sometime Israeli, a deserter in fact, who returned to the land for a short visit to check out his grandmother's will. Actually she hadn't died . . . she'd been unconscious in the hospital . . . in a coma for months. He stayed in her old house in downtown Haifa and since the war he's been missing.

ASYA: Someone behind me. Gabriel. What happened to you? YOU SENT ME TO THE WAR!! THE WAR HASN'T ENDED. What hasn't ended? Everything is ended. Adam searches for you at night . . . Maybe he'll touch me . . . leaving . . . already leaving . . .

ADAM: He wasn't killed. Not him. I'm sure he never even got to the front . . . I drive through the empty streets sometimes, walk along the wet beach. [*All actors rise from cubes and start gymnastics of old people on beach.*] A strong wind rising from the sea. An old couple in bathing suits running hand in hand along the shore. Someone taps me on the shoulder. Gabriel . . . but it's old Ehrlich . . . You still swim in the sea in the morning?

ALL: What else? For 30 years now. Every morning before work. Come . . . undress and join me in the water. [*They start moving slowly to (us) places.*]

ADAM: A light rain starts falling. Nearly 7 o'clock. I pass the old house as I do every morning now. Four months since he's disappeared. I want to break into this house. [*NAÏM crosses to (dsc).*] I need a boy. Some boy who can climb quickly . . . who wouldn't quite grasp what he was doing . . . someone who has some trust in me. [*NAÏM reaches him.*] That one. He'll be fast and maybe quiet about it. What do they call you?

NAÏM: Naïm.

ADAM: Look, I need you for a small night job. Can you sleep away from home one night?

NAÏM: No problem. I don't mind sleeping at the garage.

ADAM: No need to sleep there. You can sleep at my house. [*All the DAFYS come alive and start moving in on Naïm.*] Do you know how to keep your mouth shut?

NAÏM: Of course, I can keep my mouth shut. I can keep it as shut as you want.

ADAM: Do you know how to climb?

NAÏM [*Involuntarily glancing at the girls*]: On what?

ADAM: Not now. You'll find out soon enough. . . . Here, take 100 pounds and buy yourself some pajamas and a toothbrush.

NAÏM: Excuse me, Mr. Adam, but what pajamas should I buy?

ADAM: The pajamas aren't for me. They're for you.

NAÏM: I knew . . . I was just confused from so much happiness. [*The girls have surrounded him and are wafting him back with them.* DAFY *reaches into cube and throws him a nylon bag with pajamas inside.*]

NAÏM [*catches bag, crosses to (ds) spot.*] And for the 100 pounds I bought pajamas. . . . I was left without a dime, just a pair of crazy pajamas wrapped in a plastic bag. It started raining. I've noticed that when we're moving or walking or working they don't see us . . . but the minute we stand still they start getting all jumpy and suspicious. I was tired and wet from walking in the rain . . . wet as a cloud. I was afraid the rain would wash me into the sea . . . and I had four hours to kill till he got home . . . all the rain seemed to seep into my head and drown out my brain . . . I was ready to be counted out of the whole deal . . . even the love part. [*Crosses to (us) where* ADAM, ASYA *and* DAFY *stand waiting.*] At last, after four hours he came home.

ADAM: Great timing. You just get here?

NAÏM: Just this minute.

ADAM [*Turning to Asya*]: This is . . .

NAÏM: Naïm.

DAFY [*Crosses to (ds) spot*]: What an idiot! Why did he have to wait outside in the rain?

NAÏM [*Scraping his feet on the "door mat"*]: First I dirtied their rug with mud. Then I took my shoes off and that made things worse because my socks were torn and dirty and underneath my feet was a big black puddle and everywhere I went it followed me.

DAFY: It's not very nice to say . . . but I was reminded of the time Daddy brought me a puppy he'd found in the street. The puppy raced around the house in high spirits and immediately dirtied the floor and the carpet. He was with us for a month until we realized he was growing so fast, he was getting out of hand. [NAÏM *has been acting out her association on all fours.*]

ASYA [*To Adam*]: You brought us a donkey . . . not a dog. [*Naïm stands on two and brays.*]

DAFY: And now a little Arab . . . one of Daddy's workers. [ADAM *places cubes to create bathtub and* ASYA *stands helping* NAÏM *to undress.*]

NAÏM: There was nothing to do but dump me in the tub. The woman filled it with hot water and insisted I get in. He was thrown by all the dirt I'd brought into the house and maybe sorry he'd asked me to do the night work. [*He gets into tub and sits there. Meanwhile* ADAM *arranges the table and* ASYA *folds his overall and puts it near him and then starts searching for a change of clothes.*] I lay there in the hot water in all those sweet bubbles. Little by little I thawed out. It was nice to lie in the tub of the Jews in the middle of all the colored towels and all kinds of bottles. I don't think that anyone from the village has ever sat like this in a tub of bubbles among the Jews.

DAFY [*in spot on floor with a newspaper*]: It was very odd having another person with us on a Friday when it's always so dead here. Meanwhile mother was trying to find him some clothes. Maybe you'll try a skirt? Why not? The Scots also wear skirts.

ASYA: How dare you make fun of an unfortunate Arab?

DAFY: Just a joke.

ASYA: Keep your jokes to yourself.

DAFY: So what if he's an Arab? How does this make him unfortunate? Meanwhile Daddy found a solution.

ADAM: I gave him a hundred pounds to buy pajamas. Here, inside the bag.

DAFY: Didn't even ask if he was willing to wear the pajamas in the middle of the day. Just threw them at him.

NAÏM: I said fine, What could I say? I wanted to drown right there, I was so embarrassed. [*Starts dressing.*]

DAFY: And now we all wait for him to come out.

ADAM: I don't understand. There are others who also need to use the bathroom in this house.

DAFY: I guess he doesn't realize we have only one bathroom.

ASYA: I am really getting worried about him.

DAFY: Then Daddy opened the door and we saw him sitting there in the dark on the rim of the bathtub like a scared animal. Wearing pajamas like I've never seen in my life.

NAÏM: He started laughing and then the woman and the girl too. I tried to laugh also so they wouldn't be embarrassed but, I don't know how, the laugh turned into tears. I wanted to die. Such crying . . . from all the waiting . . . all the excitement . . . [*He moves to spot.* DAFY *puts bath into place (us),* ADAMS *fixes table,* ASYA *stays.*] Years since I cried like that . . . not even when they buried Adnan. I couldn't stop . . . like a baby . . . tears pouring like the rain was inside me. Crying and crying before three strange Jews . . . before my love, who will never be my love. In the end, I stopped, not to shame them. [ASYA *crosses over with him to table. All sit.*] I hadn't eaten since the morning and I was weak with hunger. There was a white cloth on the table and two candles lit and a bottle of wine. I didn't know they were religious. But they didn't pray . . . not even a little. Started to eat right off . . . the woman served a kind of grey meatballs . . . sweet. Meatballs to make you vomit. This woman doesn't know how to cook. She puts in sugar instead of salt. I forced myself to eat some so she wouldn't be insulted. . . . I ate a lot of bread to try to kill the sweetness. At last I swallowed all those disgusting balls . . . balls like I've never eaten before and never will eat again. Then I asked in case I ever fall into a Jewish house again: Excuse me, what do you call those grey balls?

ASYA: Oh, you call them gefilte fish. Would you like some more?

NAÏM: No, no thank you.

ASYA: Why not? Don't be shy. There's plenty more.

NAÏM: No, really no. I've had enough.

ASYA: Please have some more.

DAFY: Take these also. [*The whole family helps him.*]

NAÏM: No, please, I beg you . . . NO MORE! [*They sit, startled.*] I was still hungry so I ate more bread, which damn it, was also sweet. Suddenly I realized I had finished all their bread . . . All without order. Each for himself. When they talk to each other they don't look at one another. Such silent meals. I didn't know that Jews lived in such loneliness.

ADAM [*Looking up from his newspaper*]: Naïm, they tell me at the garage that your brother was a terrorist?

ASYA [*Shoving food on Adam's plate*]: Naïm, what does your father do? And your mother? How many brothers in the family? Sisters? What exactly does Faïz do in England? What do you know about the Jews? What exactly do you mean by the word Zionism? [*Light change. Freeze.* ASYA *and* DAFY *stand with their knives pointed and ask like army interrogators.*]

INTERROGATORS: Who were his friends? Who were his teachers?

NAÏM: We don't know.

INTERROGATORS: Tell us their names . . . their addresses.

NAÏM: I don't know. I'm sorry he was born. He's not my brother. He's not my father's son.

INTERROGATORS: What do you think about him?

NAÏM: I'm a good boy. I'm the little one. I'm a good boy.

INTERROGATORS: What do you think of him? What do you think?

NAÏM: He was just crazy. That's all. Crazy. Just crazy. [*Girls freeze.*] Something at the university. An attack on the admissions office of the university. They've taken hostages. It's he . . . Adnan came back. The army breaks in. Gunfire. They're killing him. They're killing my brother. His eyes are seeing the light for the last time. Goodbye. Madman. Goodbye. Curse him. What did he do to us? The shame. His terrible pride. My poor brother. I see his eyes inside the earth and rain falls on him. [*Light change. All continue eating.*]

ASYA: What did you study at school? How many hours of Hebrew . . . of Arabic . . . of math . . . of history . . . what history . . . How many generations of your family have lived in Israel . . . How many people live in your village . . . how many work in the cities . . .

NAÏM: She asks so many questions. As though she works in the security service. And all so serious and friendly as though it really interests her. Seems to me the first time she spoke to an Arab . . . except those that deliver her groceries or clean her streets or fill her gas tank. And I see that they know nothing about us. They don't know that we know a lot about them. That we study Bialik and the Beit Midrash and the burning shtetl and the destiny of the Jews. . . .

DAFY [*Leaves table for floor in spot*]: Poor things. What have they done to deserve it?

NAÏM: I also know some poems by heart. I can recite them. No pride of young lions shall hide there the eye of the desert nor the glory of Bashan and its choicest oaks fallen in splendor by the somber tents sprawl angry giants among the golden desert sands. . . . We are heroes! The last generation in bondage and the first in deliverance. [*Stands on cube in high excitement.*] Our hand alone, our mighty hand did cast off from our neck the heavy yoke and we raised our eyes to the heavens and they were narrowed in our eyes. . . . and who shall be our master? [*Freeze.* ADAM *and* ASYA *look forward at image of dead son.*]

DAFY: I look at Mommy and Daddy and suddenly it hits me. The boy looks like Igal. They don't realize it. They don't sense it. . . .
What did you say your name was?

NAÏM: Naïm. [*Gets off the cube.*]

DAFY: I didn't know they had such simple names. [NAIM *moves to spot. The others return table to (us) area.*]

NAÏM: Afterwards I dropped off . . . so tired after the strange day. At 11 o'clock the television was dark and they led me, like in a dream, to a room full of books and I got into a soft white bed and fell asleep . . . deep . . . deep in the heart of the Jews. [ADAM *moves into spot while Naïm moves (bs) and starts putting on overalls.*]

ADAM: At two in the morning I woke him. He was so confused he spoke to me in Arabic. He got dressed quickly in his own clothes which were now dry and stiff . . . and we went out into the cold night . . . into the empty street.

NAÏM: We drove to the lower city . . . downtown Haifa . . . and there he killed the engine in a dead-end street . . . and started to walk . . . looking from side to side all the time like a thief. I didn't know that he also broke into houses at night. I thought he made enough money in the garage. Then he stopped near an old Arab house . . . falling apart . . . dark inside and out.

ADAM: You see that apartment on the second floor with the broken shutters? Climb up there.

NAÏM: What?

ADAM: Open the shutters with the screwdriver. Don't put the lights on. Open the inside door for me.

NAÏM: So this is what it was all about. The friendly talks and the pajamas. I could cry. If my father saw me now. One son abroad . . . the other a terrorist . . . and the little one a night burglar. A successful family.

ADAM: And if someone comes I'll whistle and you'll make a run for it.

NAÏM: What would you whistle?

ADAM: What do you know?

NAÏM: Jerusalem of Gold.

ADAM: Listen. Don't be afraid. It's the house of a friend of mine who went to fight in the war and I have to find some of his papers . . . that's all.

NAÏM: I didn't answer because the lie was so naked it had a tail on it.

ADAM: Well, get a move on.

NAÏM: I started to climb. The walls were wet and slimy . . . a crumbling Arab house. Finally I got to the second floor. Smelled inside like it hadn't been aired for a thousand years. He won't find much loot in this place. Then I heard someone moving in the dark. Somebody got here before us. [*Lights candle and crosses to (ds).*] I found the house door. The bolts were fastened. I pulled them back. [*ADAM in spot with him.*] I think there's someone here.

ADAM: What? [*They step back and VADUCHA enters spot.*]

VADUCHA: My first night home after a year. Who would have believed I'd come to this? I was never afraid of living alone. Now I hear a noise from the next door. Someone came in through the window. A boy stands there looking at me . . . as though Gabriel, turned into a boy again, is wandering through the rooms as he did twenty years ago. . . . Oh, help me . . . I'm losing my senses again. But the boy is real . . . an Arab . . . I can always smell them . . . they smell of eggplant, green garlic and fresh straw. The same smell that awakened my senses before. [*ADAM and NAÏM step forward, NAÏM hiding behind Adam.*] What is it? Who are you?

ADAM: I thought the house was empty. I'm looking for Gabriel. You're his grandmother, Mrs. Arditi.

VADUCHA: Yes, I'm Arditi. You know where he is?

ADAM: I'm looking for him all the time.

VADUCHA: Where is he?

ADAM: That's what I ask myself. He went to the war and didn't return. But I'm certain that he hasn't been killed.

VADUCHA: Then he was frightened by something. He must be looked for at night.

ADAM: At night?

VADUCHA: Why are you looking for him?

ADAM: What could I tell her? That I'm looking for my wive's lover. Mrs. Arditi, I know you were in hospital, in a coma . . . when did you come back?

VADUCHA: Yesterday.

ADAM: The grandmother came back to life. But you lost your consciousness. . . .

VADUCHA: I found it again. [*Snuffs out candle and crosses to (sr) to arrange table.*]

NAÏM: After a week he pulled me from under a car.

ADAM: How are the poems?

NAÏM: How's the grandmother? I wanted to say how's Dafy but grandmother came out instead.

ADAM: Grandmother? Which grandmother?

NAÏM: The one we visited last week . . . the one who lost and found her consciousness.

ADAM: Oh, she's fine. Sends you regards. Listen Naïm, I need you for some night work with the tow truck. Would your father let you sleep in town?

NAÏM: No problem. My father doesn't care where I spend the night.

ADAM: Good. Bring your things together . . . the pajamas and all the rest. We'll start towing cars together at night. Rescue work. You and I.

NAÏM: All night?

ADAM: All night.

NAÏM: Excuse me, Mr. Adam, but where will I sleep? I don't mind sleeping at your house again.

ADAM: Don't worry, we'll find you a place. Maybe at the garage or maybe at the grandmother's. [*NAÏM crosses to (us) to take bag from cube.*] Say, that's a good idea. You'll take care of her and she'll take care of you. [*They cross to (csr).*] I brought you the boy. This is . . .

NAÏM: Naïm.

VADUCHA: Yes, yes. This is the boy who came in through the window. *Keef chalek ya walad? (Translation: How are you, boy?)*

NAÏM: All right.

VADUCHA: *Deer Balak! (Translation: If you please!)*

ADAM: Naïm will stay with you and help me look for Gabriel.

VADUCHA: Come in, come in and try not to notice how dirty the place is.

ADAM: What are you saying? Everything shines here.

VADUCHA: This is clean? You should have come forty years ago and see what clean means. Here you could eat off the floor. [*Takes Naïm's bag.*] What's in this bag? You didn't bring me bugs? What's this? [*Extracting eggplant.*] The Turks already left the country.

NAÏM: I don't know what's in there. Maybe Mama . . .

VADUCHA: Then tell mama thank you . . . just next time not to mix food with clothes or there'll be cockroaches in your pockets. Where did you steal those pajamas? The towel you don't need . . . throw it straight to the dirty wash. Good, we'll go over the clothes later. Meanwhile go take a bath. You hear me? [*She places cube for tub and holds towel around him for him to strip.*] Yallah! Don't dirty the bathroom. This isn't a hotel and I'm not going to wash the floor three times a day. What are you getting excited about? I've already seen it all. Naïm, I've arranged a room just for you. But here you'll sleep alone. Without donkeys . . . or goats . . . alone. [*NAÏM resignedly crouches in tub.*]

ADAM: The poor kid was getting used to the idea that every time he entered a Jewish home they sent him straight to the bathtub. [*VADUCHA serves demitasse.*] Don't trouble.

VADUCHA: I've already troubled. I'm not going to throw it out.

ADAM: Naïm will stay here and he can be of help . . . he's a good boy, you'll see.

VADUCHA: When they're young, perhaps. Before they join Fatah. [*NAÏM puts tub (us) and starts dressing.*] Perhaps you can help me? Tell me what is this Kissinger? Before I went to the hospital I never heard of him and now the papers are full of him.

ADAM: He's a key personality in this part of the world . . . the American Secretary of State . . . a Jew.

VADUCHA: A Jew? Impossible! Maybe he's a convert? Isn't he ashamed to make so much trouble?

ADAM: It's not so bad. . . .

VADUCHA: What's not so bad? Read what they say about him. Tell me, can't someone speak to his father? [*NAÏM comes to table.*] Sohada!

NAÏM: What Sohada?

VADUCHA: Why so fast? Come let me see how well you washed. Behind the ears isn't a part of you? Next time, I'll wash you. Don't look so surprised. . . . I've washed bigger boys than you. Now sit down and drink. [*Goes to bring another cup.*]

ADAM: Naïm sat quietly and read the paper. I've noticed before how calm he is . . . he has extraordinary ability to adapt himself to new surroundings.

VADUCHA: What's this? He reads Hebrew or plays games with us?

ADAM: Naïm has graduated high school. He knows Bialik by heart.

VADUCHA: What does he need with Bialik? We're ruining our Arabs. Soon they'll stop working and start writing poetry. . . . But if he can read then maybe he can read to me. My eyes tire so fast and there's lots of interesting articles in the papers.

ADAM [*Rising*]: You see, Naïm, you'll have interesting work here.

VADUCHA [*Rising to him*]: Going already? Drink some more coffee. . . . What time do I put him to bed?

ADAM: He's a big boy now. He can put himself to bed.

VADUCHA: Will you be coming tonight to get him? . . . I wish I could join you both. So kind of you to think about me . . . not forsaking me like all the others . . .

ADAM [*Hugging her*]: A smell of baby soap came from her. [*Leaves.*]

NAÏM [*To spot*]: I decided I wasn't going to get involved with her. I didn't come here for politics. I came here for love. Her cooking was good. Real, spicy Arab food. I didn't know whether to clear the dirty dishes from the table. I didn't want her to think I was a handyman. I wanted her to know right away that I was a mechanic who boarded with her . . . not a servant. But she was so old . . . red eyes . . . groaning with each step . . . almost crawling on the floor so bent over. . . . She must be more than seventy because father is seventy. Suddenly I was afraid she'd die on me. . . .

Maybe you want me to clear the table?

VADUCHA: Sit quietly. [*Climbs painfully onto cube.*]

NAÏM: Tell me what you want and I'll do it.

VADUCHA: *Eenta sachich walad taeeb. (Translation: You're a good boy.)*

NAÏM: Smiling at me with that death smile. . . . You can speak to me in Hebrew. . . . You don't have to work so hard.

VADUCHA: Then you'll forget your Arabic and your father will be mad at me.

NAÏM: I won't forget. There are still some Arabs left in Haifa. [*Crosses to table, sits and each takes paper and reads.*] What a house! No radio, no television . . . just newspapers. What a drag . . . sitting opposite each other like an old married couple.

VADUCHA: What's the time?

NAÏM: Seven . . . Every five minutes she asks . . .

VADUCHA: What's the time?

NAÏM: Seven.

VADUCHA: God must be having a good joke on me . . . at the age of 93 I'm taking care of a little Arab. I know he'll grow up to be an ass like all the rest. You can't let them out of your sight for a minute. Too bad Adam didn't bring me a Jewish orphan and I could have performed a mitzvah before I died. I see a handsome boy sitting alongside me like the little grandson I had years ago and there's light in the house again. But then night fell and I saw the two of us were alone in the house and I started thinking . . . he's not a child . . . he's a big boy . . . his face is dark and threatening . . . he could steal my gold coins . . . He could . . .

Naïm, read me what Rosenblum writes here on the first page. Maybe when he reads I can sense his intentions from his voice.

NAÏM: So I read to her. Something about all the Arabs wanting to destroy all the Jews.

VADUCHA: That's what was missing . . . to put the idea right into his head.

NAÏM: I want to destroy you?

VADUCHA: So sweet when he asked that question . . . full of sweetness.

NAÏM: I look at her . . . those red eyes . . . really scary . . . that white face . . . a witch.

VADUCHA: Then I got the idea of asking him to kiss me. If he kisses me he won't be able to raise a hand against me at night and I can sleep in peace.

NAÏM: And then she said something wild . . . really weird . . . where did she get the idea?

VADUCHA: Come, give me a kiss.

NAÏM: I thought I would pass out. But I didn't want to argue the first night.

VADUCHA: He couldn't refuse an old lady. He got up, brushed my cheek with his soft mouth . . . maybe fifteen years since I got a kiss so sweet.

NAÏM: Her cheek tasted like a dried tobacco leaf. [*Moves to spot while she puts cubes back (us).*] Through the windows of my room I could see the harbor lights. Really beautiful. Tonight I'll see my love in a dream. And I did see her, but not in a dream. [*He crosses to* ADAM, *who is bringing his cube (ds) to make the tow truck.*]

ADAM: Every night I tell myself . . . this is insane . . . but I can't stop. So we go out at night . . . Dafy and I picking up Naïm and driving off to the night life Israelis who've broken down on the roads. [NAÏM *and* DAFY *bring cubes behind him and sit. They start driving with starts and stops, turns, etc.*] Israel in a fitful, dreamless sleep . . . months since the end of the war and the land is still uneasy . . . men wandering the roads searching for something . . . some account to be settled. And I with the two children behind me, the light flashing above my head, searching for an old car, model 1947 . . . for a man who disappeared in the war. Absurd.

NAÏM: We're like a firemen's crew . . . or better than that . . . a tank unit. The first time I got in and saw her I nearly fell out. She's the boss. Her father does what she wants. But what she wants she herself doesn't know. We sit so close together I wear my thinnest clothes to feel her better. . . . How are you?

DAFY: Great! How's the grandmother?

NAÏM: Fine. Why don't you eat more?

DAFY: I'm not fat enough for you?

NAÏM: You fat? Maybe you use too much sugar.

DAFY: Do you hate us very much?

NAÏM: Hate who?

DAFY: Us, the Israelis.

NAÏM: We are Israelis, too.

DAFY: No, I mean the Jews.

NAÏM: Not so much now, since the war when we beat you, we hate you less.

DAFY: But your brother the terrorist, the one that jumped from the university . . .

NAÏM: I told you he was crazy.

DAFY: And you, do you hate us?

NAÏM: I? I never . . .

ADAM: Enough. Quiet back there. Look for a little blue Morris model 47.

NAÏM: But there's no such car. I know it's all a dream.

ADAM [*Stops with a start. Freeze*]: In a ditch at the shoulder of the highway, a car cut clean into halves. A nightmare of an accident. Two parents and a child. The child killed. The parents on the critical list. I flash the light on to see the shattered windows, bloodstains on the seats, a child's shoe, a little sock. My head spins, my stomach turns, in a moment I shall black out.

DAFY: At night I share the real life while the kids in my class are dreaming. Lately I've been feeling completely cut off from the rest of the class . . . and just today we had a class with the new math teacher, Baby Face, the real teacher was killed in the war . . . and I missed him horribly. Baby Face and I hated each other at first sight. And today he came into the class and jumped on me first thing. And then he takes a notebook out of his briefcase . . . the notebook of the teacher who was killed . . . with all our names and marks on it . . . and he said I can't understand how you rated such a high mark from the last teacher. I shouted at him don't you dare talk about him . . . it's a pity you weren't killed instead of him.

ADAM: We're not going out anymore at night. [*They start returning to places and* ASYA *moves (sr) with her cube.*]

DAFY *and* NAÏM: Why?

ADAM: It's over. No point to it anymore.

DAFY: You've given up?

ADAM: Almost.

DAFY: And Mommy?

ADAM: She'll also give up.

ASYA [*She starts dreaming the dream and it becomes physicalized with all the actors moving through it*]: An afternoon sort of country, the sun strong and low in the sky . . . short fat stalks of corn growing all around. Dafy is pregnant. She sat among the corn stalks and a seed entered her. Adam brings a doctor. They'll take that thing out of her womb . . . a fieldmouse . . . a nightmare. Only they know how to do this. They will save the mouse. Dafy breaks away from them and runs to me . . . clutches me . . . shaking both of us. [*DAFY shaking her awake.*]

BOTH: What mouse? What are you talking about?

ASYA: You woke me in the middle of a dream.

DAFY: What dream?

ASYA: A real nightmare . . . I dreamed about you . . . Nonsense. Were you awake when the principal called?

DAFY: Yes.

ASYA: Still can't sleep nights? Are you in love? How do you get through the night alone?

DAFY: It's not too bad. When I go out walking the streets at night it's very interesting.

ASYA: You what?

DAFY: What you heard.

ASYA: You know what can happen to a girl walking the streets at midnight?

DAFY: At two o'clock in the morning. The streets are empty then.

ASYA: Dafy, enough!

DAFY: What's the big deal? What can happen to me?

ASYA: Dafy, stop it!

DAFY: I don't go far. Just to the corner where Igal was killed and back again . . . But you told me . . .

ASYA: Who told you?

DAFY: Daddy.

ASYA: When?

DAFY: Some time ago. [*ASYA crosses to start making bed with pillow and sheet, also places cube with Dafy's bra, panties and stockings on it.*] What is there to hide? Why can't I know? Daddy said he was killed on the spot and didn't suffer at all. You think he did suffer?

ASYA: What difference can it make now? Drop it.

DAFY: I wish he'd been killed.

ASYA: Who?

DAFY: Schwartzy.

ASYA: Enough, Dafy.

DAFY: All right then, just wounded . . . just paralyzed from the neck up so he can't open his mouth again . . .

ASYA [*Slapping her*]: I told you enough.

DAFY: Do you think he'll expel me from school?

ASYA: Would he be justified?

DAFY: Yes . . . he probably would.

ASYA: Then he'll expel you. Never mind. We'll find another school.

DAFY [*Moves to bed and starts taking off jeans*]: I'm so tired. I never before felt such a sweet tiredness. My other cheek burned as though it had also been slapped. It's more than seven years since she touched me. She covers me and sits beside me as she used to years ago. It's such a pity to go to sleep now . . . and even as I'm thinking it I fall asleep. [*ASYA to cube. NAÏM rises, crosses to her.*]

NAÏM: I know there's no one home but I ring the door bell anyway . . . wait . . . ring again . . . wait . . . ring for the last time . . . no answer. Ring for the very last time . . . knock . . . put the key in the lock . . . one last ring . . . and . . . I open the door. The house dark . . . nobody home . . . I'll write him a note and go . . . First one look at her room . . . lie down on my love's bed and go. [*He returns to door in slow motion and her version starts.*]

DAFY: A ring at the door. Who can it be? Another ring. I'm not getting up. If it's the mailman, let him leave it in the mailbox. Another ring. A knock . . . it sounds as though somebody is trying to force the lock . . . A short ring and the door opens . . . [*NAÏM now acts out her version of him as a thief.*] Somebody prowling in the house. Light footsteps. Now he's coming straight at me . . . *imaleh* . . .

NAÏM: [*Stops in freeze*]: There's someone here . . . Dafy lying in bed in the dark room. Her blonde hair spread all over the pillow. She's alone in the house. Too late . . . She saw me.

DAFY: It's only Naïm. Daddy's given him a key to the house. The sweet little Palestinian Problem turns a deep red.

NAÏM: It's only me. I thought there was no one home. Are you sick?

DAFY: No, I'm not sick . . . I didn't go to school today. Did Daddy send you for something?

NAÏM: Yes . . . no . . . I wanted to tell him something.

DAFY: Tell me.

NAÏM: What can I say? They're sure to find out about the key and then I'm done for.

DAFY: Tell me.

NAÏM [*Coming (ds)*]: What can I say to her? I love you? I've always loved you? [*Moves back.*] The grandmother is dying and I came to say I'm resigning.

DAFY: The prime minister tenders his resignation . . . from what?

NAÏM: From the job. I've no strength left.

DAFY: Strength for what? You'd think he'd been working hard lately. How funny he is . . . so serious. At least give a tiny smile . . .

NAÏM: To take care of her.

DAFY: What a pig! He's taking care of her. And Daddy said she was taking care of him . . . that she'd fallen in love with him. I thought it was she who was taking care of you.

NAÏM: What nerve! It's not true.
She really sets me off. Suddenly I feel faint. My breath stops. Her little feet sticking out from the sheet. When she leans over I see something soft and white where her bra should be. I'll kill her. [*Covers her feet with the sheet and freezes.*]

DAFY: His eyes are crazy. That sexy voice with the cute accent. He'll go up in fire in another minute. Poor thing is in love with me. I know. But his pride . . . his celebrated pride . . . I must keep him, calm him down, before he runs out on me.

Maybe you'll sit for a minute, if you can spare the time. You can resign a bit later.

At last . . . a smile. Looks for a chair. Covered with clothes. Sits on the edge of the bed . . . Something warm and solid keeping its distance. Silence. He sits with his head down, searching for words.

NAÏM: Is school over already?

DAFY: For me.

NAÏM [*MOVES to spot*]: She understands nothing. She'll never understand. What hurts me. How lonely I am. With her father and mother. In this beautiful house. Lying in her bed. No worries. What does she know about life? [*Moves back.*] Suddenly she smiles at me. A long kind of smile . . . I love her more and more. Maybe there's hope after all?

DAFY: Maybe you'll sit for a minute. If you can spare the time. You can resign a bit later.

NAÏM: So sweet. I look for a place . . . the chair full of clothes . . . stockings, brassieres, panties . . . things that make me weak and dizzy [*trips over chair into bed*] and feel from afar something warm and soft. She better stop smiling or I'll do something to her to make her sorry she smiled like that. What's she doing? Her legs on me . . .

Is school over already?

DAFY: For me . . . they expelled me . . . I told one of the teachers off and the principal expelled me.

NAÏM: What a strange one. She's really off balance . . . Noticed it before.

Why didn't you beg his pardon?

DAFY: You think I'm crazy?

NAÏM: The heat she gives off. Her little tits peeping out. I need to be brave . . . not to give up. [*Freeze, grabbing her foot.*] And if I grabbed her and kissed something . . . what more could happen to me. I've already quit, anyway.

DAFY: He's so close. The smell of straw on him. His smooth dark skin. I just need a little courage . . . not to give up now. [*Grabs him and they roll onto floor and freeze.*] And if I grabbed him and kissed him, what more could happen? He's already quit, hasn't he? This wanting, coming from deep inside me. Let me grab, hug, be just a little brave. Suddenly I need to pee. Really must . . . [*Jumps up.*] Just a minute. [*Strips under sheet (us) and then returns.*]

NAÏM: The small one burns . . . hard as a rock. In a minute I'll be all wet. That's it . . . Arab . . . get up and go. But I can't. I must calm down. Before I make a mess of it. She's back . . . all fresh and smelling of flowers. I must go.

DAFY: So I grabbed hold because I was afraid he'd leave me and he held me and then we kissed . . . a deep kiss . . . like in the movies . . . and he smelled like straw and tasted of pineapple and chocolate . . . and I tore off his clothes so he wouldn't be dressed with me almost naked. [*They tear apart and stand facing (ds) at each other end of the bed and then following, there is a physicalization of their act . . . each alone.*] I said come and be my lover. Because I don't want it to hurt.

NAÏM: It's wonderful. So fast. Already? Is that it? God I'm really doing it.

DAFY: But he did hurt me. I couldn't stop him. Enough. Stop now! Oh, he's so sweet.

NAÏM: This . . . this is it . . . this itself . . . and those tits . . . like hard little apples . . . a little girl . . .

DAFY: *Imalle!*

NAÏM: [*Almost simultaneously*]: That cry! What am I doing? Inside . . . really inside her. Just like I thought it would be and yet different . . . Why doesn't she say something?

DAFY: No way to stop now. This is it. I'm sure I'm the first of the girls. If Osnat and Tali knew . . . that it's good . . . like a dream . . . so deep in me . . . the smooth movement . . . it's all so terribly serious . . .

NAÏM: This is happiness. This is the greatest happiness. More than this there can't be . . . nor need be. Ahhh . . . [*Falls onto bed.*]

DAFY [*Covers herself with sheet still standing*]: He groans like an old man. Like someone else inside me. Good or bad . . . no way to know. What are you thinking?

NAÏM: Nothing.

DAFY: It's not possible not to think.

NAÏM: Good, I'm thinking of the old woman.

DAFY: What about the old woman?

NAÏM: She must have died in the meantime.

DAFY: How old is she?

NAÏM: Over ninety. I wish I could live to be that old.

DAFY: When did Daddy give you the key?

NAÏM: He didn't.

DAFY: But you used it today.

NAÏM: That's my key.

DAFY: Yours?

NAÏM: The first time he sent me here . . . the day we met . . . I had a key made.

DAFY: Why?

NAÏM: I just wanted a key to this house.

DAFY: Because of me?

NAÏM: Also because of you.

DAFY: Because of who else?

NAÏM: Good. Only because of you.

DAFY: They can put you in jail for that.

NAÏM: Let them . . . Somebody is coming into the house. [*Goes to chair to dress. She throws sheet over him.*]

ADAM: What's this? What's going on here? Pulling down the blinds in the middle of the day . . . the whole house dark . . . Naïm standing in the corner . . . pulling on his clothes . . .

DAFY: Daddy, don't hurt him. He's not to blame. Daddy, have pity on him.

ADAM: What's she shouting about? That child's not normal. I'm the one who needs pity in this house. Driving in my sleep for two days and nights . . . I move closer to see if it's really Naïm and what he's doing here.

DAFY: Daddy, let go of him. He came to say he's resigning.

ADAM: Resigning! From what are you resigning?

NAÏM: From all of it. From working for you.

ADAM: Now tell me . . . exactly . . . what happened to the old lady. Where is she? I called and no one answered.

NAÏM: So I think she's dead . . . already since yesterday . . . she's all paralyzed . . . doesn't eat . . . doesn't talk . . .

ADAM: So why did you leave her?

ASYA [*Entering*]: What happened?

ADAM: We're going down to see . . .

ALL: The old lady . . . [*Put cubes into (us) places and sit. All in beginning position sitting (us) and telling us the story.*]

VADUCHA: And now . . . reverse. The body lost and only thoughts remain. Hands . . . gone. Legs . . . gone. Face . . . gone. I don't want to die. Why now, if I got this far? Why not a few more years? He came through the window, the little bastard. They're not as stupid as they were when the state was born. He thought I had already died . . . put a sheet over me . . . then, afterwards, tried to feed me . . . to put bread in my mouth. So sweet, the little bastard, sweet and dangerous. Oh, lord of the universe, my eyes sink into darkness . . . too bad about me . . . too bad for I am dead . . . too bad for I am not—

ADAM: We left her with papers scattered all over . . . sticking to her body . . . shrouded with newspapers . . . I finally grasped what happened between Naïm and Dafy. He became a little lover during the year. I spread open the map on the car wheel . . . check the distances from here to the border. We speed north . . . passing through Acre and Naharya . . . suddenly . . . [*They all stand on cubes in various search positions.*] Searchlights . . . roadblocks . . . frontier guard . . . WHO ARE YOU? WHERE ARE YOU HEADING? IDENTITY PASSES! They send us back, showing the way to his village. [*All sit.*]

NAÏM: This is it.

ADAM: I try to start the car, but the engine's dead. The lights dim. The battery is absolutely dead.

NAÏM: He could have killed me. I don't care if they don't let me see her. I'll remember her a thousand years. He lifts the hood of the engine and tries to start it. Doesn't move. Stuck. Let him work a little. He forgot how to work. A good man but worn out. And they made poor Adnan so crazy . . . you can love them and also hurt them. People will wonder what happened to Naïm that at last he's full of hope.

ADAM: The smell of fields all around me. A sky full of stars. A side road. Out of repair. Somewhere in the Galilee. [*All stand on cubes.*]

NAÏM: Standing beside an old dead car from '47 and no one to save me. I should call Hamid. But I don't move. [*All start moving slowly (ds) into path of collision.*] Wrapped in silence. A deep quiet. As though I were . . . deaf. [*Freeze in positions of warding off collision. Remain frozen until darkness.*]